495 GOLF LESSONS by ARNOLD PALMER

DIGEST BOOKS, INC., NORTHFIELD, ILLINOIS

- *Instruction by* **Arnold Palmer**

- *Editorial Supervision by* **Earl Puckett, P.G.A.**

- *Production Manager:* **Deborah James**

- *Publisher:* **Sheldon L. Factor**

Copyright © 1973 by Arnold Palmer Enterprises

Copyright © 1961, 1962, 1963, 1964, 1965, 1966, 1967, 1968, 1969, 1970, 1971, 1972 by National Newspaper Syndicate, Inc.

All rights reserved, including the right to reproduce this book or portions thereof. Printed in the United States of America.

Published by Digest Books, Inc., 540 Frontage Rd., Northfield, Ill. 60093

ISBN 0-695-80402-2

Library of Congress Card Number 72-97512

TABLE OF CONTENTS

SECTION ONE—Problem Shots

Accelerate Club on Short Shots	7
Keep Your Head Still—Especially if You Wear Glasses	7
Forced Swing Ruins Timing, Hence Speed	8
Lazy Legs Cause Hooked Shots	8
"Trigger" Your Grip With Your Right Forefinger	8
Accuracy Calls for Square Stance	8
Alter Stance to Draw or Fade Shots	9
Finish "Quick" Into the Wind	9
Step Into Shots to Aid Weight Shift	9
How to Fade and Draw to Save Pars	9
How Ball Position Affects Your Shot's Direction	10
Move Right Shoulder Down and Under to Correct Pulls and Slices	10
"Tight" Right Elbow Solves Many Problems	10
Swing Hard . . . Low Scores Depend on Action	10
Bend From Waist for Upright Swing	11
Watch for the Divot Mark	11
To Achieve Timing, Practice	11
The Squarer the Clubface, the Straighter the Shot	11
How to Hit the "Hogan" Fade	12
Know How to Slice When You Want To	12
Swaying Robs Power	12
Closed Stance May Aggravate Slicing	12
A Simple Drill to End Shanking	13
Straightening Sliced Shots	13
Hitting Behind Ball? Accentuate Leg Action	13
Watch Out for "Loose" Lies in the Rough	13
Left-Hand Position at Impact Influences Direction	14
Here's the Right Address Position	14
Let Your Head Turn With Your Shoulders	14
Waggle Your Way to Improved Golfing	14
Weight Centered for Balance	15
Your Left Heel	15
Keep the Right Knee Bent	15
For Smoother Swing Avoid Grounding Clubhead	15
Minimize Distinction Between Long and Short Irons	16
Use "Clockface" to Draw or Fade	16
Weight on Heels in Downswing	16
How to Execute the Intentional Hook	16
"Blocking Out" Causes Hooking	17
Choke Up and Aim to the Right	17
What Causes Sliced Shots?	17
Pick a Target When Practicing	17
Pre-Cocking Head Aids Turn	18
Here's Knee-and-Arm Position at Address On Target	18
Correct Stance Adds Power to Swing	18
Why Spinning Balls Fly Higher	19
Check Shaft Flex When Buying Clubs	19
Short Backswing for Short Shots	19
Rough-Shooting Calls for "Floater"	19
Golf Distance Determined by Club Speed	20
Swinging Easy—A Difficult Habit to Break	20
Keep Your Weight "Inside" Your Feet	20
Grip Firmly, Effortlessly	20
Proper Coiling Requires Straight Left Arm	21
For Straighter Shots, Avoid Fanning Clubhead on Takeaway	21
Visualize Golf Balls as a Clockface	21
Hit on "Through" the Ball	21
Avoid Raising and Swaying: Here's How	22
"Cushion" Your Follow-Through	22
A Good Way to Add Distance	22
Sharp Clubhead Descent Needed From Buried Lie	22
"Looping" and How to Cure It	23
Key Driving Pointers	23
Hit Down on Teed Iron Shots	23
Headwind Requires Swing Adjustment	23
"Extend" Yourself on Tee Shots	24
Fit Your Clubs to Your Swing	24
Three Causes of Topped Shots	24
How Far to Hit With Each Club?	24
Downhill Lies Call for Special Techniques	25
Get Height When Shooting to Elevated Green	25
Strengthen Wrists and Forearms	25
A Success "Secret"	25
Don't Let the Hands Wander	26
Find the Stance Width Best for You	26
Two Important Swing Concepts	26
A Good Thought for Successful Swings	26
My Backswing is too Fast	27
Avoid Careless Clubhead Placement in Iron Shots	27
Preserving Your Power	27
Straight Left Arm—Must It Be?	27
Achieve the Tight Elbow Position	28
Cure for Pulled Shots	28
How to Execute the Intentional Slice	28
Right Hand Must Also Hold Firm	28
How to Hit Shots High or Low	29
A "Hero" Shot From Hardpan	29
Accurate Clubface Alignment—A Must	29
How to Check Your Position at the Top	29
Stress Still Head on Tight Shots	30
Learn What to Expect From Your Clubs	30
Avoid Deep Cut From Soggy Turf	30
Proper Grip Aids Accuracy	30
Keep Your Head Back	31
Build a Firm Left Side	31
Quick Weight Shift Builds Power	31
Look at Your Finish to Determine Earlier Mistakes	31
"Delayed Hit" Might Work for You	32
Stretch Into a High-Finish Position	32
Swing Slower if Hands Separate	32
Minimize Backswing on Short Shots	32
Keep Your Clubhead "Inside" the Target Line	33
High Hands—Low Scores	33
"Thinking Man's" Shots	33
Lowering Heel Aids Weight Shift	33
Make Upright Swing on Shots From Rough	34
Don't Overdo Hand Action	34
Take Your Hands Out of Your Takeaway	34
Play Short of Flagstick When Green is Soaked	34
Play Full Shots Opposite Left Heel	35
You Can Slice With a "Hook" Grip	35
If You Slice, Check Your Address Position	35
Get the Most From Your Equipment	35
Two Principles for Good Gripping	36
Ball Placement in Relation to Stance	36
Start the Club Back "Square"	36
Good Timing Increases Distance	36
Increase Consistency the Musical Way	37
Be Sure to "Finish" Your Backswing	37
"Low, Down" Golfing Advice	37
"Head Up" for Longer Drives	37
Keep Left Ear "Over" the Ball	38
Maintain a Left Side Lead	38

Ladies, Stand Tall at Address	38
Swing the Club With Your Feet	38
Toe Out Right Foot to Lengthen Backswing	39
For Those Extra Yards of Distance	39
Are You Swinging "Over the Ball"?	39
Look Back at Hands When Addressing Ball	39
Sand Wedge Best for Shallow Cuts	40
Your Clubs Determine Your Swing	40
Beware of Downwind Shots	40
"Hit Down" for Height	40
Your Club Should Lie Flat	41
Try a 5-Wood	41
Flat Swing Prime Cause of Shanking	41
Iron-Shot Distance Can Be Over-Emphasized	41
Keep on Target Line	42
Distance for Women	42
Hip Positioning Has Great Effect on Shot Direction	42
Three Ways to Check Swaying	42
Palms Align for Straighter Shots	43
Check Yourself in a Mirror	43
A Difference Between Duffers and Experts	43
Coil Up in the Backswing	43
Uphill or Downhill, Weight Belongs on High Foot	43
Extend Left Arm for Swing Consistency	43
Downswing Path Must Be Straight	44
Lower Left Heel First	44
Left Hand Guides Your Shot	44
Finish Swinging with Elbows Close	44
Another Key to Distance	44
Hands Lead on Long Iron Shots	44
Special Clubs Can Correct Your Troubles	45
Closed Clubface Offsets Ball Slip	45
Helpful Hint for Proper Turning	45
Level Your Swing on Long Iron Shots	45
Three Ways to Top; Avoid Them All	45
Long-Iron Shots Too Rough From Rough	45
Slower Backswing May Add Distance	46
Use Divot Mark to Aid Accuracy	46
Save the Woods Until Last	46
"Nailing" Can Be Fatal	46
Retain Wrist Cock Into Hitting Area	47
Keep Weight to the Left on Shots From the Rough	47
Avoid "Right-Hand Take-Over" at the Top	47
Wood Shot Recovery	47
Don't Be Too Tidy in Hazards	47

SECTION TWO—Strategy

Keep Records to Help Analyze Your Game	48
Use a Tee When Playing the Par-3	48
Strike Sand First, Turf Second	49
Warm Up With Feet Together	49
Stress Accuracy on Rainy Days	49
When to Gamble, When to Pass	49
On the Course, Play to Score Well	50
There Are Times When You Must Retreat	50
Drive Away From Trouble	50
A Great Way to Deflate Opponents	50
Making the Ball Back Up	51
Keep Track of Fairway Hits	51
When in Doubt Play Short of a Hazard	51
Know the Rules and Save Strokes	51
Plan Stance While Approaching Ball	52
Some Handy Tips About Selecting Clubs	52
Play Short of Flagstick When Green is Soaked	52
Plan Ahead	52
Be Careful of Loose Impediments	53
Play All Chip Shots to Same Landing Area	53
Count Your Clubs	53
Pre-Plan Your Golfing Approach	53

Don't Be Misled by Wind	54
Check Pin Position Before Cutting Dogleg	54
Why Pros Emphasize Yardage to Center of Green	54
When the Going Gets Rough	54
Plan Your Round and Lower Your Score	55
Sacrifice a Few Yards, Save a Few Strokes	55
Plan Shot to Use All of Fairway	55
Practice As You Play	55
Know the Rules About Repairing Greens	56
"See" Your Shot, Then Make it Happen	56
A Time to Play Safe	56
Avoid Playing Alongside Water	56
Club Choice Can Make or Break Your Shot	57
Golf Courtesy Pays Off	57
Casual Water Rule Can Save You Strokes	57
Usually You Charge; Sometimes You Don't	57
Visualize Flagstick in Safe Position	58
Score Better With New Grips	58
Check Pin Position Before "Charging"	58
Elevated Tee or Fairway Adds Up to Greater Distance	58
Do Your Own Thing	59
Play Faster, Play Better	59
Let the Wind Work for You	59
The Advantage of Being the Underdog	59
Plan Ahead and Break a String of Bogeys	60
Don't Be Greedy on Tough Holes	60
When Pressure Builds, Don't Tighten Up	60
An Aid in Judging Distance	60
Golf Has Its Psychological Side	61
Watch Good Players	61
Visualize Only the Target Area	61
Imagine the Flagstick in the Bunker	61
Don't Over-Club on Water Holes	62
Approach Shots Call for Pre-Planning	62
Let Sound Judgment Prevail in Some Cases	62
Play It "Straight" on Doglegs	62
When to Use "Too Much" Club	62
The 4-Wood Calls for Finesse	63
Don't Gamble on the Early Holes	63
Avoid Swing Changes Whenever Possible	63
Hit Full Iron Shot Into Guarded Green	63
Playing Short Can Be Good Golf Strategy	64
When to Leave the Driver in the Bag	64
Swing Smoothly Into the Wind	64
Hold Balance Into Headwind	64

SECTION THREE—The Swing

How to Take Proper Aim	65
How Grip Affects Backswings	65
A Tip for Producing Maximum Speed	66
Pour Right Hand Into the Shot	66
Firm Left Side Aids Accuracy, Distance	66
Finish in Balance	66
Take a Cut at a Dandelion	67
Keep a Level Head During Your Swing	67
Head Turns in Backswing and Downswing	67
The Right Swing Plane for You	67
A Talk on Timing	68
Swing Clubhead Straight Back From Ball	68
Start Your Swing With a Forward Press	68
Address the Ball With Hands Forward	68
Swing the Clubhead	69
One Way to Achieve Grooved Swing	69
Turn Your Back to the Hole	69
Swing is a Matter of Coordination	69
Flat Finishes Can Finish Your Game	70
Ground That Flying Right Elbow	70
Extend Impact Zone for Better Direction	70
A Crucial Stage of the Swing	70

The Golf Swing is Still a "Swing"	71
Tip for Longer Shots	71
Learn to Coil Up on the Backswing	71
Countdown for Lower Scores—4, 3, 2, 1	71
Put Your Hands in the Power Position	72
Ever Try a 6-Wood?	72
Keep Hands Unified at Top of Swing	72
Take Club Back Low	72
Bend From the Waist Throughout Your Swing	73
Defining Shoulder "Tilt" and "Turn"	73
Wide Swing Increases Distance	73
Practice Builds Confidence	73
Sweep Long Irons With Firm Left-Hand Grip	74
Retain Knee Flex Throughout the Downswing	74
The Best Way to "Loop"	74
Pull Clubhead With Back of Left Hand	74
Your Club Can Point the Way to Fine Results	75
How to Prolong Wrist Cock on Downswing	75
The "Inside" Feeling Pays Off	75
Speaking of Stance	75
How Fast Should You Swing Back?	76
Bend Slightly at Knees and Hips	76
Vardon Overlap Has Great Effectiveness	76
How Ball Position Affects Height of Shot	76
Play Ball Off Center of Clubface	77
Push Off Right Foot to Aid in Weight Shifting	77
Look at Target "Over" Your Left Shoulder	77
A Good Way to Check Your Grip	77
Return Right Elbow to Right Hip	78
Try Left-Arm Swing to Improve Timing	78
Learn to Hit Hard and Hit Squarely	78
Torque Action Increases Clubhead Speed	78
Left Knee Controls Hip Turn	79
Retain Knee Flex During Swing	79
Position Feet for a Powerful Swing	79
Make Big Turn, Short Backswing	79
Swing the Clubhead	80
The Backswing Must Be Unrestricted	80
Keep Hands "High" at Address	80
It Pays to Check and Recheck Your Grip	80
"Straight" Left Arm Doesn't Mean "Rigid"	81
Kick Left Knee in During Backswing	81
It's All in Your Hands	81
Shoulder Turn Helps Shot Accuracy	81
Take Your Right Hand Out of Your Backswing	82
Look Back at Hands When Addressing Ball	82
Proper Hand Position Sets Stage for Proper Downswing	82
Full Shoulder Turn Increases Distance	82
Swing "Wide" to Hit Far	83
Stay Down With Your Shots	83
Hold "Impact Position" Through to Your Finish	83
Golf is "Backhanded" Game	83
Point Chin Behind Ball for Freer Shoulder Turn	84
Keep Your Hands "Quiet" at Top of Backswing	84
Widen Swing Arc for Extra Distance	84
Here's Correct Golf Swing Wrist Action	84
Checkpoints for Proper Posture	85
How Much Practice?	85
The Modern Backswing	85
"Plane" Facts	85
Stay "Over the Ball" During Backswing	86
Setting Up to the Ball	86
Three Grip Choices; Take One	86
Two Ball Positioning Systems	86
Three Fingers That Control Your Swing	87
Set Up to Ball "At Attention"	87
How Your Grip Affects Your Shots	87
Right Grip With Right Hand	87
Keep Wrists High and Ready for Action	88
You Need Plenty of Leg Action in Backswing	88
Lady Golfers Have Knee Troubles	88
Roll Inside on Left Foot	88
Pull With Your Left Side on Downswing	89
For a Well-Timed Swing	89
Tip for White Collar Golfers	89
Body Turn Opens and Closes Clubface	89
Proper Shoulder Action Can Keep Ball on Target	90
Shaft and Swing Length Determine Speed!	90
How Backswing Tension Produces Downswing Power	90
Take a Look at Your Swing Plane	90
"Aim and Fire"	91
Address the Ball With Elbows in Close	91
The Pause that Refreshes	91
Align Bottom Edge of Clubface	91
Swing Arms Freely	91
Free Your Mind of Theory	91
Bow-and-Arrow Principle Adds to Force	92
Do Your Shafts Match Your Swing?	92
Straight Down the Line	92
Ladies, Swing Your Arms—Fast	92
Imagine How You Want to Feel at Impact	92
Things to Look For in the Mirror	92
Point Your Knees for Proper Footwork	93
Swing Club Target-to-Target	93
Extend Left Arm for Wide Backswing Arc	93
A Key to Timing and Distance	93
Extend Your "Flight Path"	93
Uncock Wrists in Hitting Area	93
Start Downswing With Pulling Action	94
Don't Press for Extra Yardage Into Strong Wind	94
Here's to a High Finish	94
In Golf, It's "Cool" to Keep Warm	94
Ladies, More Power to You	94
Hold Head High to Lengthen Backswing	94

SECTION FOUR—The Short Game

Accuracy: Prime Goal on Short Shots to Green	95
How to Pinpoint Short-Iron Shots	95
Proper Backswing for Short Shots	96
For Short-Iron Improvement	96
Finish Short Shots With Clubface Skyward	96
High-Lofted Pitch to Green Has Undesirable Effect	96
Extend Arms for Crisp Pitch Shots	97
Play Your Chip Shots as if They Were Long Putts	97
Know-How Needed On Short Approach Shots	97
Aim Approach Shots at Top of Flagstick	97
Shorter Clubs Need Shorter Swing	98
Wrists Firm When Chipping	98
Putt When You Can	98
The Pitch-And-Run—A Handy Shot to Know	98
Advance Hands on Chip Shots	99
On Short Shots, Weight Stays to Left	99
The High Fade Approach Shot	99
Chip With Appropriate Club	99
Shots to Play Slow But Firm	100
Pitching Wedge—A Stroke Saver	100
Learning the "Cut" Shot	100
The Importance of Planned Approach Shots	100
Avoid High Loft on Short Shots	101
Land the Ball on the Green	101
Lob Shot for Quick Stops	101
Swing Arms Freely and Smoothly	101
Play Run-Up Shot to a Banked Green	102
Hints for Shooting From Thick Rough	102
Strike Ball First on Iron Shots	102
A Quick Way to Lower Your Scores	102

For Better Chip Shots	103
How to Make a Tough Shot Look Easy	103
Handy Shot on Par-5 Holes	103
Wedge-Shooting Calls for Slow, Smooth Swing	103
Employ the Handy "Lob Pitch" Shot	104
How to Play Shot to Elevated Green	104
Plan Approach Shots to Allow Simple Putts	104
A Useful Shot to Know	104
Increasing Short-Iron Accuracy	105
How to Approach Approaching	105
Bank on the "Bank Shot"	105
Chip Shot Landing	105
The Short and Soft Wedge Shot	106
Short Irons and Backspin— Your Golfing Teammates	106
Chipping Practice Can be Fun	106
Back-Up to Lower Scores	106

SECTION FIVE—Putting

Check the Grass on Sidehill Putts	107
Systematize Your Pre-Swing Moves	107
Watch Putter Strike the Ball	108
Left Wrist Firm for Accurate Putting	108
Play Sharp Side-Hillers as "Speed" Putts	108
Stroke Out Towards Target	108
"Topple" Your Putts to the Bottom of the Cup	109
Developing a Sense of Distance for Long Putts	109
How Grain Affects Direction of Putts	109
Check Slope From Side of Line	109
Two Schools of Thought on Putting	110
"See" Your Putts Before You Stroke	110
Be a "Square"	110
When Your Putting Goes Sour	110
Don't Use Same Stroke Length on all Putts	111
Note General Slope When Approaching the Green	111
Get the Most Out of Pre-Round Putting Practice	111
Do Your Own Planning on Putts	111
Don't Over-Allow on Long Putt Rolls	112
Improve Putting With Smaller Target	112
One Hand Faces Other in Proper Putting Grip	112
A Cure for Pushed Putts	112
When the Pressure Builds	113
Consider Your Fellow Golfers	113
Stress Distance on Long Putts	113
Accelerate Stroke on Short Putts	113
Backstroke Technique in Putting	113
Grooving Your Stroke	114
Here's to Accurate Putter Alignment	114
A Putting-Practice Technique	114
Learn From Your Mistakes on the Green	114
A Useful Tip for Better Putting	115
There's a "Sweet Spot"; Find It	115
Sight Putts From Over the Ball	115
Feel "Inward" When Putting	115
Allow for More Break on Downhill Putts	116
Stroke Firmly on Return Putt	116
Strike Putts at Bottom of Arc	116
When to Putt From Off the Green	116
Sloping Putts are Tricky	117
Putts Should Roll, Not Dribble	117
Go to School on the Greens	117
"Grain" Can Offset "Break" on Putts	117
Putting Tempo, Smooth and Accelerated	118
Putting Calls for Sweeping Stroke	118
Steady Head is Key to Sound Putting	118
A Quick Way to Guide Putting Stroke	118
The Power of Positive Putting	119
Three Ways to Effective Putting Grip	119
Putting Right on Target	119
Putting Problems? Try an Arm Stroke	119
Strike All Putts in Same Spot on Putterface	120
Have Confidence in Your Putting Line	120
Improve Your Chances for Sinking Putts	120
A Simple Aid to Better Putting	120
The "Plumb Line" Method of Judging Putts	121
Putting Stroke Takes Practice and Finesse	121
Don't Move Outside Putting Target Line	121
Effective Putting, Uphill and Downhill	121
Practice Straight-In Putts	121
Accurate Focusing Cuts Down Risk of Pushed and Pulled Shots	121

SECTION SIX—Sand Shots

Proper Club Makes Sand Shots Easy	122
Splash—Don't Blast—From Sand	122
Let Your Lie Determine Where Club Enters Sand	123
How to Play That Long Shot From Sand	123
Vary Clubface With Lie of Ball in Sand	123
Try Practicing Sand Shots in Slow Motion	123
Buried Sand Shots Don't Call for Brute Strength	124
The Sand Shot and the Firm Left Wrist	124
The Long and Short of Sand Shot Play	124
Firm or Soft Sand? Swing Technique Must Differ	124
Alter Stance When Sand is Wet	125
Setting Up in Sand	125
Playing Sand Shots From Hilly Lies	125
"Sit Down" on Sand Shots	125
Slide Knees on Shots From Sand	126
Avoid Crossing Over Hands on Sand Shots	126
"Square" Clubface on Buried Lies	126
Clubface Angle Determines Depth of Sand Cut	126
How to Escape From Sand on First Try	127
Use Sufficient Loft From Deep Bunkers	127
Play Long Bunker Shots as if From Fairway	127
Sand Problems Intensify on Wet Course	127
Turn Out Left Toe on Shots From Sand	128
How to Judge the Depth of Your Cut on Sand Shots	128
Hit Sand Shots Twice as Hard	128
Where Situation Allows, Hit Sand Shots as Fairway Irons	128

SECTION ONE

PROBLEM SHOTS

How to Cure What Ails Your Golf Game.

ACCELERATE CLUB ON SHORT SHOTS

A common fault among high handicap golfers is their failure to make the clubhead accelerate into the ball on short shots to the green.

Frequently you see these players take an exceptionally long backswing (illustration #1) and then sort of let the clubhead limply drop down to the ball. The usual result is that

the club cuts into the turf behind the ball, and they "chilidip" the shot.

Short shots require a firm stroke into the ball. Keep your swing smooth and rhythmical, but keep your backswing less than full (illustration #2) and accelerate the clubhead into the back of the ball, striking it just before the club cuts into the turf.

If you make this short, accelerating stroke, with your wrists firm at impact, you will soon discover that more frequently you are hitting the ball squarely and with better control of the distance it will fly.

KEEP YOUR HEAD STILL— ESPECIALLY IF YOU WEAR GLASSES

In the ideal golf swing, the head would remain perfectly still throughout, yet not restrict, a full shoulder turn. In some cases it may help if the head turns slightly with the shoulders —but only slightly; a motionless head is still the ideal.

It is especially vital that golfers who wear glasses avoid any head movement. Not only does

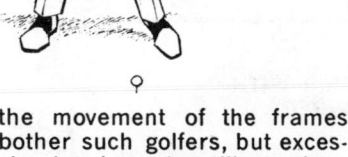

the movement of the frames bother such golfers, but excessive head turning (illustrations

#1 and 2) will cause the line of vision to switch from being through the glasses to outside the glasses—from in-focus to blurred.

If you wear glasses, address the shot while looking through the center of your glasses. Don't tilt your head. Then keep looking at the ball through the center of your glasses throughout your swing (illustration #3). This is the only way for golfers with glasses to play consistently well.

1—PROBLEM SHOTS

FORCED SWING RUINS TIMING, HENCE SPEED

The key to maximum distance on shots is to hit the ball as squarely as possible, and with as much clubhead speed as possible.

The golfer who forces his swing loses out on both counts: he doesn't contact the ball squarely, and he destroys good timing, the key to top clubhead speed.

Some golfers, like myself, can swing "fast" and still obtain good results. But most players will hit the ball farther, more often, if they actually slow down their swings. This slowing down allows their body and legs to play a more prominent role in the building of clubhead speed.

I suggest you at least try a slower, smoother, better-timed swing this year. If you do so, and stress square contact with the ball, the extra distance will occur automatically.

"TRIGGER" YOUR GRIP WITH YOUR RIGHT FOREFINGER

One of golf's most common faults is holding the club too much in the palm of the right hand. The fingers should dominate the grip, not the palm.

Hold the club so that the right forefinger wraps around the underside of the shaft. As if you are triggering a pistol. By assuming this position, it is likely that the rest of your right-hand grip will be sufficiently in the fingers.

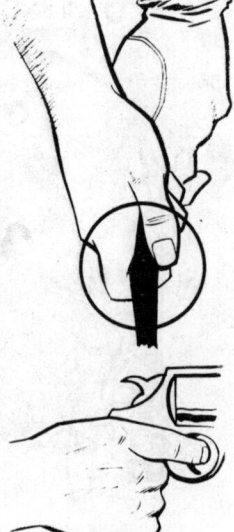

The left hand controls the club and holds it more in the palm. But the role of the right hand is more sensitive. Hold the club gently. And remember, never let your forefinger "squeeze the trigger."

LAZY LEGS CAUSE HOOKED SHOTS

Do many of your three-quarter iron shots finish to the left of target? If so, you probably suffer from a common golf ailment known as "lazy legs."

It's quite natural that your leg movement would slow down a bit on these less-than-full shots, but this is something you should guard against.

When the legs work too slowly or incompletely in the down-swing, the right hand tends to crawl over the left prematurely. This closes the clubface and produces hooked and pull-hooked shots.

The problem will resolve itself automatically if you simply remember to finish your hip turn through the ball.

ACCURACY CALLS FOR SQUARE STANCE

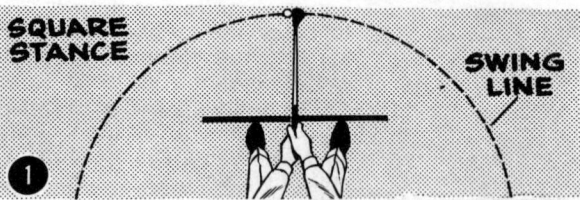

The square stance, in which a line across the toes parallels a line from ball to target, is best for shot accuracy.

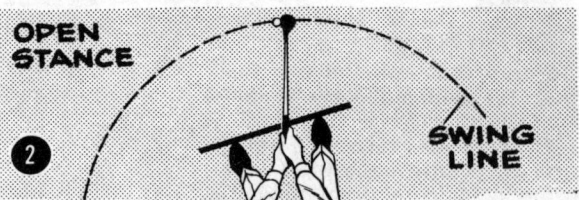

In the illustrations we have (1) a square stance with the toe parallel to the shot line; (2) the open stance with the toe pointing to the left of target, and (3) the closed stance with the toe line pointing to the right.

Of these three stance positions, the clubhead moves along the target line for a greater distance in the first drawing than in the other two. I think you will agree that the stance which keeps the clubface on line for the longest distance is the one that will give you more straighter shots, all other factors being equal.

1—PROBLEM SHOTS

ALTER STANCE TO DRAW OR FADE SHOTS

Intentionally fading shots to the right or drawing them to the left is accomplished by a slight alteration in your stance.

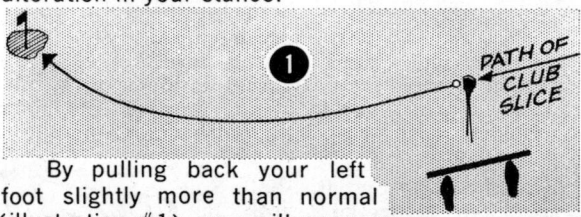

By pulling back your left foot slightly more than normal (illustration #1), you will open your stance. This causes your clubhead to cut across the ball from the outside and imparts a clockwise slice spin to the ball. A slight fade will result.

The opposite occurs when you pull your right foot back farther than normal (illustration #2).

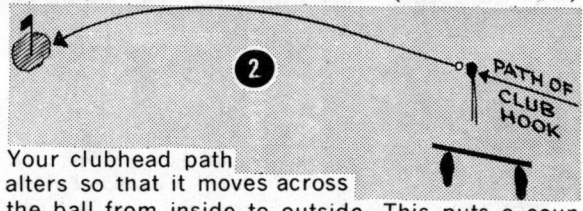

Your clubhead path alters so that it moves across the ball from inside to outside. This puts a counterclockwise hook spin on the ball and produces a slight draw.

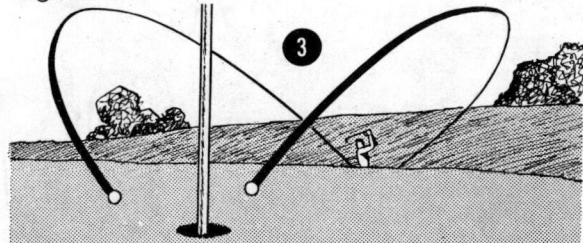

Whenever you alter your stance in this way to fade and draw shots, your clubface must be "looking" straight ahead when it meets the ball. If it should be "looking" to the right or left of the target, your shots will curve—or push or pull—too far offline.

STEP INTO SHOTS TO AID WEIGHT SHIFT

Many golfers find it difficult to shift their weight onto their left foot at the start of the downswing. Instead they fall back onto their right foot, and usually misdirect the shot.

If you have this problem, I suggest you imagine that you are a baseball player striding into a pitch. Actually take a small step toward the ball as you hit practice shots. Don't worry about missing the ball. Merely try to get the feeling of shifting your weight to the left BEFORE you start to return the club to the ball.

In a short time you'll find yourself making a proper weight shift without actually stepping foward.

FINISH "QUICK" INTO THE WIND

Shots into the wind must be struck low, crisp and straight. The best way to achieve this type of shot is to (1) use a slightly less-lofted club than normal, (2) choke down on your grip slightly, and (3) finish the shot as soon as you can after impact.

Regarding the third point, you must strike the ball solidly, with your left wrist very firm. This will shorten your follow through and keep the ball driving low and forward.

The only danger on this shot is that you might fail to clear your hips as you move through the hitting area. This would cause the clubface to close and hit the ball left of target.

HOW TO FADE AND DRAW TO SAVE PARS

Many a par can be saved if a golfer knows how to intentionally hook or draw and slice or fade his approach shots. It really is a fairly simple thing to maneuver the ball if you follow this two-step technique.

First, position your clubface behind the ball so that it faces the target (see arrows in illustration).

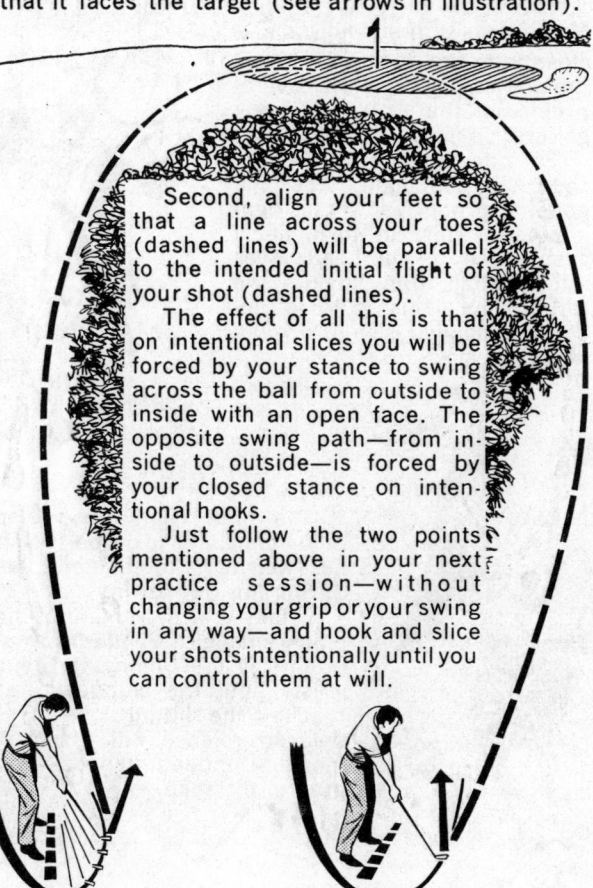

Second, align your feet so that a line across your toes (dashed lines) will be parallel to the intended initial flight of your shot (dashed lines).

The effect of all this is that on intentional slices you will be forced by your stance to swing across the ball from outside to inside with an open face. The opposite swing path—from inside to outside—is forced by your closed stance on intentional hooks.

Just follow the two points mentioned above in your next practice session—without changing your grip or your swing in any way—and hook and slice your shots intentionally until you can control them at will.

1—PROBLEM SHOTS

HOW BALL POSITION AFFECTS YOUR SHOT'S DIRECTION

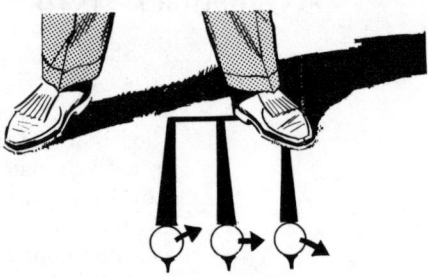

The positioning of the ball in your stance has a direct effect on the accuracy of your shot.

If you play your shots too far back in your stance, you will probably hook to the left or push to the right.

If you play your shots too far forward, say opposite your left toes, you will probably slice shots to the right or pull them to the left.

Position of the ball affects shot direction because it largely determines the positioning of your body at address. If you play the ball too far back in your stance, you will be forced to address the ball with your hips and shoulders "closed"—this encourages hooking. The farther forward you play the ball, the more your hips and shoulders are forced into an "open" or slice position.

If you are slicing to the right, try playing the ball back inside your left heel on your drives. If you are hooking, try positioning the ball opposite your left heel.

"TIGHT" RIGHT ELBOW SOLVES MANY PROBLEMS

Returning the right elbow close in to the right side during the downswing can solve several problems that plague many golfers.

For one thing, returning the right elbow in tight forces the golfer to properly lower his right shoulder. This, in turn, helps assure that the clubhead moves into the ball from "inside" the target line. This is good insurance against slicing or pulling.

The tight right elbow also helps the golfer to properly shift his weight onto his left side during this downswing.

Finally this movement of the elbow enables the golfer to properly delay the unhinging of his wrists until the clubhead has reached the hitting area. This delayed release will result in more clubhead speed—and greater distance.

MOVE RIGHT SHOULDER DOWN AND UNDER TO CORRECT PULLS AND SLICES

If you pull shots to the left or slice them to the right, your fault may be in your shoulder turn on your downswing.

If your shoulders turn on too-level a plane (illustration #1), you will force your clubhead out beyond the ball. You will put a slice spin on the ball if your clubhead is facing straight ahead at impact. If it is looking left, you will get a pulled shot, or maybe a pull-hook. At any rate you will have a flat finish position (illustration #3) with your hands very low.

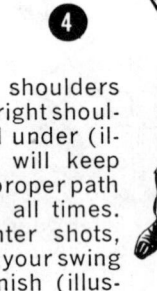

If you tilt your shoulders properly so that your right shoulder moves down and under (illustration #3), you will keep your clubhead on a proper path —inside the ball at all times. You will hit straighter shots, and you will complete your swing with a nice high finish (illustration #4).

SWING HARD... LOW SCORES DEPEND ON ACTION

Until the finish of the swing, none of your weight should be concentrated on the outside of either foot.

At the address for any full shot, feel the weight along the insteps and along the inner side of either leg.

As the club is swung away, more weight goes to the inside of the right foot -- never the outside. As you swing back to the ball, have a feeling of "pushing off" the instep of your right foot. At finish, of course, the weight finally goes to the outside of the left foot.

1—PROBLEM SHOTS

BEND FROM WAIST FOR UPRIGHT SWING

It is so true in golf that your swing—and its success or failure—is largely determined by your address position.

For instance, in illustration #1, I have made what I consider to be a nice upright backswing. Note how my hands have moved well up above my left shoulder. I am properly coiled and in good position to deliver a forceful blow to the ball.

However, it would be very difficult for me to reach this top-of-the-swing position if I had not bent properly from the waist when I addressed the ball (illustration #2). Only by bending from the waist fully, and with my back relatively straight, so that my hands were about under my chin, could I properly turn my shoulders on a sufficiently vertical plane to provide the upright backswing.

TO ACHIEVE TIMING, PRACTICE

When your timing goes sour, the cause is probably due largely to starting your downswing solely with your hands and arms.

I suggest that, to cure bad timing, you hit some practice balls with a short-iron club, such as a 9-iron. Concentrate on starting your downswing with your lower body, as I am doing in the illustration.

Soon you will feel that good timing coming back into your swing as your wrists automatically begin to uncock at the proper time in the hitting area.

WATCH FOR THE DIVOT MARK

Head movement on the downswing has ruined many golf shots: don't let it hurt your scores.

When you move your head on the downswing, you alter the path of your clubhead. If you lower your head, you will probably hit fat shots. If you raise your head, you may top the ball.

To help keep your head still, I suggest you look for the divot mark to appear on your iron shots. On woods and putts, try to see the clubface strike the ball.

This simple gimmick will save you many missed shots. It will also put negative thoughts out of your mind by forcing you to concentrate on positive action.

THE SQUARER THE CLUBFACE, THE STRAIGHTER THE SHOT

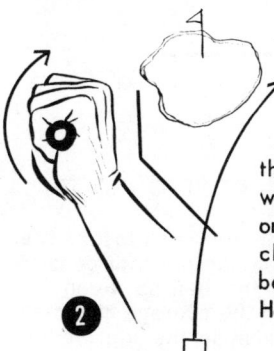

In illustration 2, the golfer has turned his hand upward so that wrinkles appear on the top side of the wrist. This positioning opens the clubface, causing sliced shots to the right.

In illustration 1, we see that the golfer has bent his hand downward so that wrinkles will appear on the underside of his wrist. This closes the clubface so that it will be looking to the left at impact. Hooked shots will result.

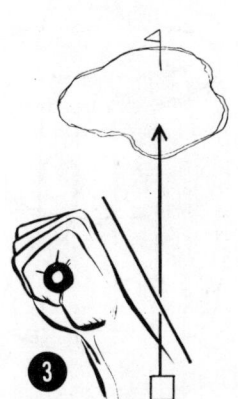

Most golfers will have best shot consistency if they employ the position shown in illustration 3. The forearm and back of the hand form a straight line. This usually indicates a "square" clubface that will produce generally straight shots, all other things being equal.

1—PROBLEM SHOTS

HOW TO HIT THE 'HOGAN' FADE

Most amateur golfers would prefer never to hit another shot that curved in a slice pattern. However, there is much to be said in favor of a high fade approach shot. This shot curves slightly from left to right. It sort of floats down onto the green and settles very quickly. Believe me, when the greens are hard or when the putting surface is raised or if there is a wind at your back, the high fade approach, which Ben Hogan executes so masterfully, is well worth having in your arsenal.

To hit this shot, you first address the ball with your feet, hips and shoulders all turned slightly to the left—but with your clubface still looking at the target (illustration #1). This address position causes your club to cut across the ball slightly, producing the fade.

Also, play the ball forward farther than normal in your stance (illustation #2), up near your left heel. This will give your shot extra height.

Finally, be sure that your right hand does not cross your left during or shortly after impact (illustration #3). Such crossing over would close the clubface and cause a low pull-hook to the left.

KNOW HOW TO SLICE WHEN YOU WANT TO

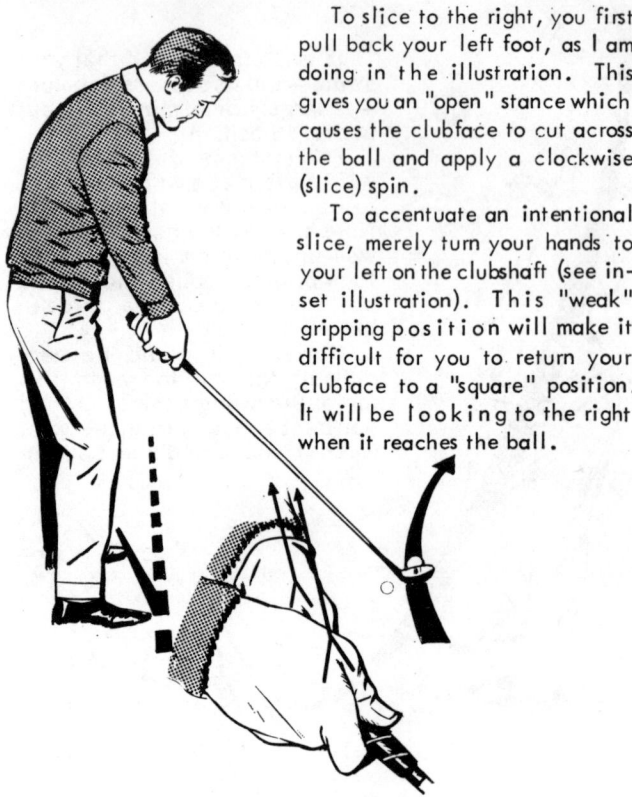

To slice to the right, you first pull back your left foot, as I am doing in the illustration. This gives you an "open" stance which causes the clubface to cut across the ball and apply a clockwise (slice) spin.

To accentuate an intentional slice, merely turn your hands to your left on the clubshaft (see inset illustration). This "weak" gripping position will make it difficult for you to return your clubface to a "square" position. It will be looking to the right when it reaches the ball.

CLOSED STANCE MAY AGGRAVATE SLICING

First, a closed stance may cause a blocking out by the left side on the downswing. This forces the clubhead to slice across the ball. Second, a closed stance may cause the golfer to swing the clubhead across the ball to the left (illustration #1) in an unconscious effort to offset the closed alignment of the feet to the right of target.

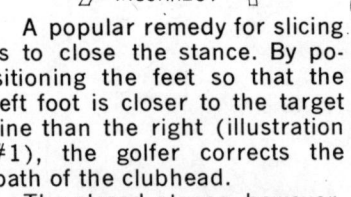

A popular remedy for slicing is to close the stance. By positioning the feet so that the left foot is closer to the target line than the right (illustration #1), the golfer corrects the path of the clubhead.

The closed stance, however, may—under certain conditions—merely aggravate the slice.

At best, the closing of the stance to offset slicing is a compensation. I strongly suggest that anyone who slices—or hooks—consistently, begin the corrective process from a square stance (illustration #2) in which the feet are equi-distant from the target line.

SWAYING ROBS POWER

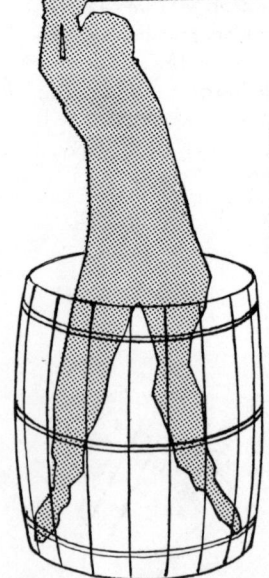

One of the key reasons that golfers on the pro tour consistently hit the ball so much farther than the average club player is because the touring pro seldom sways. He tries never to slide his body to the right on his backswing, or to allow his head and shoulders to slide to the left on his downswing. He knows that swaying will rob his swing of much of its power.

I think that the average club golfer will add distance—I know he'll become more accurate—if he can avoid swaying.

I suggest you imagine swinging while standing in a barrel, as I am shown doing in the illustration. Try to avoid letting your body hit the sides of the "barrel."

1—PROBLEM SHOTS

A SIMPLE DRILL TO END SHANKING

One major cause of shanking—striking the ball on the hozel instead of the clubface—is the tendency to shove the club forward with a very tense right hand and arm. This shoving action pushes the heel of the club into the ball before the clubface has a chance to square itself to the target.

Learn to relax the right hand and arm during the downswing. Merely practice tossing golf balls forward with a sidearm—almost underhanded—movement. Make sure that you hold the ball at the end of your fingers. Then merely SWING the arm back and forward. Feel the naturalness of this movement when the arm remains relaxed.

Transfer this same motion to your golf swing. Retain the relaxed right arm. Suddenly you'll be swinging the club; not shoving it. Your shanks will disappear.

HITTING BEHIND BALL? ACCENTUATE LEG ACTION

Golfers of every ability level occasionally hit behind the ball on key shots (illustration #1). If this problem persists in your game, I suggest you stress foot and leg action in your downswing.

Striking the turf behind the ball — hitting "fat," as they say—usually is caused by failure to shift enough weight onto the left foot on the downswing.

Good legwork is the answer in making this weight shift properly. As you begin to move into your downswing, drive your knees to the left (illustration #2) while keeping your upper body in position. This leg action will tend to "level out" the path of your clubhead in the hitting area, and the clubface will move squarely into the back of the ball.

STRAIGHTENING SLICED SHOTS

The golfer in illustration #1 has moved into a position at the top of his swing that will probably produce a sliced shot. If your tendency is to slice, check yourself to see if there is a similar break between the back of your left hand and forearm.

If such a break exists, you are moving into what we call an "open" position during your backswing. This encourages slicing. To straighten your shots,

move into a "square" position at the top (illustration #2) in which the back of the left hand and forearm form a straight line.

To encourage reaching a square position at the top—and thus at impact—try to keep your clubface looking at the ball for a longer duration on your takeaway. Keep it square to the line for the first couple of feet of your backswing, just as many golfers keep their putter blade facing the ball (illustration #3) during their backstroke.

WATCH OUT FOR 'LOOSE' LIES IN THE ROUGH

When the ball rests in deep grass in the rough, it is very easy to accidently move it as you address the shot. The ball usually rests on some of the long grass and is easily dislodged.

Should this happen while you prepare to shoot, you are obligated to assess yourself a one-stroke penalty.

To avoid such a penalty, practice addressing such shots without grounding your clubhead in the grass (illustration No. 2), just as you would if you were playing out of a hazard.

1—PROBLEM SHOTS

LEFT-HAND POSITION AT IMPACT INFLUENCES DIRECTION

Ideally, the golfer's left hand will return to practically the same position at impact that it was in as he addressed the ball. That way, if the clubface were facing the target at address, then it should also be looking in that direction at impact.

However, many golfers try to strike the ball by leading with the butt end of this hand, as if they were swinging a hammer. This hand position will open the clubface to the right and produce sliced shots.

For consistency, I suggest you address the ball with the back of your left hand either facing the target, or looking slightly skyward. Then "backhand" your shot so that this hand is in a similar position at impact.

LET YOUR HEAD TURN WITH YOUR SHOULDERS

Too many golfers restrict their swings unnecessarily by keeping their head rigid on their backswing and downswing. A rigid head inhibits a full and free turning of the shoulders.

In the illustrations, you will note that my head turns quite a bit during my swing (note position of the "boxes" around my head).

Though I advocate a turning of the head, I oppose any raising or lowering or sideways movement. Such movement throws your clubhead out of

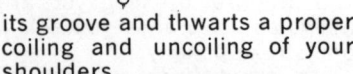

its groove and thwarts a proper coiling and uncoiling of your shoulders.

You will note, in the illustrations, that my head remains behind the ball throughout my swing. Make especially sure that your head doesn't slide forward of the ball on your downswing.

HERE'S THE RIGHT ADDRESS POSITION

If a player stands up to the ball with his legs too stiff (as in illustration #1), he will probably be unable to shift his weight properly during his swing. Often this stiff position will cause players to sway laterally to their right during the backswing.

If a golfer crouches and bends over too far at address (illustration #2), he will find it difficult to swing without raising or lowering his upper body.

Proper address posture finds the golfer bending slightly at his knees and waist, with his back fairly straight -- as if he were about to sit down on a high stool (illustration #3).

WAGGLE YOUR WAY TO IMPROVED GOLFING

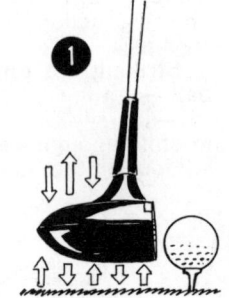

The movement of your clubhead during your waggle more or less previews the path your clubhead will take at the start of your backswing.

Therefore, raising and lowering your clubhead (see illustration No. 1) during your waggle might cause you to lift your clubhead abruptly on your takeaway.

Instead waggle by moving the clubhead backward and forward behind the ball, more or less in the same groove it will assume during your swing (No. 2). Your takeaway should find the clubhead moving straight back from the ball and low to the ground. Your waggle should follow this same patter.

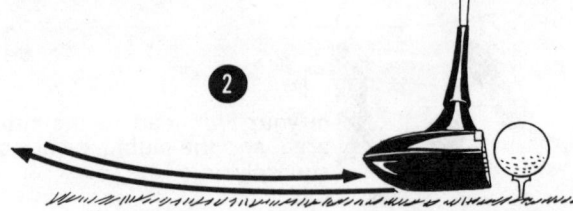

1—PROBLEM SHOTS

WEIGHT CENTERED FOR BALANCE

To stay in balance throughout the swing, try to keep your weight centered. Here's what I mean: At address (see #1), you should feel a downward pressure on the inside of both feet. Also angle inward with the right knee to keep the weight pressure on the inside of the right foot.

Then, on the downswing (see #2), this inside weight concentration is again pronounced. You push off on the instep and the right knee again angles inward, toward your target.

YOUR LEFT HEEL

Many golfers go awry when they lift their left heel improperly on their backswing. An improper heel lift directly affects your shots.

In illustration #1, we see a golfer who has virtually no heel lift. I think that it is fine to keep any lifting of this left heel to a minimum, especially on short iron shots, but only if a minimum of lifting doesn't re-

strict your action. This golfer has been restricted. He has practically no hip or shoulder turn. His backswing is little more than a mere lifting of his arms. He will generate very little power or control.

In illustration #2, we see the "toe-dancer." By raising high on his toe, he also restricts his turn somewhat. More im-

portant, he throws his weight forward and loses balance.

In illustration #3, I demonstrate a proper lifting of this left heel. Actually all I do is roll this foot to the right. My heel does lift slightly as I roll onto the ball of the foot. This brings the knee in to point behind the ball, thus freeing the hips and shoulders for a full turning.

KEEP THE RIGHT KNEE BENT

In a way it is a shame that the men on the pro tour do not play in shorts as do many of the women professionals. If you ever have the opportunity to watch these women perform, pay special attention to the position of their right knee as they swing, as shown in these illustrations of Mickey Wright in action.

Mickey's right leg remains bent forward at the knee throughout her swing. In fact both knees are slightly flexed until the very finish when the left leg straightens.

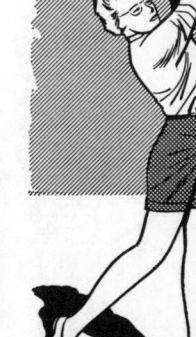

Many golfers have the misconception that the right leg should stiffen on the backswing. This is incorrect. True, it should not bend to the right, for this would promote a swaying, instead of a coiling, of the hips. Yet, it should remain bent forward at the knee to provide maximum freedom of foot and leg movement.

FOR SMOOTHER SWING AVOID GROUNDING CLUBHEAD

If your swing feels rough and jerky, or if you sometimes stub your clubhead during your takeaway, here's a gimmick that is sure to help:

Instead of grounding your club behind the ball at address, merely start your swing with the clubhead already a fraction of an inch off the ground.

By not dragging the sole of the club along the ground during the takeaway, you avoid stubbing.

You will also experience a new sense of swinging your arms smoothly and freely during your stroke. Finally, without the club resting on the ground, you'll be forced to hold it with just the correct amount of grip pressure.

This maneuver will seem strange at first. You'll fear mishitting the ball. I know, however, that it will all feel perfectly normal after just one or two practice sessions.

1—PROBLEM SHOTS

MINIMIZE DISTINCTION BETWEEN LONG AND SHORT IRONS

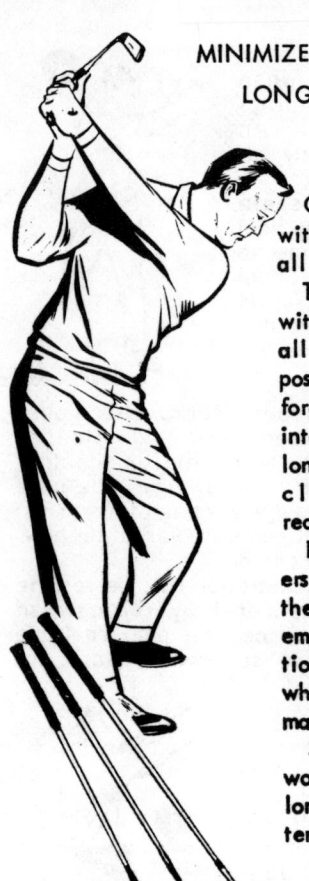

Golfers will have best success with the long irons if they swing all iron clubs about the same.

The tendency is to swing harder with the long irons because we all know that these clubs are supposed to produce longer shots. We forget that this distance is built into the clubs because they are longer and, thus, generate more clubhead speed. They don't require a more forceful swing.

In trying to swing harder, golfers overemphasize the muscles of the shoulders and arms. They de-emphasize good foot and leg action on long iron shots. That is why these shots cause trouble for many players.

So emphasize good foot and legwork the next time you practice long irons. But swing at the same tempo you'd use on a shorter iron.

USE "CLOCKFACE" TO DRAW OR FADE

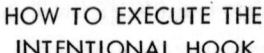

To intentionally fade a shot from left to right, or draw it from right to left, imagine the ball as being a clockface. Now hit all of your shots with the clubface looking toward the "9".

Then, if you want to fade the shot, strike the ball at "2 o' clock." This will impart a slight clockwise spin to the ball and produce the fade. If you hit the ball at "4 o'clock," again with the clubface looking at the "9", you will apply a slight hook, or draw, spin to the ball. By striking the ball at "3 o'clock," the shot will tend to fly straight.

WEIGHT ON HEELS IN DOWNSWING

During the downswing, centrifugal force practically makes it impossible to hit consistently good golf shots unless your weight is set back toward your heels.

When the golfer "rotates" during his downswing, this force causes an outward pull on the club (see arrow in illustration).

Unless this centrifugal force is offset, obviously bad golf shots will result. To balance the effect of centrifugal force, address the shot with most of your weight tending toward the heels throughout the backswing and downswing (see arrow in illustration).

HOW TO EXECUTE THE INTENTIONAL HOOK

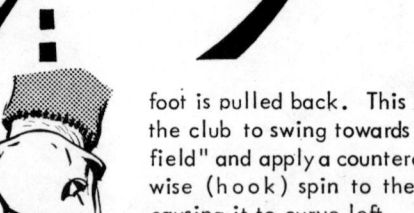

The techniques used to hook shots intentionally are actually "faults" of grip and stance that many golfers inadvertently apply in their normal game.

To hook intentionally, you can apply either or both of two alterations. In the full-figure drawing, I am addressing the ball in a closed stance -- my right foot is pulled back. This causes the club to swing towards "right field" and apply a counterclockwise (hook) spin to the ball, causing it to curve left.

The drawing of my hands shows them turned too far to my right. This will cause me to close my clubface in the hitting area so it will be looking to the left -- in a hook position -- at impact.

1—PROBLEM SHOTS

"BLOCKING OUT" CAUSES HOOKING

Stopping or slowing hip or leg action through the hitting area (Illustration #1) usually causes badly hooked shots that start to the left and then curve even farther in that direction.

Most golfers experience this problem on an uphill shot, when the hill itself makes it difficult to

clear the lower body. It may also occur on "punch" shots in which the club moves sharply downward into the turf, minimizing follow-through with the hips and legs.

If you tend to hit hooks or pull-hooks to the left, I suggest you open your stance slightly so that your hips can turn freely and lead your hands through the hitting area (Illustration #2).

WHAT CAUSES SLICED SHOTS?

Illustration #1 diagrams a major cause of sliced shots. Note that the line of the swing finds the club moving across the target line in the hitting area. This puts a cut on the ball that causes it to spin clockwise and thus move from left to right.

Illustration #2 shows the typical address position of one who slices. Such a golfer naturally aims to the left to "play for my slice." By so aiming, how-

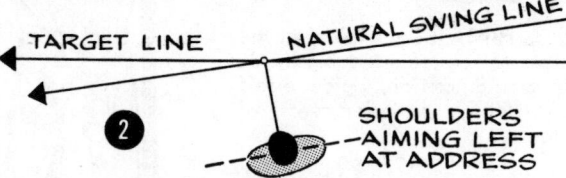

ever, he aligns his shoulders in a manner—facing to the left—that encourages exactly the same swing line that causes slicing. He is, in effect, provoking a slice by allowing for it.

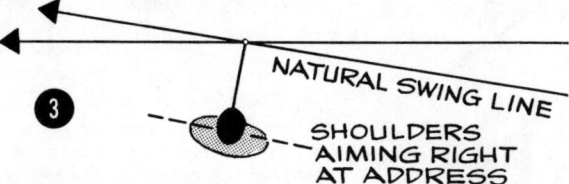

Golfers who slice would be much better off by aligning their shoulders to the right (illustration #3) so that their natural swing line puts an opposite—or hook—spin on the ball.

CHOKE UP AND AIM TO THE RIGHT

When you find you must play a shot in which the ball rests "above" your feet on a sidehill lie (see illustration), I suggest you follow two simple procedures.

First, choke up a bit on the club. This shortening of the grip compensates for the fact that the ball, being on the sidehill, is actually higher than normal and thus closer to your hands.

Second, aim a bit to the right of the target. The ball will have a tendency to pull to the left from such a lie. Aiming to the right of target will bring it in towards the flagstick.

As for the swing itself from such a lie, try to make it just as you normally would on a shot from level ground.

PICK A TARGET WHEN PRACTICING

Practicing without a pre-determined objective is usually less beneficial than not practicing at all. You might as well stay home and talk to your wife.

I think it is especially important that you aim at a target on every shot you strike. Select a tree or a marker in the distance and strive to lay your shot directly on that line. You can make a game of it by seeing what percentage of your shots actually finish within the confines of an imaginary "fairway."

Practicing without a target is bad. It tends to make you sloppy in your swinging and gets you out of the habit of aiming your shots. Next you'll discover that you are not aiming for a specific landing spot during actual play.

1—PROBLEM SHOTS

PRE-COCKING HEAD AIDS TURN

There is a young fellow on the professional tour who seems to be making quite a reputation for himself – name's Nicklaus.

Young Jack coincidentally hits a golf ball out of sight, and I'm sure one big aid to his unusual shot distance is the way he pre-cocks his head before swinging.

If Jack were to address the ball in a normal manner, (No. 1), his chin might impede the full turning, down and under, of his left shoulder on his backswing.

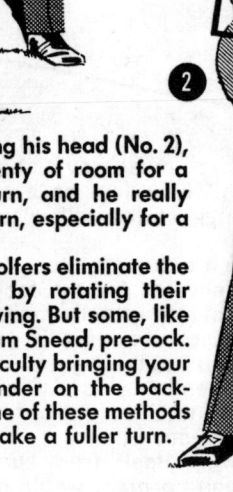

By pre-cocking his head (No. 2), Jack leaves plenty of room for a full shoulder turn, and he really gives it a big turn, especially for a man so husky.

Most good golfers eliminate the "chin problem" by rotating their head as they swing. But some, like Nicklaus and Sam Snead, pre-cock. If you have difficulty bringing your left shoulder under on the backswing, I think one of these methods will help you make a fuller turn.

ON TARGET

Correct alignment for any shot is a must.

Look at today's illustration; all the elements of proper stance are listed for you. As you can see, the target line is the line cutting through the ball and pointing toward target.

The line right-angling the target line is the ball line. Paralleling the target line is the foot line.

To all these lines, add actual foot position and you're ready for shots on target.

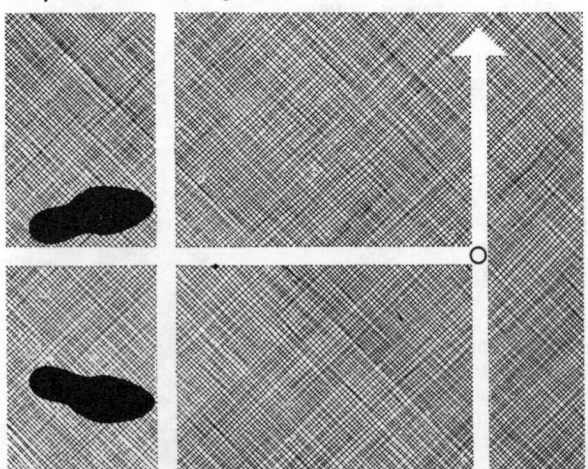

HERE'S KNEE-AND-ARM POSITION AT ADDRESS

The crouched position at address (No. 1) encourages a lifting of the body and head and a straightening of the knees during the swing. Naturally, this produces mis-hit shots.

At address stand with your knees only slightly bent and your arms hanging straight with no bend at the elbows (No. 2). The left arm especially should be extended. This will give you, over-all, a more upright address position. Your body will be in more or less the same position at address that it will assume at impact.

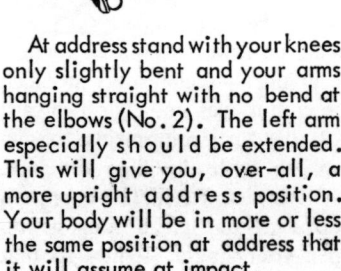

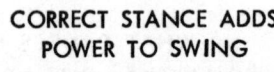

CORRECT STANCE ADDS POWER TO SWING

The diagrams give you all you should keep in mind when you first stand up to the ball. Keep these three elements in mind, and your swing posture will be smooth and well-balanced.

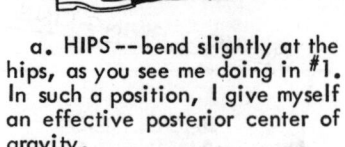

a. HIPS -- bend slightly at the hips, as you see me doing in #1. In such a position, I give myself an effective posterior center of gravity.

b. FEET -- as shown in #2, I keep them about a shoulder-width apart to give my swing balance.

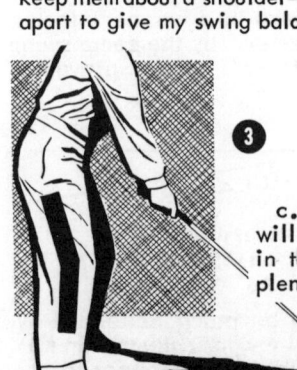

c. KNEES -- look at #3 and you will see that my knees are flexed. In this position I can count on plenty of leg action in the swing.

1—PROBLEM SHOTS

WHY SPINNING BALLS FLY HIGHER

A little basic physics can help simplify the golf swing.

Illustration #1 shows a non-spinning ball cutting through the air. The lines above and below the ball represent airstreams passing over and under the ball at equal speeds. The air pressure, likewise is the same above and below the ball.

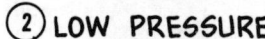

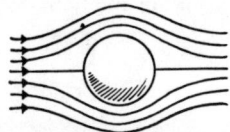 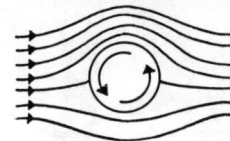

In illustration #2, however, we see that the ball is spinning. Note that the airstreams above the spinning ball move faster than below it. Thus the pressure above the ball is lower. The ball moves from high to low pressure and will rise.

The point of all this is that for a shot to rise, the ball must have backspin. It is impossible to hit a shot with topspin or overspin and expect it to do anything except nosedive.

SHORT BACKSWING FOR SHORT SHOTS

A common fault among novice golfers is taking much too long a backswing on shots from within, say, 40 yards of the green. After taking a long backswing, they let the clubhead "coast" into the ball. In short, such golfers are regulating the length of the shot by the force of the swing, rather than its length.

Failure to accelerate the clubhead into the ball produces a sloppiness and loss of club control. Scuffed or topped shots result.

In the illustrations I am hitting a wedge shot of about 30 yards. Note that my backswing is short – the hands barely reach hip height

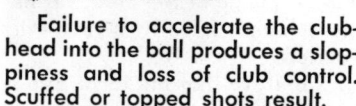

– and then I gradually accelerate the speed of the clubhead as it moves into and through the ball.

Learn to regulate the distance you hit these shots by the length of your backswing. Thus, you will be able to strike at the ball with about the same force on all shots, regardless of their length. You will not only hit these shots more squarely, but you will also develop a more sensitive touch.

CHECK SHAFT FLEX WHEN BUYING CLUBS

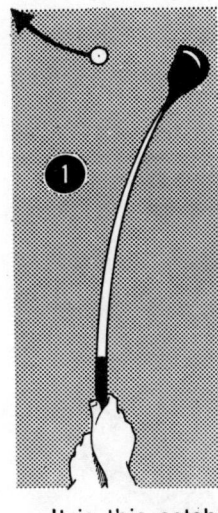

Clubshafts come in various degrees of flexibility and selecting the proper flex can greatly increase both distance and accuracy.

In the normal golf swing, the clubshaft, bending slightly forward, leads the clubhead during much of the downswing. As the hands enter the hitting area, however, the clubhead "catches up" with the shaft, before falling back again when it encounters the resistance of the ball.

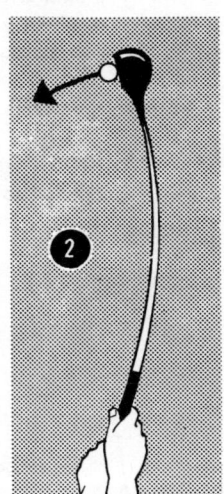

It is this catching up of the clubhead in the hitting area that can add some extra distance to your shots. It also serves to square the clubface to the target line. If the clubhead doesn't catch up (illustration #1), a slice will result. If it catches up and passes the shaft, the shot will hook.

You should choose a shaft that fits your swing—one that is whippy enough to spring the clubhead into the ball, yet stiff enough to allow a consistent squaring of the face. Generally, slow swingers will get more distance with a "soft" shaft, while hard hitters will need a stiffer shaft to provide better accuracy.

ROUGH-SHOOTING CALLS FOR 'FLOATER'

Hit behind the ball when you find yourself near the green with the ball lying low in deep grass.

Merely play this shot as you would play an explosion shot from sand. Play the ball forward in your stance as you would on a sand shot, as illustrated, and then swing so that the clubhead enters the turf behind the ball.

The best club for this shot is a pitching wedge or a 9-iron. Such a club will float the ball out of the rough and onto the green so that it will settle quickly.

1—PROBLEM SHOTS

GOLF DISTANCE DETERMINED BY CLUB SPEED

If you swing in a wide arc, your clubhead will move faster than if you swing in a small arc. Since the distance of golf shots is determined largely by clubhead speed, it should be obvious that a wide swing arc will produce more distance than will a small or shorter arc.

To increase the width of your swing -- and, thus, your distance -- you must stress a straight left arm throughout your backswing and downswing (see illustrations #1 and #2) and a straight right arm on your follow-through.

As you swing in a wide arc, make certain your head remains near the center of your "wheel"; don't let it move out towards the "rim."

SWINGING EASY – A DIFFICULT HABIT TO BREAK

Many golfers do not drive the ball as far as they should because they do not swing at it as hard as they can.

Somewhere along the line, many golfers discover they can hit the ball squarely more frequently if they do not swing hard. They lose the will to hit the ball hard. Swing-

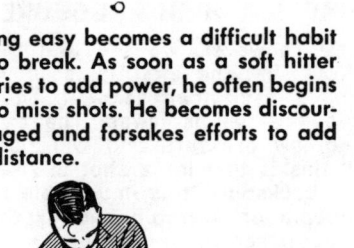

ing easy becomes a difficult habit to break. As soon as a soft hitter tries to add power, he often begins to miss shots. He becomes discouraged and forsakes efforts to add distance.

I say that almost any golfer can learn to hit the ball hard and squarely. In fact, many golfers who hit the ball hard have difficulty meeting it squarely if they try to swing easy.

Learning to hit the ball hard requires a whole new mental outlook, along with considerable practice and instruction. But I think the serious golfer should make plenty of effort in this direction.

KEEP YOUR WEIGHT "INSIDE" YOUR FEET

The figures on the left and right in the illustration show the golfer in the all-too-familiar "sway" position—away from the target on the backswing, towards the target on the downswing.

The sway robs your swing of power. It prohibits you from fully coiling on your backswing and releasing on your downswing. The sway also moves the club out of its proper path, thus causing miss-hit shots.

To prevent swaying, you should never let your weight shift to the outside of your feet. It should shift to the instep of your right foot during your backswing and onto, but not outside of, your left foot on your downswing.

GRIP FIRMLY, EFFORTLESSLY

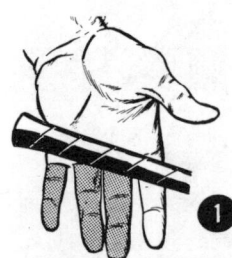

How "firm" should your grip be? Certainly firm enough to disallow any slippage of the club, yet not so tight that it restricts your wrist action.

I believe that the ideal grip is one that allows the golfer to hold the club firmly--without any conscious effort.

Obviously, this requires strong hands. Specifically it requires great strength in the last three fingers of your left hand (see the shaded fingers in illustration #1). These fingers will be the first to let go of the club at the top of your swing (illustration #2).

To strengthen these fingers, squeeze the steering wheel of your car with them, as tightly as you can, for about 10 seconds each time you drive. This simple exercise will do more for your game than any single drill I can imagine.

1—PROBLEM SHOTS

PROPER COILING REQUIRES STRAIGHT LEFT ARM

No golfer can realize maximum power on his shots if he fails to keep his left arm straight during his backswing.

Note the golfer in illustration #1. He has lifted his arms and hands, instead of swinging them upward to the top. Hence the bending of the left arm. Such a backswing lacks sufficient tension in the back and legs to produce a powerful reaction, or release of force, on the downswing.

In illustration #2 I am showing the properly straight left arm at the top of the swing. As a result my muscles are primed to release with force.

You will be surprised just how much physical effort is required to keep your left arm straight throughout your backswing. You will probably notice a definite shortening of your swing. But don't be discouraged. Your swing should be no longer than you can make it with a straight left arm.

FOR STRAIGHTER SHOTS, AVOID FANNING CLUBHEAD ON TAKEAWAY

The golfer in Illustration #1 has fanned open his clubhead during his takeaway, an error that is all too familiar among club golfers. Fanning the club open on the takeaway necessitates rolling it closed on the downswing, if you are to hit a square shot. All this manipulation leaves a big chance for error.

I suggest you take the club back without any conscious rotation of the clubface—in either direction—with your hands (Illustration 2).

It will help you make this "one-piece" takeaway if you simply concentrate on keeping the back of your left hand looking in the same direction it was facing at address. Try to hold this hand position until your clubhead begins to move inside the target line.

HIT ON 'THROUGH' THE BALL

We all know (or should know) that it's best to swing the club "through," rather than "at," the ball. This cuts down on the chances that you will "quit" on the shot before the ball is on its way.

To help you swing "through" the ball, imagine that the ball is stuck on the clubface with a piece of gum. You want to get the ball off the club. Therefore you throw the club "through" the ball and out towards the target (as I am doing in the illustration) in hopes that the ball will shoot off from the clubface.

VISUALIZE GOLF BALL AS A CLOCKFACE

There seems to be considerable confusion among golfers as to where the club should contact the ball during impact. I think it might help if you would visualize the ball as being a clockface (see illustrations).

On iron shots you want the club to contact the ball before it cuts

into the turf – in other words, just before it reaches the lowest part of its arc. This is known as "hitting down on the ball" and it produces good control of the ball's flight because it encourages backspin.

I suggest you try to meet that ball at 10 o'clock on your iron shots.

On wood shots you want the clubhead to sweep into the ball at the lowest point of its arc. Therefore, hit the ball at 9 o'clock on all wood shots.

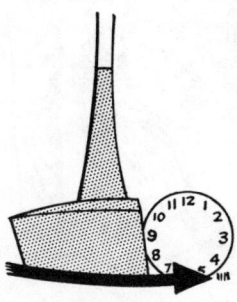

1—PROBLEM SHOTS

AVOID RAISING AND SWAYING: HERE'S HOW

Swaying and raising the body during the backswing will, of course, destroy any player's sense of balance.

As for me, I find that if I grip with my hands turned too far to my left (see #1), I feel as if I want to raise my body on the backswing.

By the same token, when my hands grip too far to my right, as in #2, I tend to sway laterally to the right on the backswing.

To counteract these tendencies, I imagine the clubface as simply being an extension of my right palm. In this way, both the right palm and the clubface are facing in the direction of the target. In this way I'm assured of a balanced swing.

A GOOD WAY TO ADD DISTANCE

Experienced golfers who feel they need extra distance off the tee should look closely at today's illustrations of Tony Lema's swing. These drawings clearly indicate the prime source of Tony's dramatic power – an extremely full shoulder turn on the backswing, coupled with a big hip turn on the downswing.

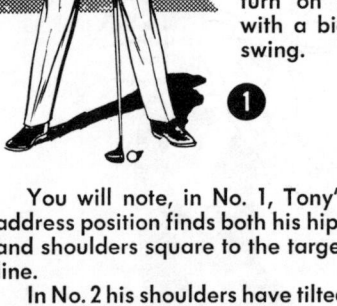

You will note, in No. 1, Tony's address position finds both his hips and shoulders square to the target line.

In No. 2 his shoulders have tilted and turned at least 90 degrees, yet his hips have turned only slightly.

In No. 3 the ball has been struck. Tony's hips have already turned much farther to his left than they did to his right during the entire backswing.

A full shoulder turn stretches your muscles on your backswing. A quick and full hip turn on the downswing stretches them even more. The result is a tremendous release of clubhead speed during impact.

'Cushion' Your Follow—Through

1. THINK THE FOLLOW-THROUGH ISN'T TOO IMPORTANT? HEAR THIS. IT IS MY FIRM BELIEF THAT A GOLFER WHO DOES NOT HAVE A FULL FOLLOW-THROUGH FIXED IN HIS MIND'S EYE BEFORE HE STARTS TO SWING WILL NEVER ACHIEVE THE CLUBHEAD SPEED HE IS CAPABLE OF BEFORE AND AT IMPACT. MUSCLES WHICH EXPECT A LIMITED OR JERKY FOLLOW-THROUGH SIMPLY WON'T RESPOND ON THE DOWNSWING.

2. WHAT HAPPENS IS THAT THE GOLFER UNCONSCIOUSLY SLOWS DOWN HIS SWING BEFORE IMPACT IF HE THINKS ABOUT A SHORTER FOLLOW-THROUGH. SINCE CLUBHEAD SPEED IS WHAT PRODUCES DISTANCE, YOU CAN SEE THE RESULT.
THE LEAST HARMFUL EFFECT WILL BE A SHORTER SHOT -- IT MIGHT ALSO TAKE OFF IN ANY WAYWARD DIRECTION.

3. BY A "CUSHIONED" FOLLOW - THROUGH, I MEAN ONE IN WHICH THE HANDS LITERALLY SINK TO A FINISH.
THE BEST FINISHES, AS THE ONE ILLUSTRATED, SEE THE RIGHT ARM STAY FAIRLY STRAIGHT RIGHT TO THE END. HOWEVER, THE LEFT ARM COLLAPSES ONCE THE HANDS GET ABOUT SHOULDER HIGH, AND CONTINUES TO DO SO UNTIL THE HANDS SWEEP OUT AND THEN UP TO A FINAL POSITION WELL ABOVE THE HEAD FOR A FULL DRIVE FOLLOW-THROUGH.

SHARP CLUBHEAD DESCENT NEEDED FROM BURIED LIE

To dislodge the ball from a depressed lie, your clubhead must be descending sharply as it comes into the ball (note solid line in illustration). If the clubhead is not descending sharply (dotted line), it may strike the turf behind the ball or catch only the top part of the ball.

You will achieve the upright swing if you retain more weight than normal on your left foot throughout your swing, especially during your backswing. The weight distribution to your left causes your clubhead to raise quickly on the backswing and descend sharply on the downswing.

1—PROBLEM SHOTS

"LOOPING" AND HOW TO CURE IT

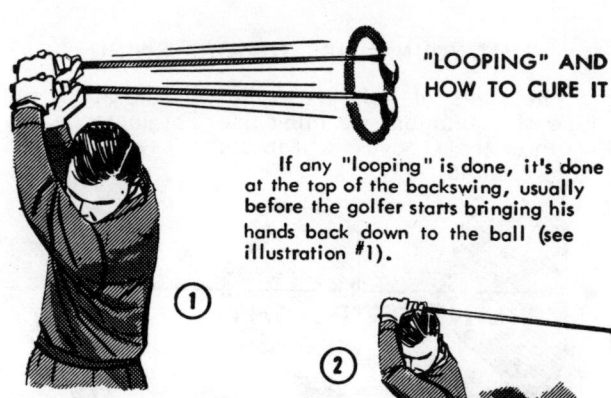

If any "looping" is done, it's done at the top of the backswing, usually before the golfer starts bringing his hands back down to the ball (see illustration #1).

The golfer who loops has failed to find a consistent way of reaching the top of his backswing and of starting back down. His hands wobble at that point, and there's no telling from which point he will begin his downswing. His swing naturally is different every time.

Keep your hands perfectly steady at the top, as shown in illustration #2. With such steadying, you'll be able to move the clubhead back to the ball in a better, more predictable pattern.

KEY DRIVING POINTERS

For best driving results, address the ball with the feet parallel to the target line, as I am doing in #1, and make sure the clubface moves into the ball along this target line. Address the ball with your left hip and shoulder turned a bit more to the right if you are slice-prone. Hook "experts" should turn the left hip and shoulder to the left.

But keep a square stance nevertheless.

Furthermore, position the ball opposite your left instep (see #2) and feel the clubhead sweep the ball off the tee as it continues toward the target well after impact.

HIT DOWN ON TEED IRON SHOTS

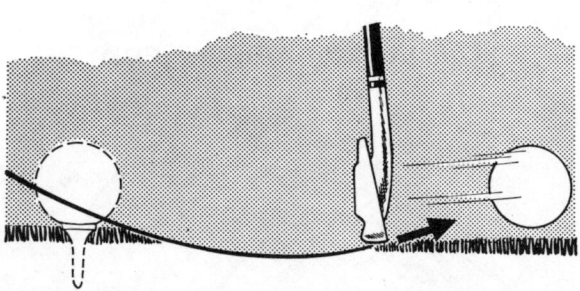

Most pros tee the ball when they play iron shots from the teeing area. Some amateur golfers seem to think it's "smart" to toss the ball onto the ground and hit the shot without a tee. This only decreases your odds of hitting a solid shot.

I think you will be much better off if you hit these teed iron shots just as you would if the ball were in the fairway. That is, hit down on the ball, contacting it first before you take your divot (see illustration). A firm downward blow into the ball will help you preserve the firm left side and firm left wrist you need for good control on these shots which emphasize direction rather than maximum distance.

HEADWIND REQUIRES SWING ADJUSTMENT

I'm swinging a 4-iron in both of the above illustrations, but illustration No. 2 shows the backswing I employ in a headwind.

When you must hit iron shots into the wind, you want the ball to fly low, where it will be less affected by the wind than if it flew high. You want the shot to be well-controlled because a headwind tends to increase any sidespin on the ball, thus accentuating a hook or a slice.

Achieve a low-flying shot by using a less-lofted club than normal. Also, less height is yours if you play the ball a bit farther back than normal in your stance. Since a less-lofted club, say a 4 iron, will fly farther than a more lofted club, say a 6 iron, you must shorten your swing slightly when using the less-lofted club.

23

1—PROBLEM SHOTS

"EXTEND" YOURSELF ON TEE SHOTS

The drive is the one shot in golf where the emphasis is on distance as opposed to accuracy (though the latter is certainly important). The drive is also the one shot in which you want to sweep the ball without striking the turf.

One way to achieve maximum distance while sweeping the ball away is to fully extend yourself, both on your backswing and your follow-through.

Note, in the illustrations, how my hands move as far as possible away from my body, both going back and swinging through. It is this extension that (1) helps me fully stretch the big muscles of my body and legs and (2) flattens out my clubhead arc in the hitting area so that it is traveling at "ball height" for a maximum distance before and after impact.

---

3 CAUSES OF TOPPED SHOTS

A common cause of topped shots is the tendency to bend too much from the knees at address (#1). You might think that bending your knees would lessen your chances of hitting the ball on top. But, unfortunately, the person who crouches at address has a tendency to straighten his knees during the swing. Naturally this raises the hands and the club so that it passes over the top of the ball.

The clubhead also raises and tops shots if your right elbow flies away from your side on the downswing (#2) or if your left elbow bends on the downswing (#3).

If you top shots try (1) "feeling tall" when addressing the ball,

(2) bringing your right elbow to the side on the downswing or (3) maintaining an extended left arm through impact.

Above all, let your club's loft provide height for the shot. Never feel that you must scoop the ball into the air. Sweep the ball with the woods and pinch it against the turf with a slightly downward blow on iron shots.

FIT YOUR CLUBS TO YOUR SWING

The rules of golf are quite specific about the type of equipment we must use. For instance, the width of the grooves in iron clubs may not exceed .035 of an inch.

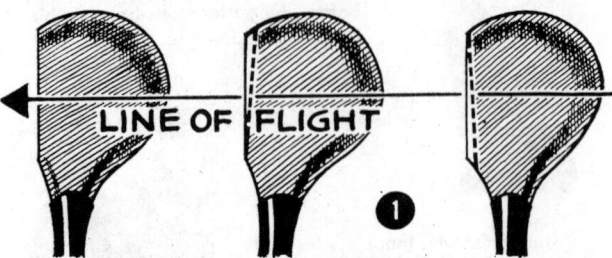

However, in one area of club-making, the rules do allow some leeway. The face of the clubhead may be turned in to a hook position or turned out to a slice position (see illustration #1). Golfers who consistently hook or slice should buy clubs that are turned either in or out a degree or so to counteract their problem.

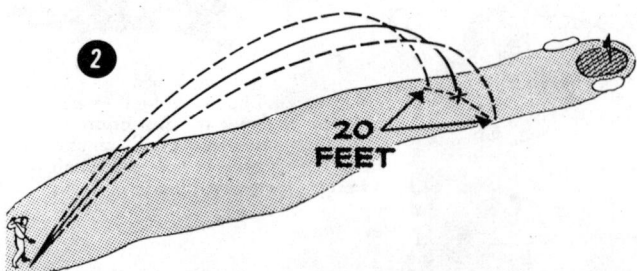

You will hardly notice a wooden clubface that is turned in or out one degree. However, this slight alteration in the club's direction of facing can account for a variation in direction of about 20 feet or more on a normal tee shot (see illustration #2).

HOW FAR TO HIT WITH EACH CLUB?

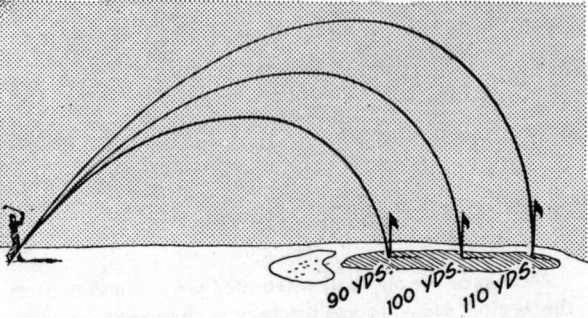

Before each tournament, the professionals mentally ascertain how far it is to the center of the green from various landmarks out in the fairway. They eliminate doubt about club selection by combining knowledge of their shotmaking ability with knowledge of the distance to various pin positions on the green.

Anyone who plays in tournaments -- even if they be merely club events -- will become a tougher foe if he follows the lead of the professionals and starts to pace off the distances his shots fly, as well as the distances from fairway to green-center.

1—PROBLEM SHOTS

DOWNHILL LIES CALL FOR SPECIAL TECHNIQUES

Here's how to defeat downhill lies:

1. Play the ball more toward the right foot.

2. Bend the "uphill" knee (see illustration #1) so hips are level.

3. Use a club with enough loft to get the ball airborne. Aim to left of target, to avoid the push or fade.

4. Let the path of the clubhead follow the ground's contour.

5. As you take backswing, keep the wrists straight for as long as possible.

6. Hit down on the ball without raising the body at impact (see illustration #3). You don't want to raise the clubhead arc, so keep down.

STRENGTHEN WRISTS AND FOREARMS

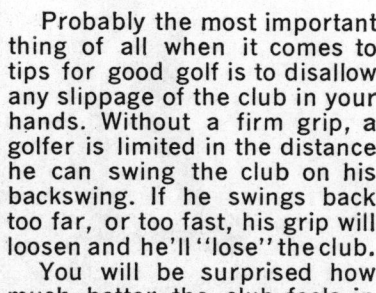

Probably the most important thing of all when it comes to tips for good golf is to disallow any slippage of the club in your hands. Without a firm grip, a golfer is limited in the distance he can swing the club on his backswing. If he swings back too far, or too fast, his grip will loosen and he'll "lose" the club.

You will be surprised how much better the club feels in your hands—how much more control you feel—after you have done some simple grip exercises over a period of 10 days to two weeks.

Merely clench and unclench your hands intermittently during the day, or in the evening while you watch TV. Having a golf club next to your easy chair, or in your office, will be especially helpful, since you can then do this exercise while actually assuming your normal grip.

GET HEIGHT WHEN SHOOTING TO ELEVATED GREEN

More height, when shooting to an elevated green, can be achieved simply by positioning the ball slightly farther forward than normal in your stance. Normally I play my 5-iron about in the middle of my stance (see illustration #1). On shots to elevated greens, I may move it forward almost to opposite my left heel (illustration #2).

Playing the ball farther forward -- while keeping the hands in their normal position -- causes the clubface to strike the ball later than normal in the swing. This means that the club will be carrying a bit more loft than normal at impact.

A SUCCESS 'SECRET'

All fine players swing the clubhead straight along the target line while the ball is being impacted on the clubface. Obviously, a shot won't fly toward the target if the clubhead isn't moving on line during impact.

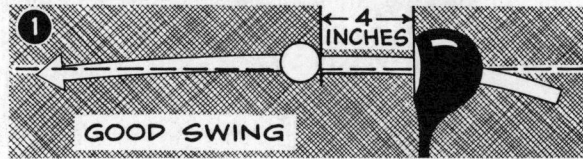

The golfer who can move his clubhead along the target line for the longest distance has the best chances of making square contact with the ball and producing a straight shot. A good swing will find the clubhead start-

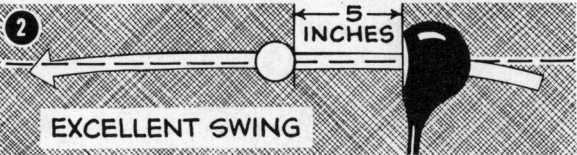

ing its move along the target line about 4 inches before the ball (#1) and continuing a similar distance beyond. Some excellent swings may move from 5 inches (#2) to as much as 10 inches along the target line, while poor swings may touch it only for an inch or two (#3).

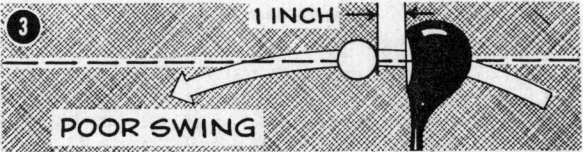

Visualize illustration #2 as you swing. Also remember to take the clubhead back from the ball on your backswing along the same path you wish it to duplicate in the hitting area.

1—PROBLEM SHOTS

DON'T LET THE HANDS WANDER

Too many golfers tend to let their hands wander on the shaft. An inexperienced player will often grip so that his right hand is too far "under" the shaft, as illustrated. He feels this gives him more power, but it only encourages using the right hand too early in the downswing and wasting power before impact.

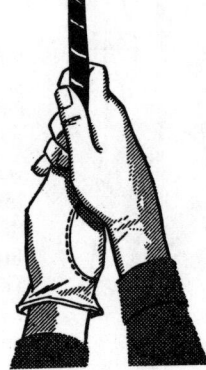

Check your grip often. Don't let that right hand slip over. The shaft should cross the left hand at the base of the fingers. After this hand is closed, place the right hand on the club so that the thumb is slightly to left of center, but still more on top than not. Keep the right thumb and forefinger close together, as shown here.

TWO IMPORTANT SWING CONCEPTS

Every serious golfer should understand the vital concepts of "clubhead path" and "swing plane." Illustration #1 shows the proper path of the clubhead in the hitting area. Note that it moves from "inside" the target line to along this line, and

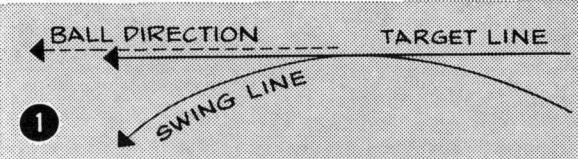

then it continues back inside. Never should it pass beyond the imaginary target line. If it does move outside, the clubhead must move across, rather than into, the ball during impact. An offline shot must result.

Illustration #2 shows how the plane of the swing—upright, normal, or flat—affects the level of the clubhead in the hitting area. If the swing is too upright, the clubhead is not at ball level long enough to assure consistently solid contact. If the plane is too shallow, the clubhead will be at ball level for a relatively long period. However, the golfer's swing will be so flat that the clubhead will not move along the target line long enough.

FIND THE STANCE WIDTH BEST FOR YOU

In general, the width of your stance on, say, a drive should normally be about the same as the distance between your shoulder blades. (See such positioning of the feet in the illustration of me at address in the lower drawing.)

However, some golfers, such as Doug Sanders (upper drawing), prefer a much wider stance.

Everybody has to find the stance width that is best for them. However, it might help you to know that a narrow stance generally allows a fuller wind-up of the hips and shoulders on the backswing. A wider stance usually produces a shorter backswing, but it also affords a wide base on which to balance yourself during the swing.

A GOOD THOUGHT FOR SUCCESSFUL SWINGS

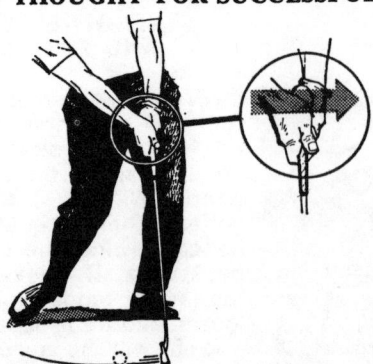

Most golfers fail to hit straight, solid shots because, for one reason or another, the back of the left hand is facing off to the right and up toward the sky, during impact.

Try to be certain that the back of this hand does face down the target line as you strike the ball. This should apply for all shots, from drives to putts.

As you address the ball and as you swing, simply think of backhanding the face of the club squarely into the back of the ball. This one thought will cause a great many other good things to occur automatically, before and during your swing.

1—PROBLEM SHOTS

MY BACKSWING IS TOO FAST

If there is one area of my swing that you should not emulate, it is my backswing. It works fine for me, but I simply take that club back too fast for most average golfers' swings.

A fast backswing destroys timing because you cannot sense the position of your hands or the feel of the clubhead. It also is prac-

tically impossible to stop an over-zealous backswing and then immediately begin the downswing without some loss of balance.

The purpose of the backswing is to put yourself into proper po-

sition for a good strong downswing. It also sets the rhythm for the swing. An abruptly fast backswing does not serve its purposes.

The next time your swing seems improper -- when your direction is bad and you seem to be hitting shots without much snap -- try slowing down your backswing. You will be surprised how readily your timing and balance return to normal.

PRESERVING YOUR POWER

In the swing of most golfers, clubhead speed has started to lessen by the time the ball is struck. Good players strive to preserve maximum clubhead speed until the clubface is on the ball. Only then does this speed decrease—as a result of the resistance of the ball itself.

The preservation of clubhead speed until impact occurs as a direct result of maintaining cocked wrists until late in the downswing (see illustration).

The wrists will remain cocked during the downswing only if the left side dominates. This side must pull the arms and, eventually, the clubhead into the ball. However, this pulling of the left side must occur with the head remaining behind the ball. There should be no lateral movement of the upper body to the left as the lower body pulls in that direction.

AVOID CARELESS CLUBHEAD PLACEMENT IN IRON SHOTS

I am always very careful to see that the leading edge of the club's sole -- not the top edge of the clubface -- is placed at a right angle to the intended line of flight (see illustrations).

Occasionally I'll even ask a fellow player to check my clubface alignment to see that it is actually looking down the target line. It's amazing how deceiving this alignment of the clubface can become. And even a slight misalignment of the face on a shot of, say, 200 yards can mean that it will fly many yards off-line.

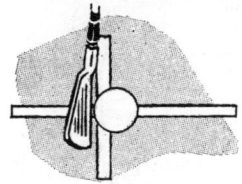

STRAIGHT LEFT ARM— MUST IT BE?

How important is it for golfers to swing with a straight left arm - one of the so-called basics of good golf? I say it's fine if you can, but not bad if you can't.

The golfer, as shown in No. 1, who can maintain a straight left arm at the top of his swing is fortunate. However if you cannot

do so without strain, forget it. Don't force yourself to keep it straight. This may lead to excessive grip pressure and tension and a hurried, jerky downswing.

It's much more important that you take the club away from the ball with a straight left arm (No. 2) to provide a wide swing arc, and that you straighten this arm when it's needed most - on the downswing and through the hitting area (No. 3).

27

1—PROBLEM SHOTS

ACHIEVE THE TIGHT ELBOW POSITION

Note in the illustrations how my right elbow barely leaves my right side.

Most golfers can achieve a tight right elbow position on their backswing by increasing the amount of their shoulder turn. The more the shoulder turn moves the hands back and up, the less the hands and arms will have to raise on their own to achieve a backswing of sufficient length and height.

Concentrate on making a full

shoulder turn and keeping your right elbow in fairly close to your side. You will find that this not only makes your swing more compact, but also provides you with a full coiling of muscles for greater distance on shots.

HOW TO EXECUTE THE INTENTIONAL SLICE

To slice to the right, you first pull back your left foot, as I am doing in the illustration. This gives you an "open" stance which causes the clubface to cut across the ball and apply a clockwise (slice) spin.

To accentuate an intentional slice, merely turn your hands to

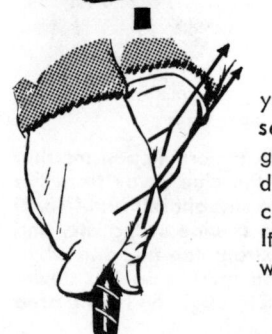

your left on the clubshaft (see inset illustration). This "weak" gripping position will make it difficult for you to return your clubface to a "square" position. It will be looking to the right when it reaches the ball.

CURE FOR PULLED SHOTS

The pulled shot differs from the push in that it flies to the left rather than to the right. It differs from the hook in that it flies on a straight line rather than in a bending curve. The pull occurs when the club, facing left, moves into the hitting area from outside the target line.

One major cause of the pulled shot is lazy footwork (#1). Here, the player has swung flatfooted and failed to transfer his weight to the left on the downswing. The resulting roundhouse swing sends the ball to the left.

For proper footwork, roll to the instep of your left foot on the backswing, lifting the heel slightly, as you see me doing in #2. Then immediately return the left heel to the ground and let the right foot roll gradually to its instep on the downswing (#3).

RIGHT HAND MUST ALSO HOLD FIRM

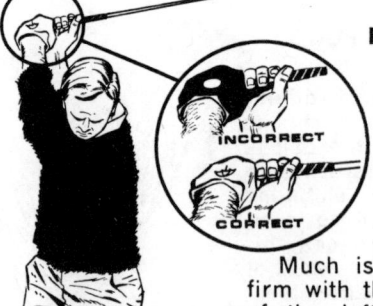

Much is said about holding firm with the last three fingers of the left hand... and deservedly so. These three fingers should control your grip on the club.

But you also must avoid right-hand slippage. If this grip loosens at the top of the backswing (see illustrations) you will tend to "hit from the top." Your hands will rush into the downswing. The usual result: a weak slapping of the ball.

Strangely, weakening the right-hand grip at the top is largely due to holding too firmly with this hand at address. Any squeezing with the right hand at address will tighten your right arm and shoulder. This tension inhibits a free backswing.

Relax your right hand at address and swing back slowly and smoothly to avoid right-hand slippage at the top.

1—PROBLEM SHOTS

HOW TO HIT SHOTS HIGH OR LOW

The position of the ball within your stance has a great deal to do with the amount of height your shot will assume. You will note, in illustration #1, how the clubface carries less loft when it strikes a ball that is played back in the stance, more loft when it meets a ball that is played farther forward.

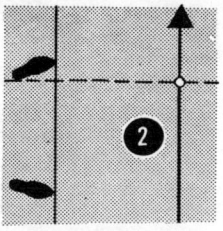

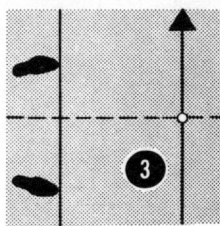

With this knowledge, it becomes fairly simple to hit shots intentionally low or high—under tree limbs or over.

If you normally play the ball opposite your left heel (illustration #2), you should play it back slightly (illustration #3) if you wish to hit low shots. If you wish to hit the ball higher, play it farther forward (illustration #4) so that you hit it on your upswing.

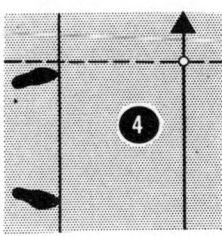

Practice these shots before trying them on the course. Sometimes an alteration in ball positioning will cause you to slice or hook until you become accustomed to the new position.

A 'HERO' SHOT FROM HARDPAN

You will win the lasting admiration of your golfing partners if you can successfully negotiate a shot from bare mud or some similar hard surface the next time the situation occurs.

On this shot you must contact the ball with your clubhead before the club reaches the lowest part of its arc. You want to hit the ball, then the ground. If the club strikes the ground first, it will bounce off the hardpan and top the ball.

To hit the ball first, make certain that it is played farther back than normal in your stance, but with your hands well forward. This positioning will reduce the effective loft of your club, so you will need to use a more-lofted club than normal to achieve much height on the shot.

HOW TO CHECK YOUR POSITION AT THE TOP

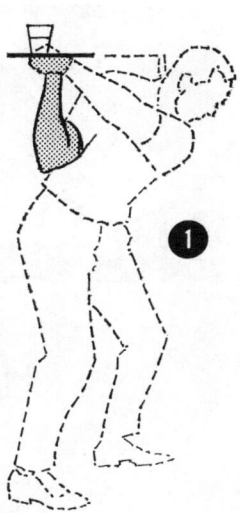

The golfer who can put himself into proper position at the top of his backswing need have little fear of badly missing a shot. The downswing is pretty much a mere reaction, a release of tension created during the backswing.

Here are two things to check about your hand position at the top. First, your right hand should be in the "tray" position, as if you were carrying a large platter of food (illustration #1). Second, the back of your left hand and the back of

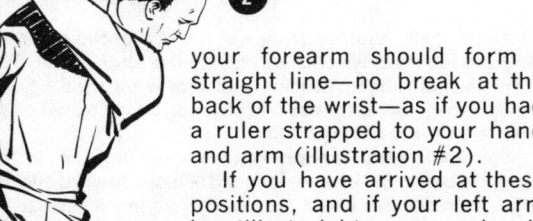

your forearm should form a straight line—no break at the back of the wrist—as if you had a ruler strapped to your hand and arm (illustration #2).

If you have arrived at these positions, and if your left arm is still straight, you need only lower your left heel and let 'er rip!

ACCURATE CLUBFACE ALIGNMENT - A MUST

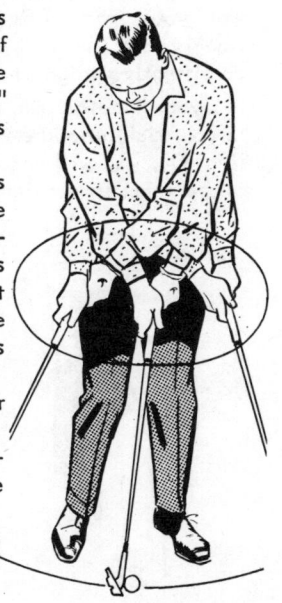

The longer the clubface looks at the target at the bottom of the downswing, the greater the chances are that it will be "square" to the target line when it impacts the ball.

Therefore, make sure the hands and arms do not roll over to the left and close the clubface before or during the time the ball is on the face. Even a very slight degree of improper clubface alignment will cause a great loss of direction on full shots.

Try to keep the back of your left hand looking at, and moving toward, the target (see illustrations), as it moves through the hitting area.

29

1—PROBLEM SHOTS

Stress Still Head On Tight Shots

The best advice I can give for playing shots from close or tight lies is to keep your head absolutely still throughout your swing. Focus your complete attention on the back of the ball and never let it waver.

Maintaining a steady head gives your swing an anchor. It's the best insurance that your clubface will meet the ball squarely despite the bad lie.

It is amazing how frequently a golfer will make exceptionally good contact on shots that appear to be difficult. The chief reason for the success of these shots is because the close lie forces players to pay strict attention to the ball.

LEARN WHAT TO EXPECT FROM YOUR CLUBS

Do you know how far you can hit a golf ball with each club in your bag?

If you have any doubt about this, and if you are serious about improving your game, then I suggest you start pacing off your normal shots. This way you will develop a valuable guide for judging distance.

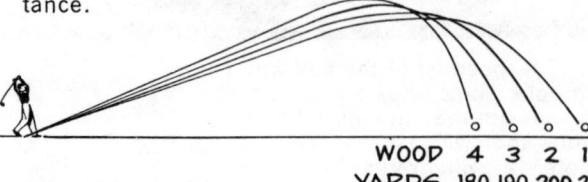

Actually this learning process is very simple. You will find that your distance varies about 10 yards per club (see sample chart illustrated here). Thus, if you learn that you hit a 5-iron 140 yards, you can assume quite easily that you will hit a 6-iron 130 yards.

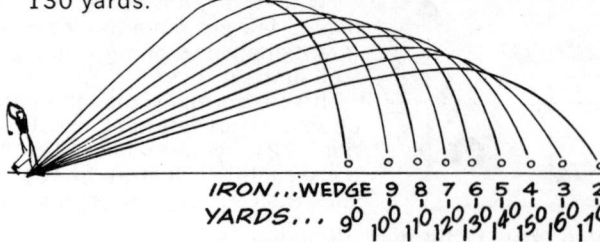

Judging distance on shots always calls for some margin of error. You have to allow a few yards on shots over hazards, for instance. But you can reduce this margin if you learn exactly what to expect from your clubs.

AVOID DEEP CUT FROM SOGGY TURF

Whereas most good golfers normally hit irons shots as shown in No. 1, taking a divot just after meeting the ball, they modify their swings to pick the ball cleanly when hitting from soggy — or even damp — turf.

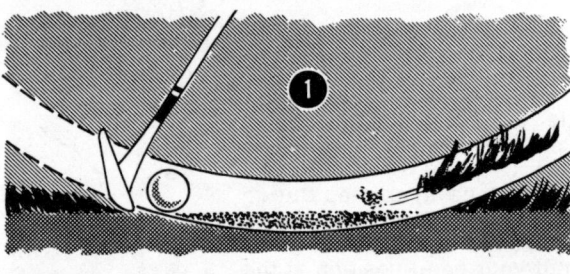

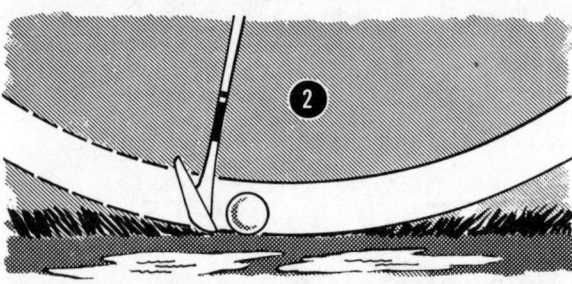

The danger in hitting from wet turf is that the clubhead may cut too deeply. This will cause the shot to fall short of its normal range. Also the ball that is pinched against wet turf will not compress as fully — and thus travel as far — as one that is pinched against a firm dry turf.

So pick the ball cleanly from the wet turf. To do this, play the ball a bit farther forward — more toward the target — than normal (as in No. 2). By playing it farther forward you will strike the ball at the bottom of your swing instead of slightly on the downstroke.

Above all, avoid cutting into the turf behind the ball.

PROPER GRIP AIDS ACCURACY

To encourage proper clubface alignment, grip the club so that the "V" formed by the thumb and forefinger of each hand points toward your right. This grip position is most likely to encourage consistently straight shots.

If your hands are turned too far to your right at address (illustration #1), you will unconsciously rotate them to the left on your

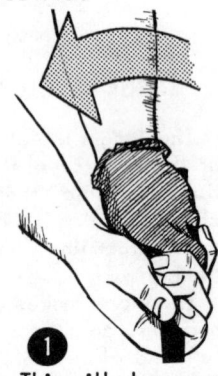

downswing. This will close your clubface so that your shots will tend to hook to the left.

If your hands are turned too far to your left at address (illustration #2), you will have trouble returning the clubface to its original position by the time it reaches the ball. You will leave it open -- facing to the right -- and sliced shots will normally result.

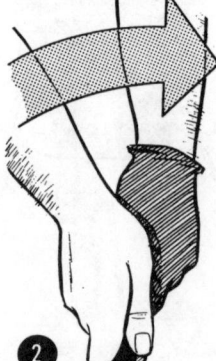

1—PROBLEM SHOTS

KEEP YOUR HEAD BACK

We are all familiar with the admonition to "keep your head down." Possibly, even better advice for most golfers would be "keep your head back."

To generate maximum clubhead speed into the ball—to achieve maximum distance—it is vital that your head remain behind the ball throughout your swing on drives. If your head slides forward with your downswing, you will rearrange the plane and arc of your swing in midstream. Loss of power will result.

Note, in the illustration, how my right side appears to be "bowed" inward as I hit the ball. This bowing effect shows that my head is still back, though my weight has shifted onto my left foot. Thus I'm hitting against a firm left side and using all the benefits I can derive from the centrifugal force of my swing.

Remember to keep your head back, but to let your weight shift forward onto your left foot.

QUICK WEIGHT SHIFT BUILDS POWER

The golfer who has active legs is likely to be a long-ball hitter.

At the top of the backswing, the good golfer shifts about 20 per cent of his weight onto his right instep. This means that at the top he carries about 70 per cent of his total weight on his right foot (illustration #1).

Then comes a quick return of this weight to the left foot (illustration #2). It all takes

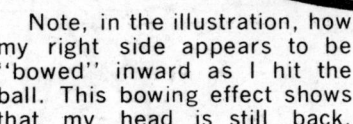

70% OF WEIGHT   30% OF WEIGHT

WEIGHT SHIFTS

place at the very start of the downswing — the quicker, the better— as the left heel lowers and the left hip begins sliding to the left.

By shifting his weight quickly, the golfer causes a further stretching of the muscles that lie between his lowered left heel and his still-raised hands. All this stretching is later released as power when his clubhead enters the hitting area.

BUILD A FIRM LEFT SIDE

There is nothing relaxed about the golf swing when it reaches impact. The lower part of your body is driving forward while the upper body stays back of the ball. The left arm has become practically rigid and the left leg is almost straight.

All this is part of hitting against a firm left side.

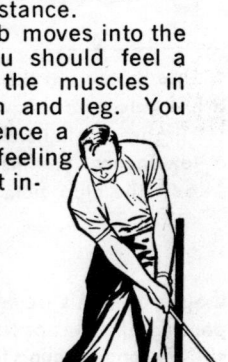

The left side must not collapse or else the shot will go awry and you will lose distance.

As your club moves into the downswing, you should feel a tightening of the muscles in your left arm and leg. You should experience a "pushing off" feeling from your right in-

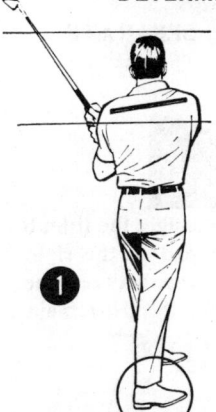

step. As your right shoulder and hip raise, your left leg will straighten.

Look carefully at the illustrations and try to build within yourself the feeling of driving forward with your lower body and holding back with your head. Then work on building a feeling of controlled tension during your downswing.

LOOK AT YOUR FINISH TO DETERMINE EARLIER MISTAKES

If your finish resembles the golfer in illustration No. 1, you probably slice a great many shots to the right, but occasionally pull one to the left.

The fact that the right foot is on the ground points up a lack of weight shift to the left on the downswing. The lack of shoulder tilt—failure to lower the right shoulder on the downswing—indicates an outside-to-

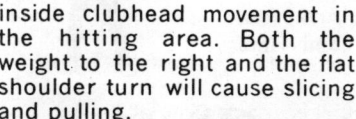

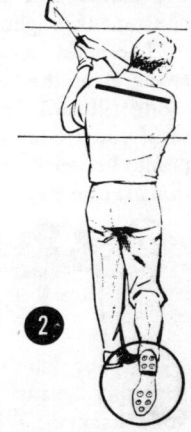

inside clubhead movement in the hitting area. Both the weight to the right and the flat shoulder turn will cause slicing and pulling.

Such golfers must shift more weight onto their left side at the start of their downswing, and they must lower their right shoulder as the club comes down. Both of these corrections will help move the clubhead straight through the ball, and thus produce straighter shots.

31

1—PROBLEM SHOTS

'DELAYED HIT' MIGHT WORK FOR YOU

Much of the fantastic power of Gary Player stems from the tremendous "delayed hit" he obtains. Check the illustrations, which were sketched from movies of Gary's swing. His left arm and clubshaft form a right angle -- 90 degrees -- at the top of his backswing. In illustration #2, Gary's hands have moved down until they are almost directly over the ball, yet his wrists are still fully cocked in the 90-degree pattern.

Thus he obtains the benefits of a full release of his wrists in the hitting area. His hands move only a few inches, yet his wrists unleash the club from 90 to 180

degrees. This tremendous outpouring of power at the very last split second accounts for his great distance. Only a player with very strong wrists could delay their unhinging so long and still square the clubface to the ball in time to hit a straight shot.

STRETCH INTO A HIGH-FINISH POSITION

A high hand position on the backswing indicates that the golfer has fully stretched, or coiled, his muscles. It stands to reason that the more fully you stretch your muscles going back, the more power you will generate on your downswing.

A high finish indicates that the golfer has properly lowered his right shoulder on his downswing and thus achieved a "delayed" unhinging of his wrists. It is this delayed hit that produces a full release of maximum clubhead speed in the hitting area.

SWING SLOWER IF HANDS SEPARATE

Study illustration #1 and note how snugly the thumb of the left hand fits against the meaty pad of the right thumb. This is the main point of contact between the two hands. For consistent shotmaking, it must remain constant throughout your swing.

The main danger point in the swing is at the top of your backswing (illustration #2). Check to see if you are holding your contact point between the hands intact (illustration #3).

If your hands are separating at this juncture, it's probably because you are swinging too fast. Slow down your backswing until you can "set" your hands into position at the top without their tending to move apart.

MINIMIZE BACKSWING ON SHORT SHOTS

A common error that novice golfers seem to make is that they take a too-long backswing on short shots. They take it way back as they would on a long shot (illustration #1) and then they sort of drop it into the ball. This produces a sloppiness of the arms and wrists that usually results in scuffed shots.

On all shots, especially short approaches and putts, the clubhead must accelerate into the ball. This acceleration is best

achieved with a short backswing (illustration #2). Keep it short and then let your clubhead speed up naturally as you enter the hitting area (illustration #3).

A short backswing and an accelerating downswing will give you the firmness of arm and wrist that you need to make square club-ball contact.

32

1—PROBLEM SHOTS

KEEP YOUR CLUBHEAD "INSIDE" THE TARGET LINE

We frequently hear and read golf instruction that refers to the clubhead's movement "inside" or "outside."

Lest this all be confusing to the reader, let me explain that "inside" refers to the area on the golfer's side of the target line (see shaded area in the drawing). "Outside" is that area on the opposite side of this line.

The best golf swing is one that never allows the clubhead to move "outside." If the clubhead should move "outside," a sliced shot to the right, or a pulled shot to the left, is likely to result.

Your clubhead will be most likely to remain "inside" if you shift your weight properly—to the right going back, to the left coming down—and tilt and turn shoulders correctly as you swing.

HIGH HANDS – LOW SCORES

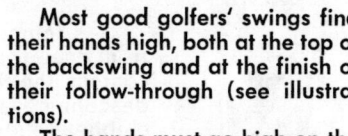
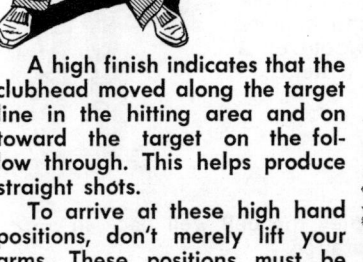

Most good golfers' swings find their hands high, both at the top of the backswing and at the finish of their follow-through (see illustrations).

The hands must go high on the backswing to help assure a full stretching of your muscles and the maximum power that such stretching produces.

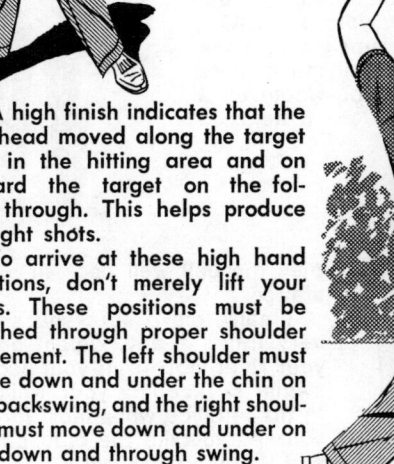

A high finish indicates that the clubhead moved along the target line in the hitting area and on toward the target on the follow through. This helps produce straight shots.

To arrive at these high hand positions, don't merely lift your arms. These positions must be reached through proper shoulder movement. The left shoulder must move down and under the chin on the backswing, and the right shoulder must move down and under on the down and through swing.

'THINKING MAN'S' SHOTS

Ingenuity and imagination play a big part in golf and the player who can improvise successfully will be a step ahead of the field. Today we have illustrated three ways to turn impossible situations into potential pars. These are shots, suggested by my friend, trick shot artist Paul Hahn, that any golfer can play.

In No. 1 we see how a golfer can dislodge his ball from a narrow rut

or washout by striking it with the toe end of his putter.

Illustration No. 2 shows one way to play a shot when an obstacle prevents a normal backswing. Just chop down on the ball and drive it back between your legs.

Illustration No. 3 shows another way to negotiate an obstacle. Strike the ball away from the hole, toward the obstacle, and then watch it rebound back onto the green.

LOWERING HEEL AIDS WEIGHT SHIFT

The golfer who falls back on his right foot (No. 1) can never be a successful golfer. It's as simple as that.

To encourage shifting of weight to the left, I suggest you make sure that the first move of your

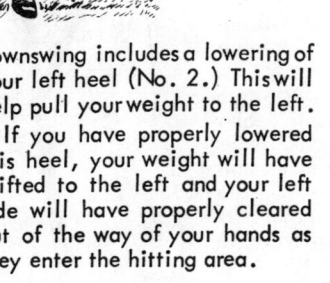

downswing includes a lowering of your left heel (No. 2.) This will help pull your weight to the left.

If you have properly lowered this heel, your weight will have shifted to the left and your left side will have properly cleared out of the way of your hands as they enter the hitting area.

1—PROBLEM SHOTS

MAKE UPRIGHT SWING ON SHOTS FROM ROUGH

It is important that on shots from deep rough your clubhead contact the ball on a sharply descending path. Should the clubhead slide into the ball from the side, it will encounter too much grass and this will slow its progress immensely.

To make the clubhead descend sharply, your backswing must also be upright. Lift the club from the ball much more abruptly than you would on a normal shot. Also, it helps to

play the ball well back in your stance.

Finally, make sure you shift very little, if any, weight onto your right foot during your backswing. By keeping your weight to the left, you will almost force yourself to take the club back and up on a steep path.

TAKE YOUR HANDS OUT OF YOUR TAKEAWAY

The "takeaway" portion of your backswing—the first several inches of clubhead movement—should originate in your shoulders. There should be absolutely no feeling that your hands are taking the club back independently of your shoulders.

Taking it back with the hands alone is liable to cause an abrupt lifting or turning of the club. This ruins your rhythm and clubface alignment.

To assure a shoulder-dominated takeaway, first imagine that your arms and a line across your shoulders form a triangle as you address the ball (solid lines in the illustration). Note that the club forms an extension of the left arm.

On your takeaway, make certain you preserve the triangle and the extension of the club from the left arm (dashed lines). You cannot maintain the triangle if you allow your hands alone to initiate the takeaway.

DON'T OVERDO HAND ACTION

When your swing is well-timed, there is certainly a feeling that the hands are pouring into the ball. However, this feeling must come as the result of a good swing. It can't be con-

sciously directed. If you make a direct attempt to hit with your hands, your right side will take over and bad shots will result.

I suggest you stress a full and rhythmical turn with your shoulders (see illustrations). Think "shoulder action," not "hand action." If your shoulder turn is correct, you will achieve "hand action" as an automatic result.

PLAY SHORT OF FLAGSTICK WHEN GREEN IS SOAKED

Normally, when the greens are wet, almost any type of well-struck shot will settle down relatively fast. You can plan to carry your shots all the way to the hole with little fear of bouncing far past.

However, this is not always the case when the greens really are soaked to the point where they are starting to puddle.

When this situation occurs, it is best to play your approach shots to land short of the hole just as you would under normal dry conditions. The reason for this is because water, at rest on the green, does not allow the ball to bite into the turf. Instead the ball "skips," just like a flat stone skips across a body of water.

Remember to hit for the flagstick when the greens are merely wet, but to allow for at least one big bounce when they are soaked.

1—PROBLEM SHOTS

PLAY FULL SHOTS OPPOSITE LEFT HEEL

Unless you are intentionally attempting to hit a low shot, I advise that you not play your drives any farther back in your stance than your left heel.

Many novice players position the ball opposite stance-center on these shots (illustration #1).

This puts their hands so far forward of the clubhead, that they cannot return it to a square

position in the hitting area. They leave the face "open" (illustration #2) and hit sliced shots to the right.

If you play these shots off your left heel (illustration #3), you will allow yourself more time to square the clubface. Straighter shots with a higher trajectory will result.

IF YOU SLICE, CHECK YOUR ADDRESS POSITION

Most beginners tend to hit the ball to the right of target. Their automatic reaction is to align themselves more to the left. As a result, shots are sliced to the right or pulled to the left.

Illustration #1 shows a typical slice position. Notice that the clubshaft goes under the right arm and over the left. This indicates that the player's upper body is aligned to the left. Invariably the clubhead will swing from outside to inside the target line during impact. This produces shots that are weak, cut to the right or pulled to the left.

When properly aligned, your clubshaft should pass over the right arm and under the left (illustration #2). From this address position you may feel that you are aimed to the right. However you will swing your clubhead squarely into the back of the ball and it will fly long and straight.

YOU CAN SLICE WITH A 'HOOK' GRIP

Most people who hold the club like player in Illustration 1A will tend to hook the ball. If they assume this grip and move into the normal impact position—with the back of the left hand facing down the target line—they will strike the ball with a closed clubface.

Sometimes, however, they will employ this hook grip but move into the ball with the butt of the left hand leading (Illustration 1B). This obviously will cause the ball to be struck with an open clubface. The result will be a slice.

I suggest you pattern your grip more along the lines shown in Illustration 2B—with the back of the left hand looking at the target. Then, if you return to this proper impact position as you strike the ball, you will hit your shots more or less straight.

GET THE MOST FROM YOUR EQUIPMENT

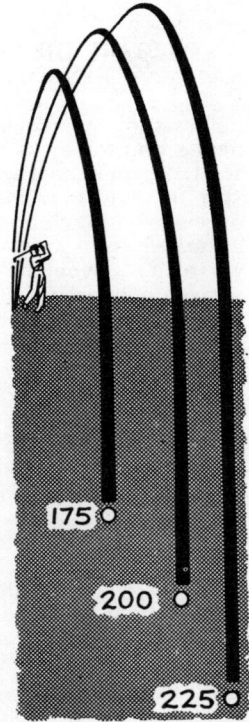

Many, many years of research have gone into the design of the modern golf club. Today's driver, for instance, is truly a precision instrument, designed to make it easier to play well. You should take advantage of this by selecting clubs that properly fit your physique and golf swing.

The illustrated chart is designed to show the type of driver you should be using. Check the distance of carry that applies to your tee shot and then note the type of clubshaft and amount of swingweight that would best suit your game.

Club manufacturers can, and will, supply you with clubs that cover a wide range of specifications. If you are in doubt about the type of clubs you need, I suggest you contact a professional golfer in your area and let him "fit" you for your next set. Properly fitted clubs can take several strokes off your scores. I know of no faster way to improve your game.

IF YOUR DRIVER CARRIES:	175 YDS.	200 YDS.	225 YDS.
DRIVER SHAFT	FLEXIBLE	REGULAR	STIFF
SWING-WEIGHT	C-6 TO C-7	C-8 TO D-2	D-0 TO D-5

1—PROBLEM SHOTS

TWO PRINCIPLES FOR GOOD GRIPPING

I hate to get specific about the grip because no two golfers have hands and fingers of the same size, shape and strength. However, I would like to point out two general principles that I feel are important for consistent golf. Illustration #1 shows these two principles, while illustration #2 points up how the grip looks when these fundamentals are ignored.

First, the hands should be as close together as possible on the clubshaft. Close unification of the hands helps keep the clubface looking at the target for a longer time in the hitting area.

Second, the hands should be more or less parallel on the club. Ideally for most golfers, the palm of the right hand should face the target, and the back of the left hand should face just slightly right of target. This hand positioning will promote a clubface position at impact that looks in the direction you intend the ball should fly.

BALL PLACEMENT IN RELATION TO STANCE

There are two schools of thought about ball placement in relation to the feet on various shots. One school (illustration #1) holds that all shots should be played opposite the left heel and that the right foot should move left -- narrowing the stance as the club's loft increases.

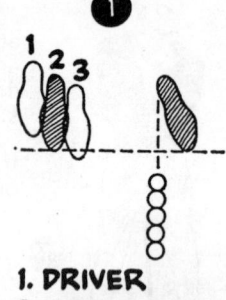

1. DRIVER
2. MIDDLE IRONS
3. SHORT IRONS

The second school holds that the ball should be played progressively farther back in the stance, as the club's loft increases (illustration #2).

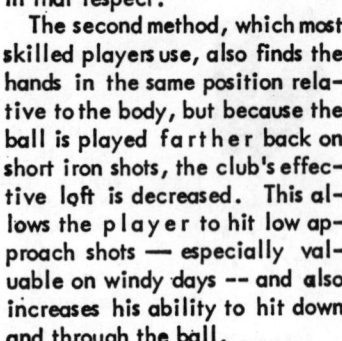

In the first method, you have the hands above the ball on all shots so that each swing is similar in that respect.

The second method, which most skilled players use, also finds the hands in the same position relative to the body, but because the ball is played farther back on short iron shots, the club's effective loft is decreased. This allows the player to hit low approach shots — especially valuable on windy days -- and also increases his ability to hit down and through the ball.

START THE CLUB BACK "SQUARE"

There should be absolutely no twisting or rolling of the hands and forearms during the start of your backswing. This sort of hand movement opens or closes the clubface unnecessarily. The golfer must reverse the movement to the exact same degree on the downswing if he is to meet the ball squarely.

During your backswing your clubface position should remain "square." To achieve a square clubface, be sure to take the club back with all parts of your body—arms, shoulders, legs—moving together as a unit.

If you do take the club back in such a "one-piece" motion, your clubface will be looking straight out (see illustration) when your hands are hip high. This is a "square" position, one that will set you off on the road to a straight shot. If the clubface looks skyward, you will slice unless you compensate on your downswing. If the clubface looks downward, you will probably hook the shot.

GOOD TIMING INCREASES DISTANCE

The swings of most professional golfers seems almost effortless, yet the ball flies so far. How can top golfers achieve so much distance with so little apparent effort? The answer is in their excellent timing.

If the swing is timed properly, the big muscles of the legs and back come into maximum play. The arms and wrists are used primarily to guide and transmit — but not originate — power.

The illustration shows me starting my downswing. The numbers indicate the order of movement that occurs when my timing is good. First the left heel lowers, then the shoulders turn, the hands start down, and finally the clubhead moves. This sequence brings my leg and back muscles into action. They are largely bypassed—wasted—if I start down first with my hands.

36

1—PROBLEM SHOTS

INCREASE CONSISTENCY THE MUSICAL WAY

If I had one wish in my golfing life, it probably would be to swing at every shot with the same smooth rhythm.

One way to help build consistent swing rhythm is to actually hum a tune as you swing. You don't have to hum aloud, but merely "think" a tune.

And make it even-tempoed and suitable to your swing.

Hum the same tune on all shots -- from putts to drives. You will be amazed how this simple practice improves rhythm, especially on those long-iron swings which occasionally get a bit jerky.

'LOW, DOWN' GOLFING ADVICE

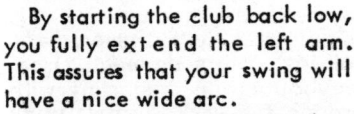

By starting the club back low, you fully extend the left arm. This assures that your swing will have a nice wide arc.

Also, the low takeaway delays the unhinging of the wrists until later in the backswing. This encourages a later unhinging in the downswing so that power is saved until impact.

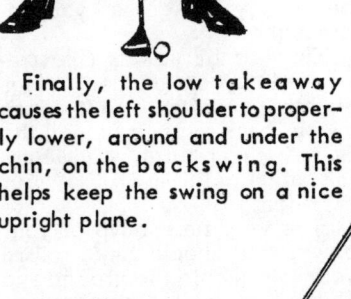

Finally, the low takeaway causes the left shoulder to properly lower, around and under the chin, on the backswing. This helps keep the swing on a nice upright plane.

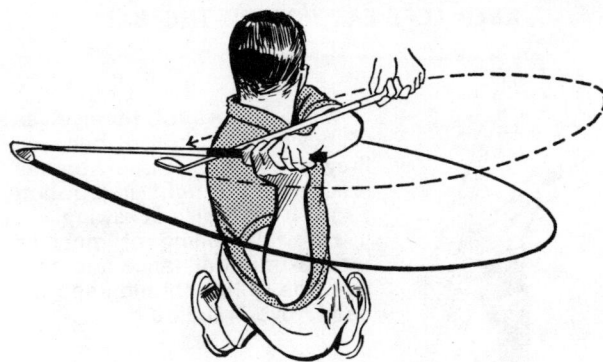

BE SURE TO "FINISH" YOUR BACKSWING

Too many golfers fail to "finish" their backswings. By this, I mean that they start down with their hands before they have made a full turn going back. The normal result is a sliced shot, or an occasional pull to the left.

The illustration shows what I mean. The dashed line shows the downswing path on a swing in which the backswing was not completed. Because the hands have started down too soon, they have thrown the clubhead outside, or beyond, the proper path. The clubhead moves into the ball from the outside, usually applying a slice spin.

The solid line shows the downswing that results from the fuller, more complete, backswing. The longer swing gives the lower body time to lead the downswing. The hands follow and automatically move into the ball from well inside the target line. During impact the clubhead is moving towards the target, instead of from outside-to-inside. Straighter, longer shots naturally result.

"HEAD UP" FOR LONGER DRIVES

Many golfers automatically reduce the length of their shots because they hunch over the ball (illustration #1). With their head down and back bent in this manner, they cannot make a full shoulder turn and completely coil during the backswing.

Address the ball with your back relatively straight but bent from the waist (illustration #2). This will put your head "up," enabling your left shoulder to pass beneath your chin during your backswing (illustration #3). The fuller shoulder turn will add to the length of your shots.

37

1—PROBLEM SHOTS

KEEP LEFT EAR "OVER" THE BALL

Many golfers rob themselves of power and control because they sway their upper bodies laterally to the right (illustration #1) during their backswing. For full coiling of muscles for maximum distance and control, the golfer should keep his head "over" the ball.

Actually, I like to think that my left ear is over the ball throughout my swing. This not only helps assure that I won't sway, but it also keeps my upper body properly "behind" the ball during my downswing.

MAINTAIN A LEFT SIDE LEAD

The phrase "left side lead" means that on the downswing, the left side should leave everything else. With a firm left side, you can increase clubhead speed and distance.

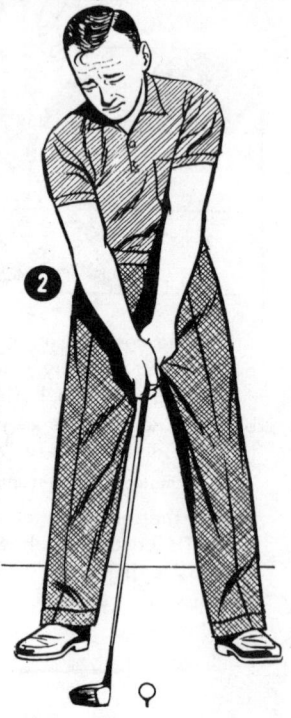

Fortunately, good golfers shift their weight quickly to the left side, thus producing this "left side lead."

Don't move ahead of the ball on the downswing, as the player in #1 is doing. This weakens the left side and cuts down on consistent accuracy. Instead address the ball on all shots, except with short irons, with your head behind the ball (as I am doing in #2) and keep it behind throughout the downswing.

LADIES, STAND TALL AT ADDRESS

The woman who addresses a golf ball with a posture as shown in illustration #1 can't help but cramp her swing. Tucking herself forward causes her hands and arms to come in too close to her body. She won't swing the clubhead back but, rather will lift it abruptly, relying too heavily on her hands and arms to engineer her swing.

I advise women especially to "stand tall" at golf, with the "derriere" extended, as in illustration #2. Keep your hands high at address. Feel your weight running back towards your heels. In this position, you women will be ready to swing smooth and fast. Your swing will not only become more effective, but also will look more graceful.

SWING THE CLUB WITH YOUR FEET

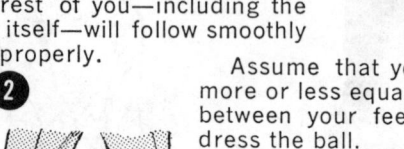

Obviously I do not intend that you take the headline on this column literally. However, many golf instructors do teach "from the bottom up," starting with proper footwork. I can't think of a better place to begin talking about the golf swing.

Two keys in the golf swing are proper weight transfer and proper balance. Both depend directly on proper footwork. If your feet and lower body move the right way at the right time, the rest of you—including the club itself—will follow smoothly and properly.

Assume that your weight is more or less equally distributed between your feet as you address the ball.

On your backswing (illustration #1), your left heel raises slightly and your left knee swings back to point behind the ball. As this occurs, your weight is shifting to the INSIDE of your right foot.

The very first move of your downswing should be to return your left heel to the ground and shift your weight back to your left (illustration #2). At the finish of your swing, most weight will be on your left foot.

1—PROBLEM SHOTS

TOE OUT RIGHT FOOT TO LENGTHEN BACKSWING

I've never felt any great compunction to extend the length of my backswing. Actually, I don't think any golfer should swing back so far that the club moves beyond horizontal at the top of the swing.

However, there are some golfers who would do better if they could move their hands a bit higher on their backswing. Freeing up their backswing turn would allow them to generate better club control and power as they start back down.

Toeing out slightly with the right foot will enable you to make a freer backswing turn. Try it if you feel your swing is too short.

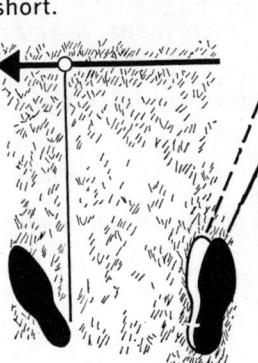

However, remember that you should feel some tension in your back and left arm at the top of the swing. If you don't, you haven't completed your backswing, and you will not derive all of the distance you are capable of generating.

FOR THOSE EXTRA YARDS OF DISTANCE

Rarely do I strive for extra distance to the point that I swing with maximum effort. You should strive to "swing within yourself."

However, on rare occasions, you may need to "let out shaft." Your opponent may be closing you out and you need a sure birdie. Or, for psychological reasons, you may want to hit it past him off the tee after he's made an especially long drive.

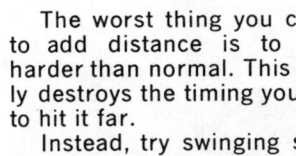

The worst thing you can do to add distance is to swing harder than normal. This merely destroys the timing you need to hit it far.

Instead, try swinging slower than normal while making a fuller shoulder turn. The bigger turn will add the power, and the slower backswing will keep you in balance and control.

Those who feel they want to add distance to their average drives can do so by practicing the slower, fuller swing, while always avoiding any lateral swaying of the upper body.

ARE YOU SWINGING "OVER THE BALL"?

Swinging "over the ball" is a common fault among all classes of golfers. Even some professionals fall into this trap on occasion.

The tendency to swing the right shoulder **around** (illustration #1), instead of **down** and around (illustration #2), on the downswing brings it more or less "over the ball." The fault brings on sliced shots, pulled shots, heeled shots — even shanks — as the clubhead is thrown out beyond the target line.

If your hands are not higher than your head at the finish of your swing, you probably are swinging "over the ball."

To correct the fault, avoid too much twisting of the hips on your downswing (illustration #1) and, instead, let them slide to the left as your right shoulder lowers.

LOOK BACK AT HANDS WHEN ADDRESSING BALL

Too many golfers "reach" for the ball at the address position. Their hands on full shots are either below their eyes or even farther out from their bodies (illustration #1).

I like to feel that I can "look back" at my hands when I address the ball. This means that the hands must be hanging fairly close to my body (illustration #2).

With your hands close to your body—about 3 or 4 inches away

on full shots—your torso will extend out toward the ball. You will be bent from the waist with your back fairly straight. Bending in this way encourages a nice full tilt of the shoulders (illustration #3) and minimizes the hip turn. A full coiling of back and shoulder muscles will result.

39

1—PROBLEM SHOTS

SAND WEDGE BEST FOR SHALLOW CUTS

Golf clubs are designed for specific purposes. The pitching wedge is ideal for playing out of deep rough; the sand wedge is best out of sand.

In the illustrations, we see the differences between a regular 9-iron (illustration #1), a pitching wedge (illustration #2), and a sand wedge (illustration #3).

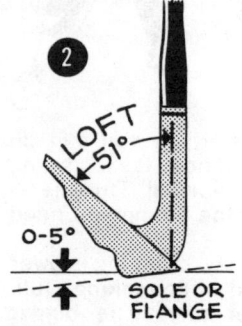

Note that the loft increases as you move from 9-iron to pitching wedge to sand wedge. Also the over-all weight of the clubhead increases.

But the most subtle—and important — change is in the amount of the club's sole that hangs below horizontal. Note

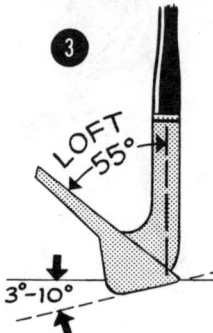

that, in the 9-iron, the sole line is about 2 degrees above horizontal. In the pitching wedge, this line is 0-5 degrees below horizontal; 3-10 degrees below in the sand wedge.

The farther the sole line runs below horizontal, the more shallow will be the cut of turf or sand that the club will take.

BEWARE OF DOWNWIND SHOTS

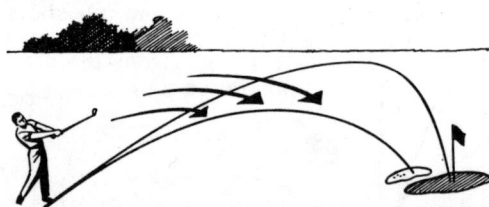

If you are hitting into a headwind, select a 3-iron instead of the normal 5-iron . . . a difference of two clubs. The shot should carry just the right distance.

Playing in the opposite direction (with the wind) calls for a different procedure. Let's say you select a 7-iron instead of the 5-iron . . . again applying a two-club difference.

This approach shot, however, falls well short of the target; perhaps in a sand trap. Somehow you miscalculated—But how?

You failed to realize that while a tailwind does push the ball forward, it also tends to "flatten" its trajectory. It "knocks down" the ball. Bear this in mind the next time you have a downwind approach shot. This is especially true in the 7-, 8-, 9-iron range where you would expect a high trajectory. Consider using more club than you would with the wind at your back.

YOUR CLUBS DETERMINE YOUR SWING

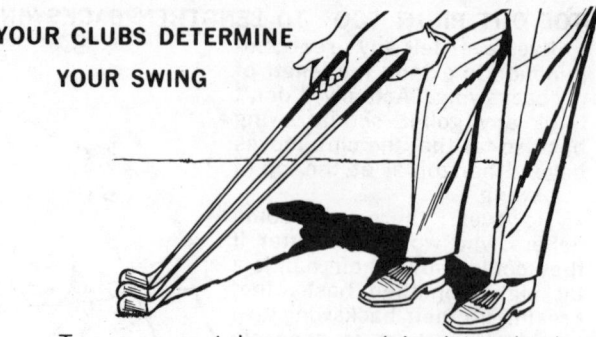

To a very great degree your clubs determine how you swing. For example, let's say a golfer has his driver toed-in a couple of degrees so that it faces to the left of his intended line. He may unconsciously compensate by opening the face during his swing.

A club that has an extremely flat lie may force a player to stand too far from the ball.

The illustration shows three irons varying in length and lie. Obviously, a golfer who carried all three irons in the same set would find it necessary to modify his address positioning three different ways.

The point is simply this:

If you are having trouble with a certain club, it may be that this club isn't properly fitted to your swing. It probably doesn't match the other clubs in your set. If you have any doubts about your clubs, be sure to let a qualified professional check them. It's possible that you can "buy" a better golf game.

'HIT DOWN' FOR HEIGHT

It does seem a contradiction in terms to say you must "hit down" when you want the ball to "get up," but that's exactly what must be done.

Notice what happens when you try to lift or scoop the ball up (#1). Such action won't cause the scored club-

face markings to rub against the dimpled surface of the ball. Result? Little backspin, a forward movement, but not much rise or height.

With a down-and-through blow, however (see #2), there's a greater amount of club-ball friction, hence more backspin, height and accuracy.

40

1—PROBLEM SHOTS

YOUR CLUB SHOULD LIE FLAT

Golfers who constantly fight a hook or a slice with certain clubs in their set should check those clubs to see that they are properly fitted as to "lie." The "lie" of a club is determined by the angle formed by the clubshaft and the clubhead. A club's lie will be either normal, upright or flat.

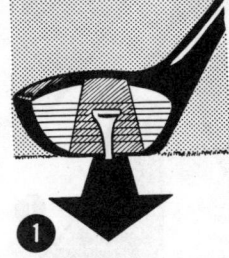

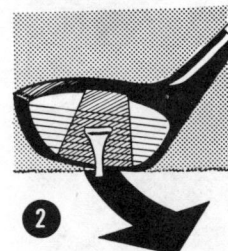

If the club's lie is normal for you, the sole of the club should rest flat on the ground when you address the ball. This is ideal for straight shots (illustration #1).

If the club rests on its heel, the lie is too upright (illustration #2). The heel will dig into the ground during your swing, and your shots will take off to the left from a closed clubface.

If the club rests on its toe (illustration #3), the lie is too flat for you. The toe will dig in, open the clubface and force your shots off to the right.

Have a friend or, better yet, your professional check the lie of your clubs as you address the ball.

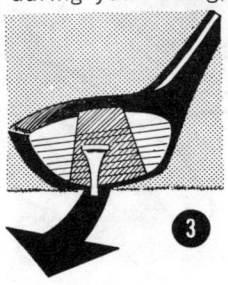

TRY A 5-WOOD

If you have trouble executing 2-iron shots properly, especially if you tend to hit your shots low, try discarding the long iron in favor of a 5-wood.

To be sure, there are advantages that the 2-iron has over the 5-wood. It is easier for a good player to control a 2-iron. The long iron is best in wind because you can keep the ball low. However, the 2-iron does not require a swing that is in near-perfect rhythm and one that will guaran-

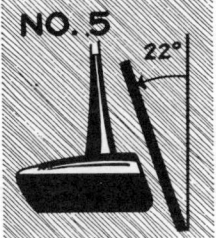

tee solid club-ball contact.

The 5-wood has slightly more loft than the 2-iron (#1). This helps you get the shot into the air and offers a larger hitting area and less trouble if the ball is not struck exactly flush.

Play the 5-wood just as you would a 2-iron—ball opposite your left heel (#2)—but sweep the ball from the grass. Don't try to pinch it with a downward blow. Swing smoothly with no back-and-forth head movement.

FLAT SWING PRIME CAUSE OF SHANKING

If you ever fall into a serious case of shanking—striking iron shots on the neck, or hosel, of the club—first check your backswing. Chances are it is too "flat." You are probably taking the clubhead back too abruptly "inside" the target line (illustration #1). This flattens the plane of your swing and causes you to return the clubhead into the ball with the heel of the club leading. The clubface lags behind.

The cure is relatively simple. You must make your backswing more upright. Take the club straight back from the ball for several inches before allowing it to move inside. An open stance, with the left foot pulled back a bit from the target line (illustration #2), will force a more upright backswing, and such a stance is suitable on at least the short-iron shots.

IRON-SHOT DISTANCE CAN BE OVER-EMPHASIZED

Success on iron shots rests primarily on producing accuracy.

This brings us to the length of backswing on iron shots. I say your backswing should be no longer than that which will give you accurate shots. Don't be ashamed to use more club and take a three-quarter swing on iron shots. Keep your swing compact and rhythmical.

The illustrations show backswings of three different lengths. I know from experience that the longest swing will give me only about 10 yards more distance than the shortest swing. And who cares? No golf professional worth his salt would sacrifice accuracy for distance on shots to the green. You shouldn't either.

41

1—PROBLEM SHOTS

KEEP ON TARGET LINE

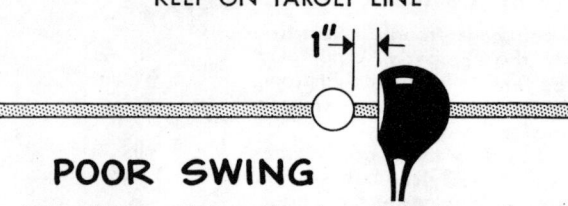

POOR SWING

Your ability to hit straight shots depends very largely on the distance your clubface travels while looking at the target in the hitting area (see illustrations). The longer your clubface looks at the target, the better chance you have to hit straight shots. Therefore, keep your clubface looking down the target line as long as possible.

GOOD SWING

The best way to achieve this is to avoid rolling your hands and forearms to the right or left on your backswing. When you roll them going back, you must perform the exact opposite maneuver on your downswing to return the clubface squarely to the ball. This is very difficult to do consistently.

EXCELLENT SWING

HIP POSITIONING HAS GREAT EFFECT ON SHOT DIRECTION

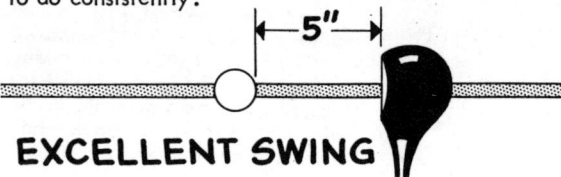

Even though your feet may be properly positioned, square to the target, you can still hook and/or slice. The checkpoint here is the hips. Are they also square?

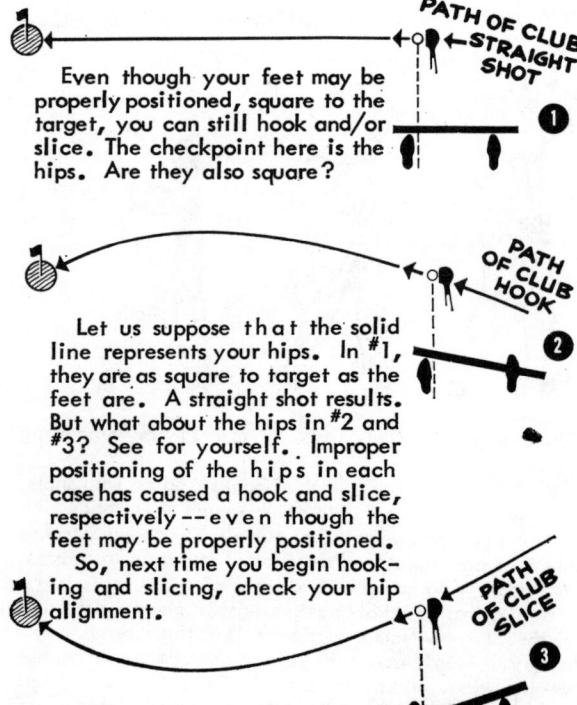

Let us suppose that the solid line represents your hips. In #1, they are as square to target as the feet are. A straight shot results. But what about the hips in #2 and #3? See for yourself. Improper positioning of the hips in each case has caused a hook and slice, respectively--even though the feet may be properly positioned.

So, next time you begin hooking and slicing, check your hip alignment.

DISTANCE FOR WOMEN

One problem that faces many golfers is the tendency to loosen their hold on the club during the swing. This problem is especially acute among women because most of the gals lack a great deal of strength in their hands and forearms.

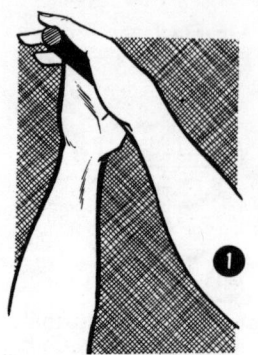

The normal result of a loose grip will be a loss of club control at the top of the backswing (#1). This not only produces erratic shots, but more often it means a loss of distance.

To maintain a firm grip throughout the swing, as shown in #2, I suggest you make sure your left thumb stays welded against your right palm (see #3). There seems to be a natural groove in the right palm to accommodate this thumb.

A firm hold on the club can and will overcome other swing errors that would normally produce bad shots.

---

3 WAYS TO CHECK SWAYING

If you feel yourself swaying or moving sideways, instead of turning on the backswing, take time off and practice your swing, using any/all of these three techniques:

a. Try swinging while looking at your head's reflection in a window. Try to keep this reflection centered in one window pane.

b. Check on hip swing by placing a stick in the ground next to your right hip. If you topple the stick with your body on the backswing, you're swaying.

c. Finally, if there's enough sun, watch your shadow while you swing. Position yourself in such a way that the shadow of your head covers an object, such as an envelope or other piece of paper. If, during the swing, the envelope moves outside of the shadow, you can tell that your head is moving laterally or up and down.

1—PROBLEM SHOTS

PALMS ALIGN FOR STRAIGHTER SHOTS

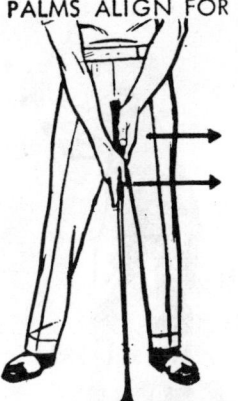

At address, the palm of your right hand and the back of your left -- like the clubface -- should be looking down the target line (see illustration).

With such a grip you can be reasonably assured of having a square clubface at impact, if your hands have returned to their original address position as you strike the ball.

Thus, a grip that aligns the palms with the clubface is best for producing straight shots.

A DIFFERENCE BETWEEN DUFFERS AND EXPERTS

A major difference between the good golfer and the duffer is the path that the hands take through the hitting area.

If you could trace this path in the duffer's swing, it would look about like the broken line in the illustration. Notice how this line describes a wide arc before impact, then comes upward abruptly.

The good golfer's hands move more abruptly downward and then extend out on a path toward the target before gradually coming up on the follow-through.

To duplicate the better golfer's hand movement, start your downswing with your legs shifting to the left and your left hand pulling the club...and controlling it...into the ball.

UPHILL OR DOWNHILL, WEIGHT BELONGS ON HIGH FOOT

Maintaining balance while swinging is a must on all shots. But special emphasis on balance is needed when you are playing shots from uphill and downhill lies. There is a natural tendency on these shots to throw too much weight onto the lower foot as you swing through the ball. This, of course, results in mis-hit shots.

A good slogan to remember is: "Keep your weight on your high foot." For right-handed golfers this means placing more weight on your left foot on uphill shots (No. 1). Retain more weight on your right foot on downhill shots (No. 2).

It is also important to play the ball farther forward than normal on uphill shots and farther back in your stance on downhill shots, as I am also doing in the illustrations.

CHECK YOURSELF IN A MIRROR

Periodically, all golfers should take a good look at their address position in a mirror. The illustration shows several things that I feel should be present. See how well your address position measures up to this ideal.

First your stance should be about shoulder-width wide—from instep to instep. This will help give you good balance.

Your feet should be toed out slightly, the left foot slightly more so than the right. This will encourage full turning on your backswing and downswing.

Your right shoulder should be a bit lower than your left, since your right hand is lower on the club than your left.

The line across your toes should parallel the line from ball to target. This "square" stance is best for straight shots.

Finally, when you play your drives opposite your left heel, your left arm and the clubshaft should be more or less continuous. This will encourage a smooth, coordinated backswing with a full clubhead arc.

COIL UP IN THE BACKSWING

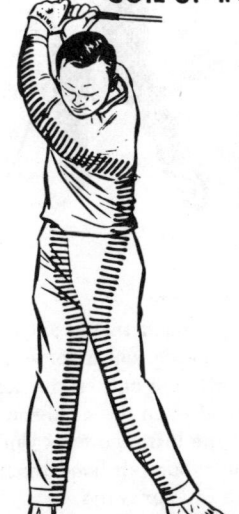

All things being equal, the greater the muscle tension created on the backswing, the greater the amount of force released into the shot.

If you have performed a proper wind-up, you should feel two ribbons of tension. One runs from the heel of the left foot, up the inner muscles of the left leg, and up the left side and left arm. The other tension ribbon runs up the inside of the right leg, across the back and to the left armpit area, where it joins the other ribbon.

If you coil, rather than sway, your body, and if you keep your head fairly steady, you should feel tension in these areas at the top of your swing.

EXTEND LEFT ARM FOR SWING CONSISTENCY

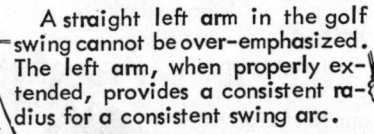

A straight left arm in the golf swing cannot be over-emphasized. The left arm, when properly extended, provides a consistent radius for a consistent swing arc.

I think it might help you keep your left arm straight if you think of it as being a spoke of a wheel. Think of this spoke as extending from its hub--the left shoulder.

When you make your swing (see illustrations), turn from the "hub" and keep the "spoke" straight.

43

1—PROBLEM SHOTS

DOWNSWING PATH MUST BE STRAIGHT

Check for two things in your grip on the club at the top of your swing.

First, your fingers should be more or less around the top of the clubshaft and your palms more or less beneath the shaft. Second, the back of your left hand should form a continuous line with the back of your left arm.

If you have a proper grip and if these two points check out at the top of your swing, your downswing should automatically assume a reasonably proper clubhead path.

LEFT HAND GUIDES YOUR SHOT

The position of the left hand on the clubshaft pretty much determines the direction your shots will fly. Basically you will have a good chance for straight shots if this hand is in the same position at impact as it was in at address.

I suggest you "memorize" the position of your left hand at address. Retain this memory throughout your backswing and downswing so you can return to it by the time you hit the ball.

I personally prefer to position this hand so that the back of it faces down the target line (illustration #1). If my clubface also faces down the target line both at address and impact, I will obtain pretty good direction on my shot. That is, if the back of my left hand again looks down the line during impact (illustration #2).

ANOTHER KEY TO DISTANCE

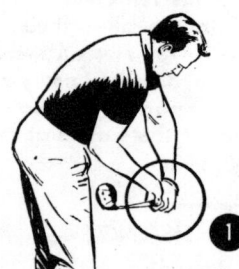

The right hand should unleash a tremendous amount of force into the ball, but only at the last split second when the clubhead is entering the hitting area. Until this time, your left hand should dominate in your swing.

Check the illustrations of me swinging into the ball. Make sure your right hand doesn't force itself into the shot until the club is approximately in the same position as in illustration #1. Then let it rip. Pour that right hand into the shot (illustration #2). Allow your right arm to straighten until it feels as if the clubhead is pulling down on your right shoulder.

The big key to distance in the swing is to time your moves properly so that your right hand comes into play at just the right time.

LOWER LEFT HEEL FIRST

Start your downswing by lowering your left heel. Nothing else must take place prior to this key move.

Lowering your left heel smoothly at the outset of your downswing automatically produces good results during your return to the ball. For example, the clubhead is kept on its proper path.

But the big advantage to lowering the left heel first is that your downswing is properly timed. It establishes an orderly sequence of movement that culminates in maximum clubhead speed at impact. The result: maximum distance.

FINISH SWINGING WITH ELBOWS CLOSE

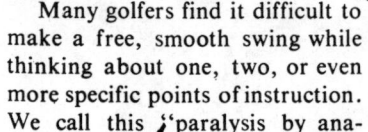

Many golfers find it difficult to make a free, smooth swing while thinking about one, two, or even more specific points of instruction. We call this "paralysis by analysis."

These golfers need what instructors call a "full-swing thought," rather than one or more "part-swing" thoughts. The full-swing thought is designed to focus the golfer's attention on something in his swing that will automatically produce good basic movement elsewhere in his stroke.

One such thought is to finish the swing in balance with the elbows relatively close together. Instead of finishing as illustration #1 depicts, think of reaching, more or less, the same close-elbow position as in illustration #2. I think you'll find that other things you may have been trying to accomplish during your swing will automatically fall into place as a result.

HANDS LEAD ON LONG IRON SHOTS

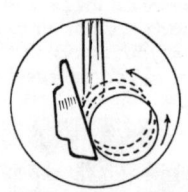

There is an unconscious feeling that seems to overcome many golfers when they play long iron shots. They look down at these shallow-faced irons and wonder if the loft is sufficient to get the ball airborne. The player holds back with his hands and throws the clubhead under the ball in an attempt to scoop it into flight.

Golfers should rely on their clubs. The loft of even the 1-iron is sufficient to apply the backspin needed to put the ball into the air. All you need is a swing that puts the clubhead squarely onto the ball.

Hit your long irons with a firm grip and a smooth, rhythmical swing. The clubs will do the rest.

1—PROBLEM SHOTS

SPECIAL CLUBS CAN CORRECT YOUR TROUBLES

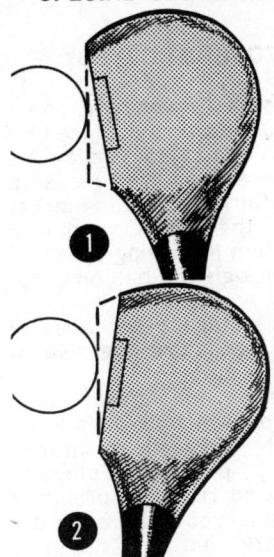

Aside from seeing that your clubs are properly suited to you in the normal areas—length, swingweight, shaft flex, clubhead lie and grip thickness—you might also consider the possibility of purchasing clubs that carry built-in hook or slice tendencies. For instance, if you are a chronic slicer, a driver with a degree of hook in the facing (illustration #1) would be in order. The opposite would apply (illustration #2) if a hook is your problem.

I would advocate a slightly hooked face especially for women, junior and senior players, and anyone else who needs every inch of distance they can muster.

HELPFUL HINT FOR PROPER TURNING

In a correct golf swing, the player TURNS on his backswing but never SWAYS.

In turning, the left shoulder lowers beneath the chin (see illustration). The left hip swings around and slightly down. The left knee moves slightly to the right. Even the head may turn a bit with the shoulders.

However, all this turning must take place around a central axis. There should be no lateral—sideways—movement to the right. This is swaying and robs the swing of power and control.

To make sure you turn instead of sway, imagine that a huge hand is pressing gently against your right side (see illustration). This hand prohibits you from swaying to the right, or even shifting your weight to the outside of your right foot.

The proper turn will enable you to feel tension in your back and leg muscles. Without this feeling of tension at the top of your backswing, you are not fully utilizing your big muscles for maximum power.

THREE WAYS TO TOP; AVOID THEM ALL

There are three ways to top a shot:

A. Bend your knees too much at address.

B. Let your right elbow fly away from your right side on the downswing.

C. Allow your left elbow to bend in the downswing.

A golfer who crouches over the ball at address tends to straighten his knees during the swing. This action raises the hands and club, so the club passes over the top of the ball.

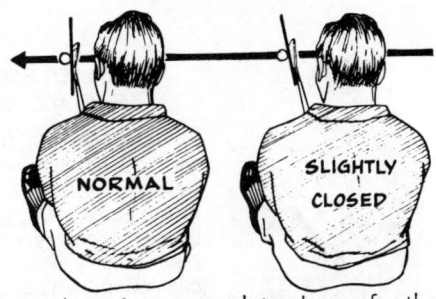

CLOSED CLUBFACE OFFSETS BALL SLIP

NORMAL — SLIGHTLY CLOSED

In wet weather, there is a natural tendency for the ball to slip off the clubface to the right in a sort of push-slice manner.

To compensate for this wet-weather phenomenon, merely address the ball with your clubface turned slightly to your left in a closed position (see illustrations). Turn the club's handle a bit to the left before you assume your grip.

This slightly closed face will offset the slipping of the ball. Thus the clubface will be more likely to fly the ball toward the target.

LEVEL YOUR SWING ON LONG IRON SHOTS

A key to solid shots with the long irons—1, 2 and 3—is to level out the bottom of your swing arc. The more level this arc—the longer it moves parallel with the ground—the better will be your chances to make solid contact.

With these shallow-faced clubs, avoid an upright swing such as you might make with a pitching wedge or 9-iron. Such a swing will bring the clubhead down to the ball on too steep a path and the club will dig too deeply into the ground (illustration #1).

The best way to achieve a level clubhead path (illustration #2) is to shift your weight smoothly to your right foot on your backswing and your left on your downswing, all the while keeping your left arm fully extended into a wide swing arc.

LONG-IRON SHOTS TOO ROUGH FROM ROUGH

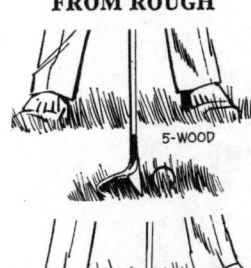

One of the most difficult disciplines in golf is to make yourself use enough loft on shots from rough. I know I can recall many instances in my own career when I lost shots — and thousands of dollars — simply because I tried to hit, say, a 3-iron shot from a 5-iron lie.

I think most golfers would be wise to simply forget about using a 1, 2 or 3 wood out of rough. The 4 or 5 wood might work occasionally since those woods do sweep the ball away with considerable loft. I'd also suggest that you never use any iron with less loft than a 4 or 5 iron. Just keep those long irons in your bag. I'll guarantee that from deep grass you can hit a 5 iron just as far as a 2 iron — usually farther.

1—PROBLEM SHOTS

SLOWER BACKSWING MAY ADD DISTANCE

The 1956 U.S. Open tournament was played over very narrow fairways at the Oak Hills Country Club of Rochester, N.Y. In an attempt for greater accuracy on my tee shots, I consciously slowed down my driver backswing. I was amazed to discover that my drives were actually traveling farther than normal.

I think the average golfer can benefit from this experience. Many amateur players actually get better distance, relatively speaking, from their middle and short irons than they do from their drives. This happens because, in striving for

accuracy on the iron shots, they actually slow down their backswing.

A slower backswing (see illustrations) can add distance for several reasons. It will produce a squarer club-ball contact more frequently. It will result in a firmer grip on the club at the top of the backswing. It will enable the player to move his weight more readily to the right on the downswing.

Save the woods until last

When practicing before a round of golf (I hope you always do hit at least a few shots) avoid the temptation to start by hitting drives. You must give your muscles a chance to loosen gradually, and hitting drives flat out could cause severe strain.

I always start with the short irons, then work gradually down to the middle and long irons, and, finally, the woods. I may stroke a few short pitch shots thereafter, as my caddie is walking in from shagging.

USE DIVOT MARK TO AID ACCURACY

Occasionally you will see a golfer unknowingly place his pipe, or a cigar, alongside his ball before he makes his shot. He carefully points the marker towards the target so that it will aid him in moving the clubhead through the ball on proper line.

This is illegal. The Rules of Golf do not allow the use of directional aids.

However, on many par-3 holes, you will find built-in directional aids—divot marks made by preceding players. There is no rule that prohibits your teeing your ball behind a divot mark that just happens to point directly to the target.

Merely tee your ball in such a position and concentrate on duplicating the original divot mark as you swing through the shot.

"NAILING" CAN BE FATAL

Golfers who heed the advice to "hit down" on iron shots may wind up "nailing" the ball instead, with a chopping downswing. This error all starts with the backswing, in which the weight never leaves the left foot (note heel on ground).

One good way to avoid "nailing" is to keep in mind that clubhead loft will get the ball into the air without additional effort on the golfer's part.

Get some weight to the left of the backswing, then bring the clubhead back to the ball so it's low to the ground just before impact.

1—PROBLEM SHOTS

RETAIN WRIST COCK INTO HITTING AREA

The so-called "delayed hit" that is so vital for producing distance on golf shots is really nothing more than the preservation of the arm-club angle you had at the top of your swing.

In illustration #1, we see that my left forearm and clubshaft form a 90-degree angle. In illustration #2, I still maintain this same angle well into my downswing.

Only in the hitting area do my wrists unhinge. My left arm and clubshaft then form a straight line at impact.

Try to consciously retain your top-of-swing angle throughout your downswing. You may be surprised with the shots that result.

AVOID "RIGHT-HAND TAKE-OVER" AT THE TOP

A common error among golfers, especially women, is allowing the right hand to take control of the club at the top of the backswing. This control then continues on the downswing and through impact.

There is no easier way to ruin a golf shot. When the right hand takes over, it often turns the hands so that the club points "across the line"—to the right of target—as in illustration #1. This misalignment of the club makes square contact difficult. Right-hand take-over also causes other mistakes ...such as "hitting from the top" (pre-mature release of energy and clubhead speed) and "coming over the ball" (throwing the clubhead outside the target line during the downswing).

In the proper swing, the right hand must never assert itself more than the left. In illustration #2, I show the ideal top-of-swing position. The absence of inward bending at the back of my left wrist indicates that this hand is still in control.

KEEP WEIGHT TO THE LEFT ON SHOTS FROM THE ROUGH

On shots from deep grass, we want the clubhead to lift more abruptly than normal as it moves back from the ball. The quicker you lift it, the less likely you will stub it in the grass and close the clubface.

This quick lifting (compare the line of a take-away with the dashed line in the illustration) also puts the club in position for a return to the ball that will be more sharply descending than normal. This further minimizes the influence of the grass on the neck and head of the club.

The danger in altering the normal clubhead path in this fashion is that you may try to lift the club solely with your hands and arms, and thus fail to make a normal backswing turn.

I suggest you try to make a normal turn, but with most of your weight remaining on your left foot. Distributing your weight to the left will force you into a more upright take-away, while you make a swing that feels more or less normal.

WOOD SHOT RECOVERY

If you hit a bad shot into the rough, then find the ball sitting sufficiently upright to allow a wood shot recovery, you will probably select your 4- or 5-wood for the shot. You must contact the ball with as much clubface loft as the club allows, and you will want to hit it squarely with a minimum of interference from the grass.

To achieve these goals, stand with the ball closer to you than would be normal with the same club from the fairway (see illustration). This will give you a more upright swing so that the club comes down squarely into the ball without sliding through a lot of grass. Also, keep most of your weight on your left foot during your swing.

DON'T BE TOO TIDY IN HAZARDS

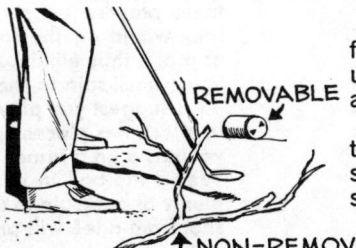

When your ball comes to rest in a hazard—either sand or water—you must be careful not to move loose impediments (natural objects not fixed or growing, such as stones, leaves, twigs, etc.). To move a loose impediment in a hazard calls for a penalty of loss of hole in match play, or two strokes in stroke play.

However, you are allowed to remove obstructions from such hazards without penalty. Obstructions are unnatural objects, such as bottles, cans, cigarettes and the like.

In either case, however, be sure that you do not touch the hazard with your club before making the shot. Grounding the club in a hazard calls for the same penalties as does moving a loose impediment.

SECTION TWO

STRATEGY

How to Think Your Way Around the Course.

KEEP RECORDS TO HELP ANALYZE YOUR GAME

Keeping accurate and thorough records of your golf game will not only add to your enjoyment, but will also help you improve. By analyzing your round each time, you will be better able to practice those areas of your game which really require your attention.

Here are some things I feel golfers should tally after each round (perhaps you can devise some sort of card that allows you to record these figures quickly and concisely):

—Number of fairways hit and missed off the tee (to determine your driving efficiency).

—Number of greens hit in regulation figures (to determine your shotmaking consistency). Regulation figures are two strokes less than the par of the hole.

—Total length of all putts made. Just add them together to determine your accuracy on the greens. You can also divide this total by the number of putts you actually took, to determine the average length of putts sunk.

—Number of times you hole out in two shots or less from off the green (to determine your chipping and pitching efficiency).

USE A TEE WHEN PLAYING THE PAR-3

Some amateur golfers simply toss aside an advantage given them by the rules when they fail to hit iron tee shots on par-3 holes from off a wooden tee. Some of these players just set the ball down and hit the shot as they would off the fairway. Others nudge it up on a tuft of grass, thus eliminating their chances of applying maximum back-spin to the ball.

I suggest you play such shots from a low-setting tee. In effect, this places the ball almost level with the ground, yet puts it on a firmer surface than even the ground itself. Teeing the ball in this manner will allow you to apply plenty of backspin to the ball. And even a slightly mis-hit shot from a tee will produce better results than it would from off the turf.

48

2—STRATEGY

STRIKE SAND FIRST, TURF SECOND

Some golfers don't know when to contact the sand on bunker shots and the turf on shots from grass.

When in a trap (illustration #1) you will normally want to swing the clubhead under the ball so that it flies out on a cushion of sand. Therefore, try to contact the sand behind the ball. Exceptions to this rule are on very long sand shots and on shots when the ball is buried or plugged in the sand.

Normally from grass (illustration #2) you should meet the ball and then the turf. This insures against sticking your club in the ground behind the ball.

Simply memorize the words, "sand first, turf second," and you'll never forget the advice I've given you today.

Stress accuracy on rainy days

On wet days the normal tendency is to swing harder on shots. The golfer senses that the wet turf will cost him distance, so he swings from the heels. Invariably he loses both distance and accuracy because of mis-hitting the ball.

I feel you should stress accuracy over distance on rainy days. First, your opponents are also going to be losing distance on the soggy fairways. Second, off-line shots are doubly penalized; wet rough is especially treacherous, as are damp sand traps.

Remember that every time you reach a fairway off the tee, you've gained an advantage over your foes, especially on rainy days.

WARM UP WITH FEET TOGETHER

Here's a suggestion for pre-round warm-up sessions on the practice tee...hit a few shots with your feet together. Don't go for distance; just try to hit it squarely.

This drill will result in your swinging in good rhythm. If you don't "wait" for the clubhead, you'll find yourself off balance.

After a few shots, proceed to your normal stance for the rest of your warm-up. But maintain the same rhythm that you needed when your feet were together.

WHEN TO GAMBLE, WHEN TO PASS

A typical "time for decision" is shown in the illustration. Should the golfer gamble by hitting for the flagstick (Position No. 1) or should he avoid the risk and shoot for Position No. 2?

I say that his decision should rest on several factors.

Those factors suggesting he shoot for the flagstick include: (a) confidence he can make the shot; (b) the competition is match play; (c) success probably will rattle his opponent; (d) it is early in the round; (e) it is late in the round and he is losing; (f) confidence he can make a reasonable birdie putt.

Those factors suggesting he aim for Position No. 2 and accept two putts include: (a) doubt that the odds favor his success in hitting Position No. 1; (b) the competition is stroke play; (c) missing Position No. 1 could ruin a good round; (d) doubt that he could sink the birdie putt from Position No. 1; (e) a par will win the hole; (f) succeeding holes offer better birdie chances.

2—STRATEGY

ON THE COURSE, PLAY TO SCORE WELL

There is a time and place to work on your golf game. The time is during practice sessions; the place is on the practice range.

Never experiment during actual competition. On the course, your only objective is to shoot the best score possible.

Don't think about your swing while playing. If you do, you will score badly and become discouraged. More important, your swing will suffer. Attend to your swing on the practice tee, not on the course.

DRIVE AWAY FROM TROUBLE

Most golfers cannot count on a straight tee shot most of the time. Yet, these same players fail to take heed to an important golf maxim when they drive on holes guarded by trouble. This maxim is: "Always drive away from trouble."

In other words, tee up on the side of the tee that is closest to the trouble. If you see rough or out-of-bounds on the right, drive from the right side of the tee. However, aim for the center of the fairway, rather than down the right side. Thus, a sliced shot will have to bend at a much sharper angle to reach the trouble than it would have to if you had hit straight down the fairway from the middle of the tee.

The opposite holds true when there is trouble on the left. Drive from the left side of the tee and aim for the middle, rather than down the left side.

Remember: Always shoot away from trouble.

THERE ARE TIMES WHEN YOU MUST RETREAT

I guess I've taken as many chances on the golf course as any man. It just isn't my nature to play it safe.

However, there are times when even I find it necessary to exercise better judgment and take "the long way home." The illustration shows one such occasion. Here I'm chipping out into the fairway, sacrificing a stroke, rather than to risk an unplayable lie in the bushes and trees between me and the green.

Golfers would be wise to temper their spirit of adventure, on occasion, and settle for an easy bogey.

One rule of thumb I suggest most golfers follow is never to attempt a shot that they haven't practiced, or at least pulled off once, in the past. Don't ruin a whole day on the golf course with one risky shot.

A GREAT WAY TO DEFLATE OPPONENTS

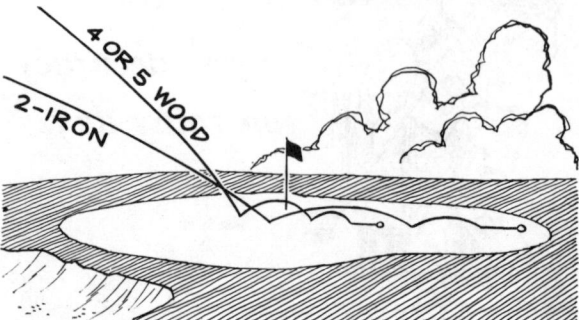

One of the most disheartening experiences in golf is watching your opponent pull a wood club out of his bag and knock the ball squarely onto the green. It's enough to take the wind out of any one's sails.

For this reason I suggest that you spend at least a small measure of your practice time hitting shots with your 4 or 5-wood. After mastering the fairway-wood approach shot, you'll have an invaluable tool for hitting to hard greens. All too often even a well-struck 2-iron will bounce forward and over such a green. A nice high fairway wood however, will settle gently on the carpet (see illustration).

2—STRATEGY

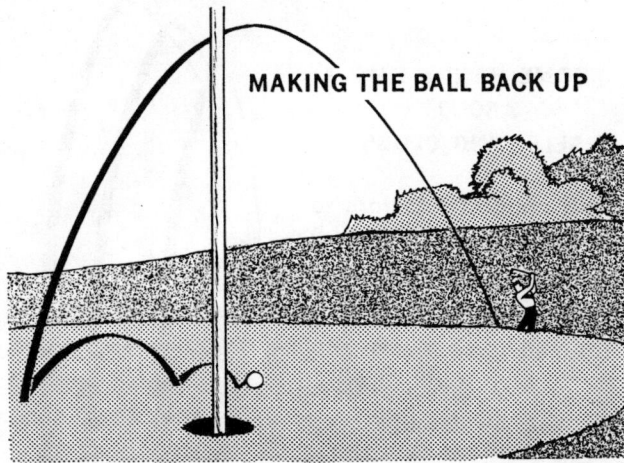

MAKING THE BALL BACK UP

One thing that always makes a golf gallery "ooh" and "aah" is the shot that lands a few feet behind the flagstick and then starts backing up towards the hole.

You too can make shots behave this way on greens of reasonable softness.

First, you must be playing an iron shot of at least 90 or 100 yards. Even the experts can't back up shots of, say, 30 or 40 yards.

Next, it helps if your ball is in a good lie on firm ground, rather than soft, lush turf.

Play the ball well back in your stance, towards your right foot. Keep your hands in their normal position, so they will be ahead of the ball.

Keep your weight on your left foot as you swing. This will cause you to lift the club quickly on your backswing and to return it sharply downward on your downswing. The sharp downstroke, made with a firm left arm and wrist, will send the ball off with enough backspin to make it pull back on the green.

WHEN IN DOUBT PLAY SHORT OF A HAZARD

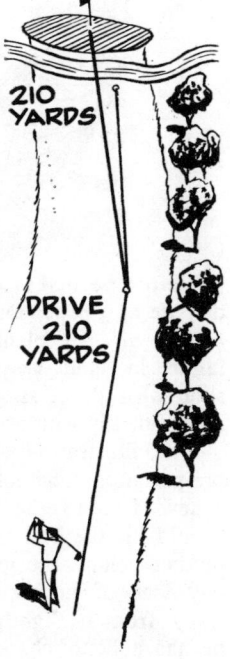

The golf hole illustrated today is typical of many that you will encounter. It's a long par-4—say 420 yards—with a hazard in front of the green. We've shown a stream here, but it could have been a bevy of sand traps or a small pond.

Whatever the problem may be, it's always wise to assess your capabilities realistically. Bear in mind that the temptation is to try to go for the green on your second shot, and thus assure yourself of an easy par or a possible birdie.

Be honest with yourself. Look back at the tee and see how far you've driven the ball. If the distance back to the tee is not greater than the distance to the green, you'd better play your second shot short of the trouble spot. I don't know many golfers who can hit their fairway shots farther than they drive. Do you?

KEEP TRACK OF FAIRWAY HITS

The professional, more so than the average club golfer, pays greater attention to the number of fairways he hits off the tee. The amateur tends to blame poor scores on hitting sand traps and missing greens. The pro, meanwhile, realizes that these errors stem from off-line tee shots.

For your game I suggest straight driving as opposed to long driving. Record the number of fairways hit during your rounds and continually strive to increase this number.

Improve your direction off the tee and you will automatically start hitting more greens and fewer sand traps.

KNOW THE RULES AND SAVE STROKES

The golfer who knows the rules can save himself strokes. A case in point is the rule governing unplayable lies.

The golfer in the illustration faces such a situation. If he were not familiar with the rule, he might assume that his only choice is to drop the ball straight back from the position it now occupies, keeping that spot between himself and the hole, and taking a stroke penalty.

This option does exist, and on occasion it's the best to follow. However, the rules also allow you to drop within two club-lengths **to either side** of the ball's original position, but not nearer the hole, again taking the stroke penalty.

This option would give the golfer in the illustration a clear shot to the hole. It would even allow him to drop onto a nice smooth lie in the fairway, if such an area existed within two club-lengths and was not nearer the hole.

51

2—STRATEGY

PLAN STANCE WHILE APPROACHING BALL

One of the most devious ways that golfers can go astray is in their shot alignment. It happens to the best players occasionally. You think you are set up and aimed toward the target; then one day someone points out that you are not.

One way to check your alignment is to visualize a line from the ball to the target as you walk up to the ball (see illustration). Also visualize a line that parallels the target line. This is the line that should run across your toes.

Then, when you address the ball, put your toes up to this second line.

This will automatically give you a square stance. If you place your clubface behind the ball at right angles to the target line, it will be facing in the direction you wish your shot to take.

PLAY SHORT OF FLAGSTICK WHEN GREEN IS SOAKED

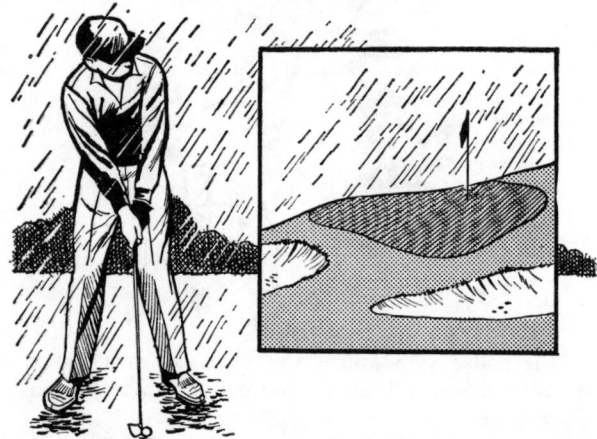

Normally, when the greens are wet, almost any type of well-struck shot will settle down relatively fast. You can plan to carry your shots all the way to the hole with little fear of bouncing far past.

However, this is not always the case when the greens really are soaked to the point where they are starting to puddle.

When this situation occurs, it is best to play your approach shots to land short of the hole just as you would under normal dry conditions. The reason for this is because water, at rest on the green, does not allow the ball to bite into the turf. Instead the ball "skips," just like a flat stone skips across a body of water.

Remember to hit for the flagstick when the greens are merely wet, but to allow for at least one big bounce when they are soaked.

SOME HANDY TIPS ABOUT SELECTING CLUBS

Two important factors to consider when buying clubs are (1) swingweight and (2) shaft flex.

Swingweight is a measurement made on a special scale that designates the weight relationship of various parts of the club. Swingweights run from C-0 to E-9, but the majority of clubs sold measure between C-6 and D-5. Swingweight measurements help manufacturers see that all clubs within a given set are similarly weighted.

Generally speaking, the stronger a person is, and the faster his swing, the higher should be his swingweight and the stiffer his shaft.

Specifically, if your best drives carry 175 yards or less, you should use a flexible shaft and a swingweight of from C-6 to C-7. If your best drive flies from 175 to 200 yards, select clubs with medium flex shafts in the C-8 to D-2 swingweight range. Those whose drives carry over 200 yards normally can obtain best results with stiff shafts and clubs with swingweights in the D-0 to D-5 class.

PLAN AHEAD

Before he makes his shot, the good golfer will anticipate any problems that might occur if he failed to pull it off. He plans the shot with this possibility of failure in mind. Once he has decided how to play the shot with the least amount of risk, he then executes it confidently with no thought of failing.

The illustration shows an example of this type of pre-planning. The golfer has deliberately aimed the shot a few feet to the left of the flagstick. Thus, if he should hit the ball too far, it still will miss the other bunker behind the green. He has, in effect, eliminated any fear of hitting into the other bunker by aiming away from it slightly. With this fear out of the way, he has a better chance of making a good swing on the shot at hand.

2—STRATEGY

BE CAREFUL OF LOOSE IMPEDIMENTS

Loose impediments, as defined in the Rules of Golf, are "natural objects not fixed or growing and not adhering to the ball." These include loose stones, leaves, twigs, worms and insects, and the like.

On the green the golfer is allowed to remove these objects. Should his ball be moved in the process, it must be replaced, but without penalty.

However, it is in the fairway or rough that you must be careful. If, say, you accidentally move your ball while removing a loose impediment within one club-length of the ball, you must take a one-stroke penalty. The same penalty occurs if your ball is accidentally moved by your partner or either of your caddies.

The best procedure is never to try to remove a leaf or similar object unless you can do so without possibly moving the ball.

COUNT YOUR CLUBS

The Rules of Golf allow you to carry only 14 clubs. Don't risk a penalty by carrying more.

It's very easy to accidentally stow an extra club (while trying out a new putter, for example) and then forget about having it in the bag.

So make a point to count your clubs before every round—especially before competition.

And count once again after the round. These days when so many players are using caddies carrying two bags, or are sharing golf cars, it's all too easy to accidentally slip a club into the wrong bag.

PLAY ALL CHIP SHOTS TO SAME LANDING AREA

There is a great deal of discussion about club selection on chip shots. One school advocates using the same club on all chip shots. I am of the opposite school which suggests chipping with the club that best fits the situation.

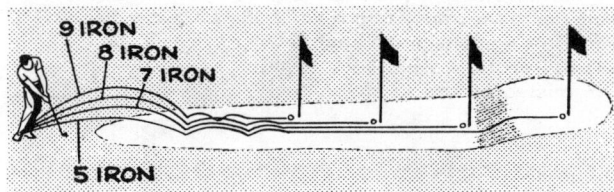

By following my technique a golfer can land the ball in the same landing area on any type of chip shot—the normal landing area being on the green just past the fringe. The club to be used depends on the distance from the landing area to the flagstick and the terrain of the intervening portion of the putting surface.

If the flagstick is far away, or if it's atop a rise in the green, you will probably run the shot up with a less-lofted club (see illustration). If the pin is near the edge of the green, you will loft the ball higher and it will settle more readily on the green.

It takes more practice to master different clubs, but the results pay off in this vital area of the game.

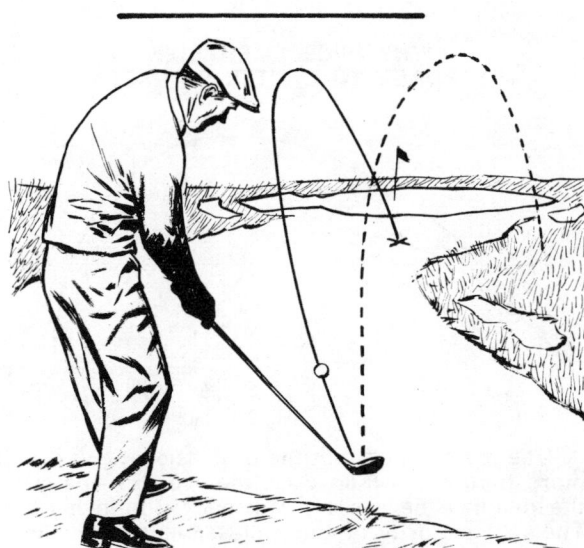

PRE-PLAN YOUR GOLFING APPROACH

The golfer should develop the type of thinking that allows a pool player to plan future shots in advance. Every time you step up to a full shot, determine where you want your ball to finish if you should miss the shot.

In the illustration we see a golfer hitting down the fairway. Let's assume that you are this golfer and that you have a tendency to slice shots.

If you are wise, you will aim to the left side of the fairway (solid line). Even if the ball slices, you will still have a shot to the green. However, if you aim for the pin and slice (dotted line), you will be in trouble.

Realize your shotmaking weakness and minimize its adverse effect by looking ahead for best position for your next shot.

2—STRATEGY

DON'T BE MISLED BY WIND

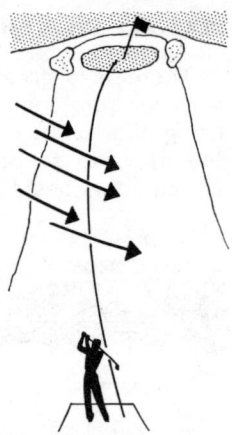

When playing in the wind, the effect of the breeze may differ from tee to green.

For instance, if you are standing on a tee that is in a valley and hitting to a green that is on a hill (see illustrations), you might be misled by the wind you feel.

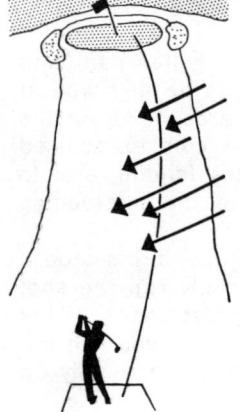

There may be a much stronger breeze blowing near the green -- near to the point where your shot will be losing forward thrust and its ability to counteract the wind.

So always check the action of the wind on the flagstick as you plan your shot. Most golfers have a tendency to underestimate the effect of the wind.

WHY PROS EMPHASIZE YARDAGE TO CENTER OF GREEN

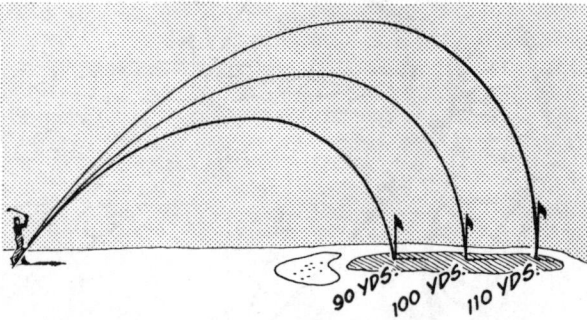

One facet of golf that the professional gives much more thought to than does the average amateur is the distance he can hit with each club in his bag. The vast majority of the professionals know almost to the inch just how far they can hit, say, a normal 5-iron shot.

And the professionals employ this knowledge effectively. Before each tournament, they mentally ascertain how far it is to the center of the green from various landmarks out in the fairway. Some, like Jack Nicklaus, actually chart the course on their scorecards or in notebooks. These pros eliminate doubt about club selection by combining knowledge of their shotmaking ability with knowledge of the distance to various pin positions on the green (see illustration).

Anyone who plays in tournaments—even if they be merely club events—will become a tougher foe if he follows the lead of the professionals and starts to pace off the distances his shots fly, as well as the distances from fairway to green-center.

CHECK PIN POSITION BEFORE CUTTING DOGLEG

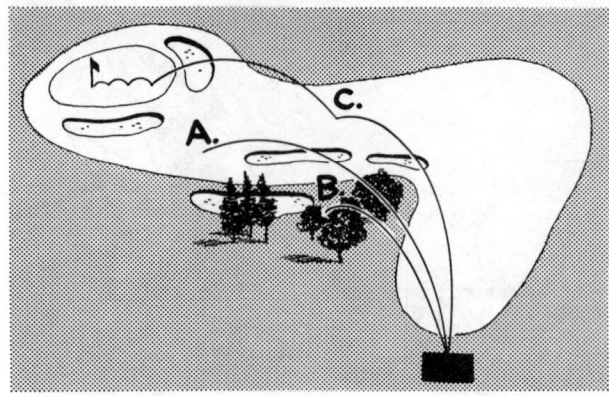

Today's illustration points up an example of thinking your way to lower scores.

It's a dogleg hole, and the golfer has the alternatives of playing safely into the middle of the fairway or of cutting across the trouble. In such cases the decision often rests on the positioning of the flagstick.

If the flag were cut into the right side of this green, the player might well cut the dogleg. He would then enjoy an open shot to the hole.

However, with the flagstick on the left, by cutting the corner to position A, he still leaves himself a troublesome shot over the sand. Of course, he might also miss the tee shot and finish in position B. In such an instance, he would probably be wiser playing safely out to position C and approaching along a clear route to the hole.

Always check the flagstick positioning before driving, especially when you are pondering how to play a dogleg.

WHEN THE GOING GETS ROUGH

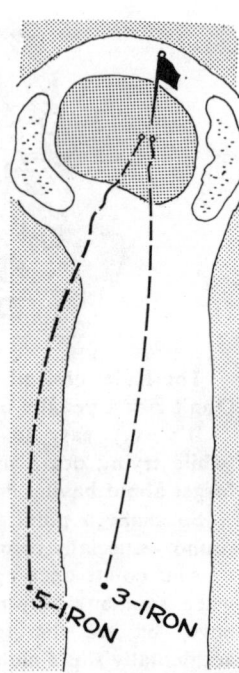

On shots from the rough, you must get the ball quickly up into the air and away from the grasping grass, therefore, you must use a club with plenty of loft. The club will loft the ball from the grass, and carry it into the fairway.

Since it is very difficult to get much backspin on shots from rough, these shots roll much farther than normal. Therefore, a 5-iron from rough may roll as far as a 3-iron from the fairway (see illustration).

54

2—STRATEGY

PLAN YOUR ROUND AND LOWER YOUR SCORE

If you shoot about 90 for an average round of golf, clear-think your way into the low 80s -- occasionally the high 70s.

First plan your round. Chances are that now you get about six pars in 18 holes. You probably get about 7 bogies, 4 double bogies and maybe 1 disastrous quadruple bogey.

Analyze what's needed to lower your score from 90 to 80. All you must do is to par one more hole. You can do that. Also change those double bogies to bogies and eliminate the bad hole.

If you are good enough to shoot 90, you are good enough to eliminate double bogies for the most part. Just think clearly on each hole and make up your mind that you won't go more than one over par. Here's what I mean:

The hole is 430 yards, par 4. Probably you cannot normally reach it in two shots. Don't try. Just keep the ball in play. Two straight shots and you'll be about 30 yards short of the green (see illustration). All you must do then is hit the ball somehwere on the green and two-putt for your bogey. You might even approach for one putt and a par.

Just keep the ball in play and the bad hole and double bogies will vanish.

SACRIFICE A FEW YARDS, SAVE A FEW STROKES

I doubt that there is a golfer alive who wouldn't gladly sacrifice 10 or 20 yards off the tee if it would save him a full shot or two.

I'm talking about using less club on tee shots which could spell trouble in the form of missing the fairway. In such situations you should always use the club that gives you the most confidence...one that guarantees a relatively straight shot. If you occasionally slice or hook with your driver, use a fairway wood, a long iron or whatever it takes to keep the ball in play.

You'll find that course architects usually do not build a lot of length into a hole with a narrow fairway. Chances are you won't even miss whatever distance you do sacrifice.

PLAN SHOT TO USE ALL OF FAIRWAY

If you are plagued by chronic hooking or slicing, you should be careful to tee your drives in position to allow yourself to use the entire fairway.

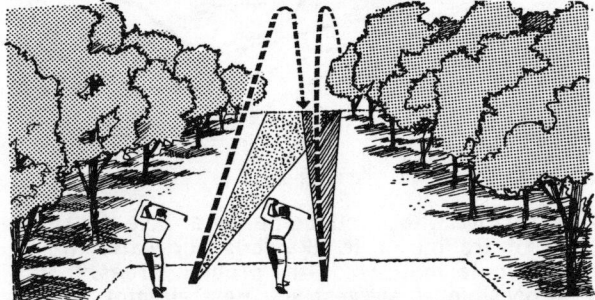

Let's assume that you slice most tee shots. If you tee your ball in the center of the teeing area and aim straight out, for the center of the fairway, you allow yourself only the right half of the fairway as a landing area (see shaded area in illustration). If you slice as might be expected, your ball may finish in trouble.

However, if you tee your ball on the left of the tee and again aim straight out, down the left side of the fairway, you allow yourself almost the whole fairway width (stippled area) in which to land the ball. Even a fairly healthy slice will merely bend back to the center or left side of the fairway.

If you have a tendency to hook tee shots, obviously you should tee up on the right side of the teeing area.

PRACTICE AS YOU PLAY

Most golfers are wasting their time on the practice tee. This is true because practice conditions are so different from playing conditions.

However, practice sessions, if properly handled, can be quite helpful. The challenge is to practice with the same attitude you have during competition.

I suggest doing this:

When you practice, imagine that you are playing your home course. Start by hitting a drive. Based on how that shot finishes, hit the same second shot that you would use on your first hole. Do the same for each of your 18 holes, always using the club you would use on the course as determined by your previous shot. Allow yourself two putts for each green and see how well you can score.

Changing from club to club may seem time-consuming, but it is an excellent way to force yourself to take your time and concentrate on each shot.

55

2—STRATEGY

KNOW THE RULES ABOUT REPAIRING GREENS

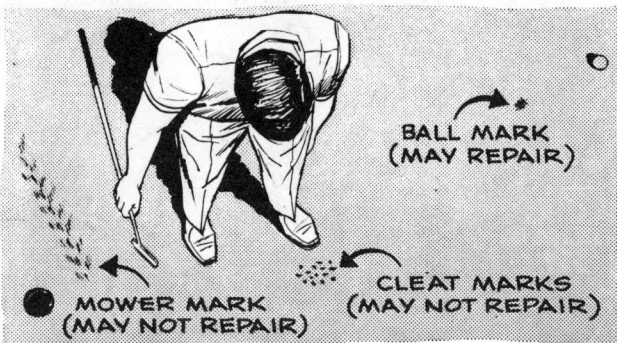

Many golfers are unaware of the rule about repairing greens before putting. You should know these rules so that you are protected against making a costly violation in a tournament.

Briefly, the Rules of Golf do not allow you to test the putting surfaces in any way. You can't brush the grass with your hand or your putter.

You cannot repair damages to a green except for marks made by balls. You cannot repair mower marks or spike marks or other such blemishes.

To be safe, remember that the only times you can touch your putting line is (1) with your putter when addressing the ball, (2) to remove a loose impediment, such as a stick or leaf and (3) to repair a ball mark.

A TIME TO PLAY SAFE

I seldom advocate playing "safe" in a golf tournament. Too often, playing safe when you are ahead turns your game into a defensive one. Pretty soon, you are thinking negatively and then you lose your lead.

However, there is one occasion in match play when every golfer should play it safe. That situation occurs when your opponent's shot flies out of bounds.

When this occurs, he has -- in effect -- handed you two free shots. Don't waste them.

If your opponent's drive has gone out of bounds, you should tee off with the club you can be sure will keep you in the fairway, even if it may be an iron (see illustration).

It may not seem sporting to resort to these tactics, but there is really nothing questionable about doing so. It's just smart strategy.

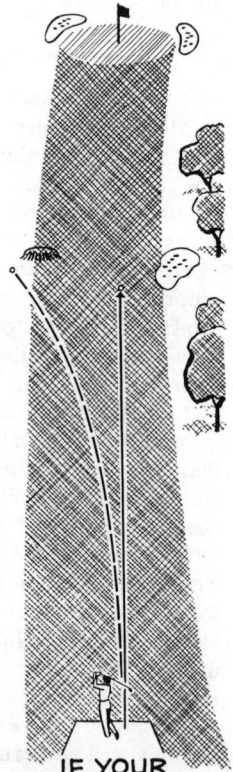

IF YOUR OPPONENT'S BALL IS OUT OF BOUNDS FROM THE TEE, PLAY IT SAFE AND USE AN IRON.

"SEE" YOUR SHOT, THEN MAKE IT HAPPEN

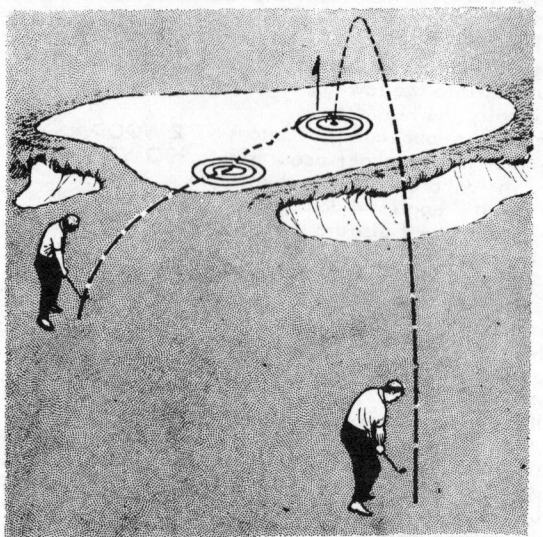

Regardless of the type of shot...putt, chip, pitch, fairway wood, etc., you should always imagine, before you play it, how that shot should look. This means actually selecting a specific spot on which you will land the ball.

By planning ahead in this manner, you force yourself into making a positive decision. You make yourself think about doing something successfully.

Positive thinking is vital in golf. Plan to make a good shot and you probably will. But if you're afraid of making a bad shot, well...as comedian Flip Wilson says, "what you sees is what you git."

AVOID PLAYING ALONGSIDE WATER

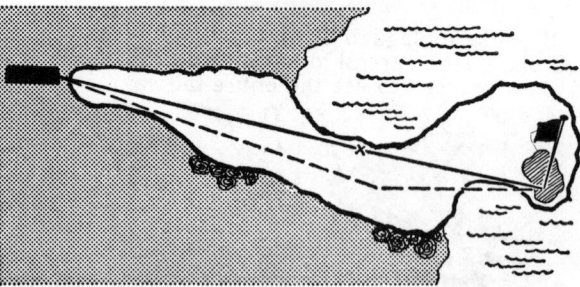

Naturally, when you come to a hole that has a lot of trouble on it, like rough or water, try to take a route that avoids the problem areas. If this is impossible, I suggest you next attempt to play **over** the trouble, rather than to skirt it. The reason for playing over trouble is that your chances of miss-hitting the shot and falling short into the problem area are probably less than the chance that you will curve the shot into it.

The illustration shows what I mean. On this par-4 hole, we have water on the left side of the fairway near the tee-shot landing area, and also on the right-front of the green.

Some golfers might drive straightaway (solid line) so as to get a straight shot into the flagstick. I'd much prefer to play away from the water off the tee—down the right side—and then come into the hole with an approach that goes over, rather than along, the water near the green.

2—STRATEGY

CLUB CHOICE CAN MAKE OR BREAK YOUR SHOT

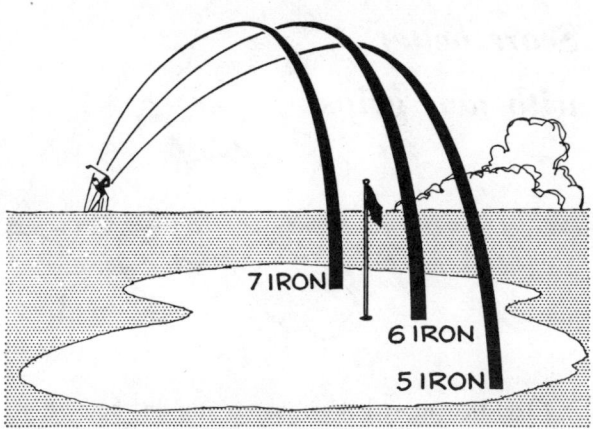

When the green runs 90-100 feet from front to back, you may have a choice of three different clubs, two of which would leave your shot either short or long (see illustration).

Some holes on your course do not allow a good view of the green from the fairway. Try to note the pin position on these greens as you play other holes earlier in the round.

If in doubt about the club selection, note where the trouble lies around the green; is it in front or behind the green? Then select a club which will keep you out of the worst trouble.

GOLF COURTESY PAYS OFF

One of the most important golf courtesy rules is this one: If you and/or your partners are moving slowly, invite following players to play right through.

It's also pretty irritating to come to your ball in a sand trap and find it at the bottom of a footprint. So, always rake and smooth out all clubprints and footprints from a sand trap before you leave it, as you see being done in illustration #2.

Don't hold anyone up. Be at the first tee, ready to play at the agreed time, and when it's your turn to hit, do so without delay. Leave the putting green promptly after holing out. You can mark your scorecard later.

Finally, park your golf cart (or car) on the side of the green closest to the next tee.

CASUAL WATER RULE CAN SAVE YOU STROKES

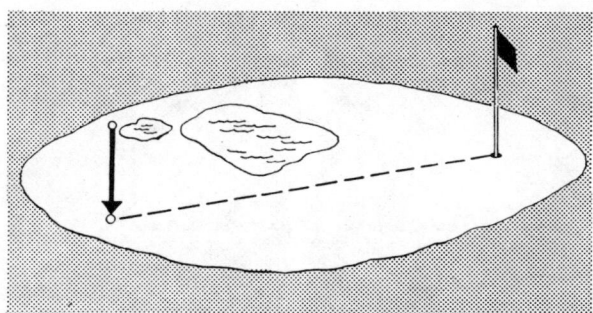

Sometimes the rules of golf can actually save you strokes. Take, for example, the rule that allows relief from "casual" (temporarily accumulated) water. Such relief is allowed whenever your ball touches such water, or if such water appears as you take your stance, or if casual water intervenes between your ball on the green and the hole.

The rules allow you to lift the ball and drop it over your shoulder into the nearest area, not nearer the hole, that affords relief from casual water.

If your ball happens to be in casual water in a sand trap, you must drop the ball to an area within the confines of the hazard to escape penalty. However, you may drop out of the hazard and accept a one-shot penalty.

I suggest that any serious golfer spend some time with a Rules of Golf book, available for 25 cents from the United States Golf Association, 40 E. 38th St., New York, N. Y.

USUALLY YOU CHARGE; SOMETIMES YOU DON'T

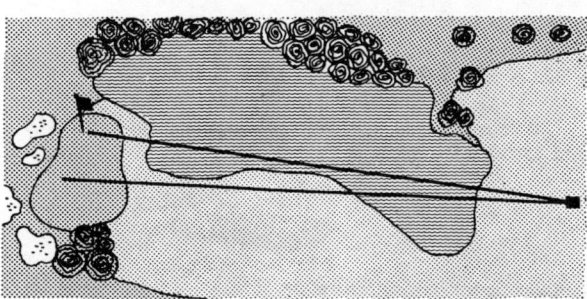

Since my reputation as a "charger" on the golf course is well-known, I suppose I should be the last one to advocate conservatism. However, there are some shot-making situations which, I feel, call for a subtle approach on the part of any golfer.

One such instance is when the pin is tucked behind the water, as on the 16th hole at the Oakland Hills Country Club outside Detroit (see illustration). When the flagstick is in this position on this hole, only a fool would go for a birdie— or only a golfer who desperately needed a birdie to remain in contention.

The safe and smart approach shot here—and on any similar holes you might encounter—is for the "meat" of the green or that portion unguarded by a hazard. If you shoot for the meat of the green, you allow yourself a margin for error. Chances are excellent that you'll get your par. Settle for that. Then charge for a birdie on the next hole.

2—STRATEGY

VISUALIZE FLAGSTICK IN SAFE POSITION

It doesn't usually pay to shoot directly for a flagstick that is positioned behind a hazard such as a sand bunker. The chances of hitting a perfect shot and setting up a birdie putt simply are not equal to the risk of catching the sand and making a bogey.

In these circumstances I find that it helps to visualize the flagstick in a safe position, well away from the hazard (see illustration). This visualization gives me a positive—yet safe—target.

By using this technique, birdie putts will be surprisingly frequent and bogies conspicuously rare.

Score better with new grips

I feel that most golfers' hands slip on the club at some point in the swing. Indications of this are the worn spots that appear on golfers' gloves.

To keep this slippage to a minimum, I suggest that active players re-grip their clubs at least once a year, preferably in the spring when cold hands make firm gripping especially challenging.

Changing grips is a simple, relatively inexpensive process that most club pros can do in their own shops.

Remember that your hands are your only link with your golf club. Give yourself every chance to make that linkage secure.

CHECK PIN POSITION BEFORE "CHARGING"

The wise golfer is the player who knows when to charge and when to fall back.

A key factor in his decision on a given hole is the positioning of the flagstick on the green. Study the two greens shown in the illustration. Then consider how many times you've shot for the pin when it was tucked into a corner behind a hazard, and how many times you've bogeyed the hole.

Also consider how many times you've had an open pin position but really haven't given your full powers of concentration on actually trying to sink your approach shot.

I think that too many times we merely shoot for the green, instead of a specific spot or area on it.

ELEVATED TEE OR FAIRWAY ADDS UP TO GREATER DISTANCE

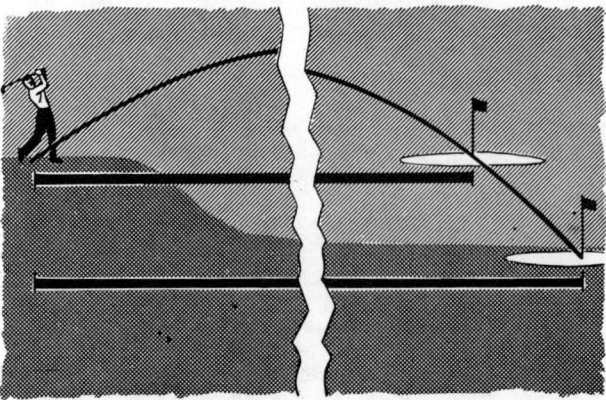

Many golfers fail to realize that a shot from an elevated tee or fairway to a green below will travel farther than will a shot to a green on your same level. The illustration shows why this is so. Note that the ball travels farther because of its extended parabola.

By the same token, if you shoot to a raised green, you can expect that the ball will not travel as far as normal.

Normally, my shots will travel about 10 feet farther if the hitting area is 20 feet higher than the green. The reverse applies to elevated greens.

This knowledge should prove helpful, especially on par-3 holes, so many of which include elevated tees or greens. Also, par-3 holes are often well-guarded by hazards or rough. Mis-judgment of distance can be especially harmful.

2—STRATEGY

DO YOUR OWN THING

If golf isn't enjoyable it shouldn't be played. For that reason I never criticize a player who chooses a somewhat unorthodox method to make a shot succeed. Golf isn't a matter of **how**, but rather of **how many**.

The illustration shows an example of how a relatively inexperienced golfer might perform better by resorting to a somewhat abnormal type of shot. This situation generally requires a high pitch that would land on the green.

But some players find it difficult to hit shots with high-lofted clubs. They feel more secure with a 4- or 5-iron. Such players should take the shot that is easiest for them. In this case it's a run-up shot with the less-lofted club.

LET THE WIND WORK FOR YOU

When the wind is blowing from the side, I believe in letting it work for me, and I think that other golfers should do the same.

Let's assume we have a left-to-right wind, as shown in the illustration. The golfer has two choices. He may (1) aim the shot to the left and let the wind bring it in to the green, or he may (2) play the ball to hook into the wind.

I much prefer the first alternative—letting the wind work for you by bringing the ball into the green. This course of action practically assures that your ball will finish no worse off than slightly to the left of the green—even if the wind quits blowing completely.

On the other hand, if I plan to hook the shot into the wind to offset its effect, and if the wind dies, or if I hook too much, my ball will finish in trouble to the left (note dotted line).

Another advantage of using the wind is allowing you to employ a normal swing, rather than requiring you to adjust for the intentional hook.

PLAY FASTER, PLAY BETTER

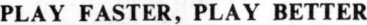

I firmly believe that most golfers play better if they don't have to sit around and wait between shots. This waiting merely increases tension and stiffness.

One way to speed play at your course is to set a good example in the use of golf cars. Whenever you share a car with another player, always drop him off at his ball and then proceed on to yours...or vice-versa if you are "away." While he's addressing his ball, drive over to yours and plan your shot. Then your partner can walk toward the car while you are playing.

I'm sure that if all golfers at your club, would follow this practice, you'd all enjoy the game much more and probably shoot better scores.

THE ADVANTAGE OF BEING THE UNDERDOG

Time and again I see the underdog in a golf match failing to see the advantage that is inherent in his role.

Let's face it... the favored player has everything to lose. The pressure is on him. No one expects the underdog to triumph.

Never think you can't beat a stronger opponent. Win a hole or two from him and then see who starts to feel the pressure.

2—STRATEGY

PLAN AHEAD AND BREAK A STRING OF BOGEYS

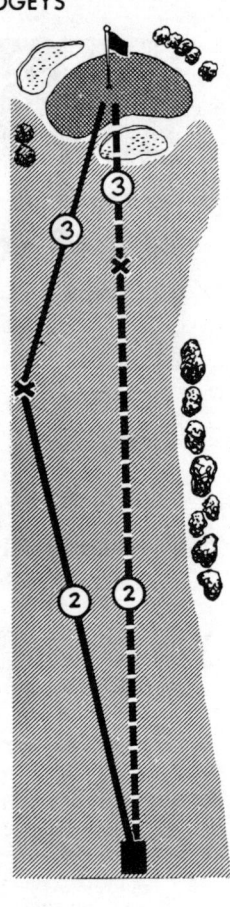

Good golfers plan their play on a hole before they hit their tee shot. The best way to break a string of bogeys is to stand on the tee and take stock of just where each shot must finish to give you a par.

As shown in the illustration, one golfer has played his second shot on this par-5 hole right down the middle. Unfortunately a bunker guards the front of the green, so he must risk a bogey or worse by playing his third shot over the sand.

The smart golfer would look at the green, the bunker and the position of the pin, and then play his second shot to the left side of the fairway. Thus, he has an open shot to the flag and a better-than-average chance for a par, maybe a birdie.

Make it a habit to plan your play on a hole before you tee the ball for your drive. This is concentration at its best.

WHEN PRESSURE BUILDS, DON'T TIGHTEN UP

When you face a shot that involves a great deal of mental strain, such as the one over water illustrated today, you might tighten your grip on the club. Tightening the grip can hinder a smooth, rhythmical swing and make your swing jerky and rushed.

If you loosen your grip slightly, but still maintain firm control of the club, you will be better able to give the shot your best swing.

There are many ways to overcome mental anxiety on such shots, but I think the best is to concentrate on some positive aspect of your swing, such as merely striking the ball squarely.

DON'T BE GREEDY ON TOUGH HOLES

There are certain holes on any golf course that are easier than others. When you come across one, grab any opportunity that might arise to make a birdie.

On the more difficult holes, however, be content with a par, or even a bogey, depending on your level of skill.

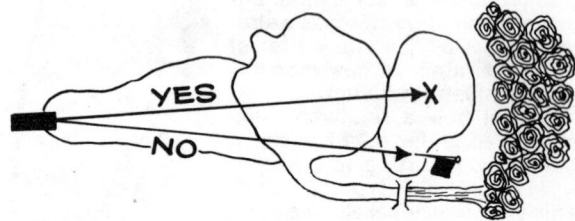

The illustration shows a good example of a hole that should be played with caution. The flagstick is on the right, which is the shallow portion of the green. It would take a tee shot of almost perfect length for the ball to finish near the hole.

On such a hole I'd probably play for a part of the green that gives me more landing area, in case my shot is too strong or too weak. I recommend that you do the same.

AN AID IN JUDGING DISTANCE

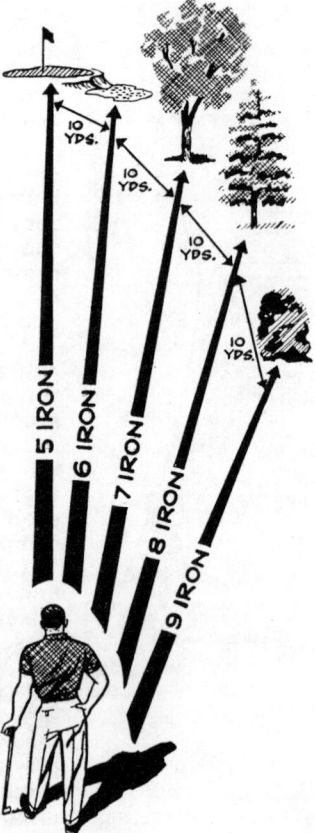

A problem shared by all golfers, regardless of their shot-making ability, is that of judging distance.

On the tour we have one advantage over the average club player. The fact that galleries often surround a green helps provide us with a better target. However, we usually compete on "strange" courses so the ability to correctly judge distance is most important.

Sometimes I use a method that we call "progression" to aid in my selecting the proper club. To judge distance through progression you first sight an object, such as a bush or tree or even a variance in the texture or terrain of the fairway, that is wedge or 9-iron distance away. Since I know that I gain 10 yards with each less-lofted club I progress to, I merely continue sighting objects, each in approximate increments of 10 yards, farther down the fairway. For each 10-yard progression, I drop down one more club. Finally I sight the green and choose the club to which I've progressed, confident that it will give me the correct distance.

60

2—STRATEGY

GOLF HAS ITS PSYCHOLOGICAL SIDE

I've noticed that good competitors often play their best when they are behind. They realize that there is nothing more demoralizing to an opponent than to steal

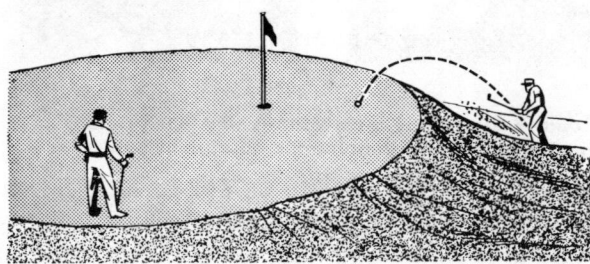

a hole he apparently has won. They seem to welcome the opportunity to come from behind.

Let's say your opponent is on the green in two shots (see illustration) and you are shooting four from the sand. Don't give up; try to hole your shot. Can you imagine how that would frustrate your opponent? It could change the whole tide of the match.

Never give up. A key shot that steals a hole is much more valuable -- from a psychological angle -- than any other well-played shot.

WATCH GOOD PLAYERS

Never pass up the opportunity to watch good golfers perform, either "live" or on television. The human being has great ability to imitate subconsciously (this talent is especially evident in youngsters) and it is possible to improve your golf swing by watching others.

You may wish to study a specific point in the experts' swing, such as the grip, stance, length of swing, etc. But this can be misleading. These specific parts vary from person to person, even among the best players. You may become confused or misled.

I suggest you watch good golfers' swings in total, rather than in part. Notice the back and forward rhythm and how there seems to be no hurried feeling. Then, the next time you play, your subconscious will tend to reproduce a good rhythm in your own swing.

If you can, play with good golfers and watch them swing. If you must play with poorer players, look away from them when they shoot.

VISUALIZE ONLY THE TARGET AREA

Most good golfers have developed to considerable degree the ability to create mental pictures. They can stand over a putt and actually "see" the line to the hole in their mind's eye. The same holds true on chip shots. They can visualize the exact spot on the green on which they wish their ball to land.

Another area of play in which the imagination can lend a big helping hand is on approach shots to the greens.

On such shots there is invariably some sort of trouble—trees, sand or water—that could adversely influence the shot (see illustration).

The wise golfer, however, learns to block out these problems from his mind's eye. Instead, he concentrates on the target area. In short, he eliminates negative factors about the shot at hand and stresses the positive goal.

IMAGINE THE FLAGSTICK IN THE BUNKER

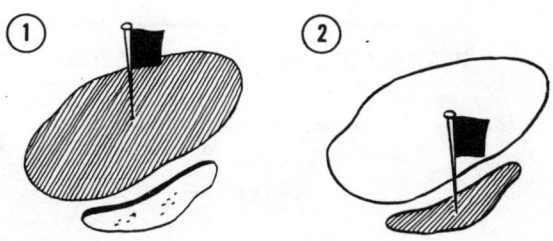

I never allow a negative thought to enter my mind when preparing to make a shot. This takes mental conditioning, but any golfer can learn to think positively.

For example, suppose you are faced with an approach shot that must fly over a sand trap (illustration #1). If you visualize yourself dumping the shot into the bunker, you probably will do just that.

Personally, I would imagine that the bunker is really the green and that the larger green is really sand (illustration #2). Now I must simply strike the ball solidly and firmly enough to clear the "imagined bunker." That's the positive thinking I've been talking about.

2—STRATEGY

DON'T OVER-CLUB ON WATER HOLES

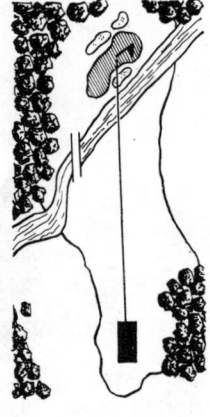

There is something about shooting to a green over water that causes most golfers to over-club. They'll select a 6-iron instead of a 7-iron and the ball flies well past the flagstick.

This is a special problem on the 155 yard, 12th hole at the Augusta National course where we play the Masters tournament (see illustration). The specific problem is Rae's Creek. If you over-club on your tee shot here, you can carry over the shallow green, into a downhill lie in a deep rough behind the putting surface.

If you find that you are continually flying the ball over the green on water holes, it may just be because of this tendency to over-club.

APPROACH SHOTS CALL FOR PRE-PLANNING

Today's illustration clearly shows why you should play approach shots to finish below the hole, so that you leave yourself an uphill putt.

The ball which runs uphill to the hole has the higher edge of the hole acting as a built-in backstop. The downhill putt, on the other hand, has little or no backstop. A putt, struck too hard downhill, has less of a chance of sinking in than an uphill putt has.

Also, remember that an uphill putt will stop closer to the hole if it misses the cup than will a downhill putt that gravity causes to roll on and on.

LET SOUND JUDGMENT PREVAIL IN SOME CASES

You will encounter some golfing situations from which it is simply good judgment to "fall back" (see illustration).

Bear in mind that the penalty for dropping back from an unplayable lie is only one stroke. Often I have seen golfers try and fail to dislodge a ball from a tough lie. That's one way that nines and tens occur.

Remember that you can sacrifice a stroke on a hole, accept your bogey and still shoot a fine score for the round. However, it is very difficult to fight back from a double or triple bogey.

PLAY IT "STRAIGHT" ON DOGLEGS

There is always a temptation on dogleg holes to "shave distance." In many instances the distance saved with even a perfect shot fails to ease the challenge of the hole.

In the illustration we see a typical example of what I mean. Note that Golfer B, who has cut the dogleg with his tee shot, still finds himself blocked from the flagstick by the sand bunker. Golfer A, who has taken the much safer route away from the trees, has an open shot to the hole.

Obviously the safe way was the best way on this hole; it often is.

WHEN TO USE 'TOO MUCH' CLUB

When making a shot to a green that is closely guarded by hazards, consider the consequences of hitting a poor shot.

A typical example is shown in the illustration. The shot calls for a long iron or wood and the green has sand bunkers on the left side and in front. Unless you strike the shot squarely, it probably will finish in the sand or, at best, short of the green.

I suggest using a longer than normal club for this shot . . . say a 2-iron instead of a 3-iron. Give yourself a chance to carry the hazards even if you mis-hit the shot slightly. If you should hit the ball squarely, it will still sit down quickly and hold the green (see arrow).

2—STRATEGY

THE 4-WOOD CALLS FOR FINESSE

Lately, there is a tendency for average and high-handicappers to substitute the 5-, 6- and even the 7-wood in place of a 2-, 3- or 4-iron. If you have trouble with the long irons, see if you can't do better with the woods.

Actually, a 4-wood can be made to do the work of a 4-iron. Choke up on the grip three or four inches (see illustration) and swing just as you would on any normal 4-wood shot. By "shortening" the clubshaft this way, you automatically cut down both the length of your swing and the shot's distance.

DON'T GAMBLE ON THE EARLY HOLES

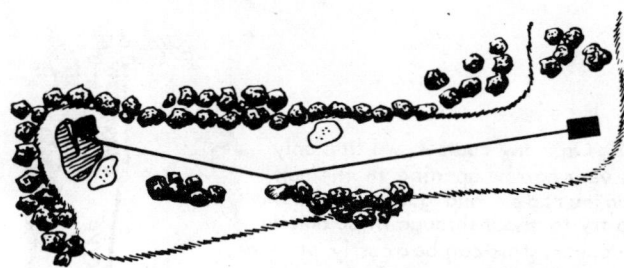

I chose the first hole at Augusta National (see illustration) to describe my method of playing the early holes in a round.

On this hole I will normally play well away from the sand on the right on my drive. On my approach shot I will play away from the sand on the left-front of the green, unless the flagstick is well beyond this hazard.

Nothing is worse than starting a round with a big, fat double-bogey. I suggest playing for a pars on the first few holes. You may get a "bonus" birdie along the way, but par should be your main objective. Later, after a backlog of good holes—and your swing feels loose and grooved, you might want to go for a few birdies.

AVOID SWING CHANGES WHENEVER POSSIBLE

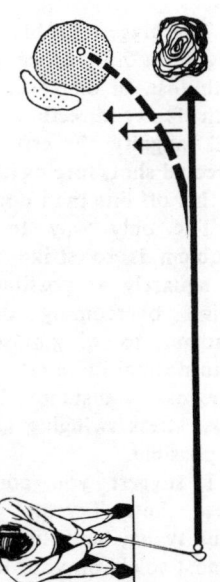

On crosswind shots you can either aim to left or right and let the wind bring in the shot, or you can alter your swing to fade or draw the shot into the force of the wind. I much prefer the former option since it involves no swing changes.

Merely select an object to the side of the pin from which the wind is blowing and hit the shot towards this object. Obviously, the force of the wind will determine how much you must alter your aim.

When playing in the wind, it is also wise to look at treetops to determine the force of the wind at that height. Often a slight breeze at ground level may be of much stronger force higher up where your ball will be traveling.

HIT FULL IRON SHOT INTO GUARDED GREEN

The illustration shows a green that is guarded on all sides by trouble. When such a green is small...such as the 7th at Augusta National shown here...you must be very careful about planning your strategy on the hole.

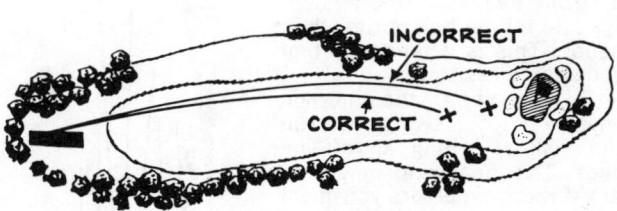

Leave yourself at least a full wedge shot on the approach. If you don't, you may not be able to put enough backspin on the ball to make it land and hold on the green.

The wise golfer will use less club than a driver off the tee in the situation. By hitting the shorter tee shot, you allow yourself the chance to put full backspin on your approach.

2—STRATEGY

PLAYING SHORT CAN BE GOOD GOLF STRATEGY

On many courses, we find only a very narrow opening to the putting surface and golfers continue to try to shoot through these narrow avenues. This can be a costly practice, especially for players who are a bit shaky on sand shots.

Play short of such greens (see illustration) unless you are reasonably certain you can carry the bunkers.

If you play short, you will still be in a good position to pitch onto the green and one-putt. You can still get a par on par-4 holes and, possibly, a birdie on short par-5s.

You will be reasonably sure of having a good lie in the fairway from which to play your next shot. If you go for the green and hit the sand, you might come up with a bad lie and ruin your round by going several over par.

WHEN TO LEAVE THE DRIVER IN THE BAG

I feel that club selection is almost as important on tee shots as it is on approach shots. You should always consider using a wood club (other than the driver) or even a long iron on any tee shot that places a premium on accuracy rather than length.

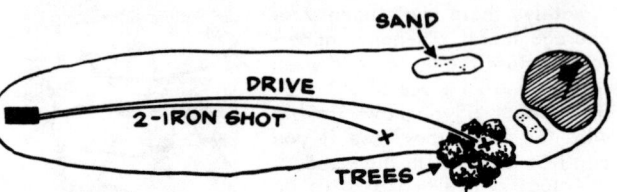

The illustration indicates what I mean. By using a club shorter than the driver, the golfer can not only lay up shy of the trouble, but he also can improve his chances of hitting the fairway.

Sacrificing some 20 yards off the tee may require your hitting a 7- rather than a 9-iron to the green. But your chances in so doing are still far greater than if you were forced to hit your 9-iron from out of sand or from behind a clump of trees.

SWING SMOOTHLY INTO THE WIND

When driving tee shots into a strong headwind, the tendency is to hit the ball harder than usual. This is a tendency that you should resist.

By changing the normal rhythm of your swing, you run the risk of hitting an off-line shot. The headwind magnifies any directional errors you might make. A shot that should slice only 10 yards may bend twice that amount because of the wind's action.

I strongly suggest that when hitting in the wind, you concentrate on striking the ball as squarely as possible. This is a positive thought that will replace the natural urge to over-swing. And it's the best way to beat the wind.

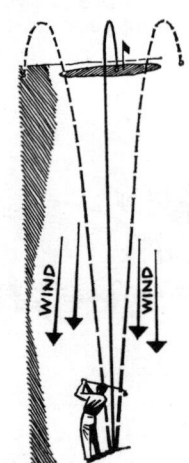

HOLD BALANCE INTO HEADWIND

The biggest problem when hitting shots into a headwind is not with loss of distance, but rather with faulty direction. The wind will magnify the error of a misdirected shot, forcing it to fly much farther off line than normal.

The only way to solve this problem is to strike these shots as squarely as possible. This requires overcoming the natural tendency to swing more forcefully than normal in an effort to negate any loss of distance. Instead you must stress swinging as smoothly as possible.

I suggest you concentrate on "balance" during these shots. Try to "grip" the turf with your feet as you swing, and finish with your weight established almost solely on your left foot.

SECTION THREE

THE SWING

How to Avoid Pushing, Shoving, Lifting and Throwing the Club.

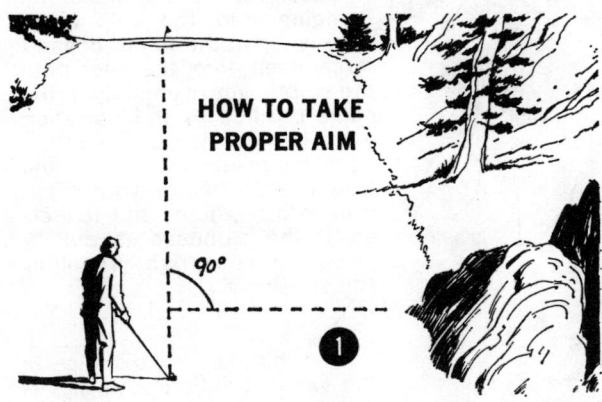

HOW TO TAKE PROPER AIM

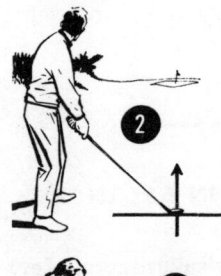

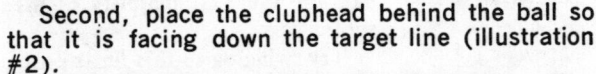

Aiming a golf shot is similar to aiming a rifle. You must not only point the gun (club) at the target, but you must also position your body to allow yourself to execute the shot properly.

You will have your best chance at proper aiming if you follow the three steps that I am showing in the illustrations.

First, approach the ball from behind and sight an imaginary line from it to the target. Square off this line at 90 degrees and extend the second line to some object at the right of the fairway (illustration #1).

Second, place the clubhead behind the ball so that it is facing down the target line (illustration #2).

Third, position your feet and your body so that you are facing directly the object you have chosen alongside the fairway.

If you follow this procedure, you will properly align not only your clubface, but also your entire body, into a perfectly square position.

HOW GRIP AFFECTS BACKSWINGS

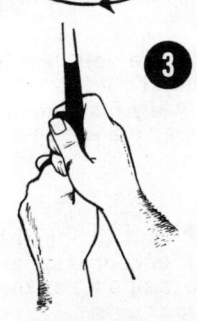

The golfer who grips the club incorrectly hinders his chances of making a proper backswing. This is shown in illustrations #1 and #2. In the first drawing, the golfer's hands are turned too far to the right on the clubshaft. From this so-called "strong" grip, the normal tendency is to turn the shoulders on a too level plane during the backswing (see illustration #2).

The result is a very flat backswing; one that forces the hips to twist too severely. This movement minimizes the activation of the big muscles of the back and legs.

Illustration #3 depicts the proper grip. Employing this method, the golfer will more likely take the clubhead straight back from the ball and continue into a proper upright backswing (illustration #4). This type of backswing will result with the shoulders turning much more fully than the hips. Consequently, those major back and leg muscles will come into play to a far greater degree.

65

3—THE SWING

A TIP FOR PRODUCING MAXIMUM SPEED

A combination of forward drive and stable head position builds a terrific force that moves down to the clubhead and produces maximum clubhead speed (see illustration).

Some better players actually let their heads move back to their right on their downswing to further increase this source of power. However, I don't advise that the average golfer try to consciously duplicate this head movement.

Make sure, however, that your head does not move forward toward the hole as your legs drive in that direction.

POUR RIGHT HAND INTO THE SHOT

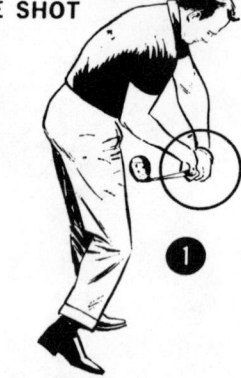

The average golfer does not apply enough right-hand power into his shots. If more golfers would learn to use their right hands properly at the correct time in the swing, there would not be nearly so many golfers slicing shots.

The right hand should unleash a tremendous amount of force into the ball, but it should do so only at the last split second when the clubhead is entering the hitting area. Until this time, your left hand should dominate in your swing.

Check the illustrations of me swinging into the ball. Make sure your right hand doesn't force itself into the shot until the club is approximately in the same position as in illustration #1. Then let it rip. Pour that right hand into the shot (illustration #2). Allow your right arm to straighten until it feels as if the clubhead is pulling down on your right shoulder (illustration #3).

The big key to distance in the swing is to time your moves properly so that your right hand comes into play at just the right time.

FIRM LEFT SIDE AIDS ACCURACY, DISTANCE

Early in the downswing when the shoulders are level across (illustration #1) the left leg may be slightly bent as the hips slide toward the target.

However, in the hitting area, when the left shoulder has raised, the left leg must be firm—almost rigid (illustration #2).

If the left leg is firm, the right shoulder will raise automatically instead of turning on a level plane. This keeps your clubhead inside the target line and encourages a solid hit. It also helps delay the unhinging of your wrists.

In short, the firm left leg forces you to turn your shoulders in a manner that will give you the best chance for an accurate and powerful shot. It also helps you keep your head behind the ball—to "stay with the shot."

FINISH IN BALANCE

Study today's illustration of my finish position and note especially how my weight has shifted onto the outside of my left foot and onto my right toe.

I think that the golfer who finishes in such balance can't help but make solid contact with the ball on the vast majority of his shots.

Try swinging to this finish position. Don't think about anything else during your swing. Merely imagine how it will feel to be in this position. See if this doesn't force you to make a better swing over-all.

3—THE SWING

TAKE A CUT AT A DANDELION

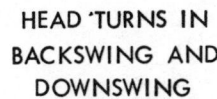

I'm afraid that because my own swing appears fast and forceful, I've given the impression that the golf swing requires a full-out blast of every living muscle and nerve in the human body. Nothing could be farther from the truth.

Let's face it, in golf we are not striking a heavy immobile object such as the tree trunk in Illustration #1. We are merely trying to make square contact with a ball that weighs less than two ounces. There is really no need to swing full force. This merely frustrates square contact.

I think most golfers would be far better off if they were to actually hit their shots with the same force they use on their practice swings. Try imagining that your golf ball is really nothing more than a dandelion. Make a smooth, full unhurried swing (Illustration #2) and see if you don't start playing more of your approach shots from the fairway instead of the rough.

HEAD TURNS IN BACKSWING AND DOWNSWING

While it is true that your head should not move laterally or up and down during the swing, the head should rotate, just as the hips and shoulders must, during the swing.

From the illustrations, you can see how and to what extent my head turns or rotates on the backswing and downswing.

Without such head rotation, my swing would become constricted, and the swing arcs would be shortened.

With lateral or up-down head movement, the swing plane and arc would be thrown out of kilter and missed hits would result.

KEEP A LEVEL HEAD DURING YOUR SWING

One of the main reasons for inconsistent shotmaking is the raising and lowering of the head during the swing.

You will note that, in the illustrations, my head remains in the same position at the top of my swing and at impact as it did when I originally addressed the ball.

If you can keep your head "level" in this manner, you will have a much better chance of returning the clubhead squarely to the ball. You will be less likely to top or scuff the shot.

THE RIGHT SWING PLANE FOR YOU

Swing plane is a little understood, but highly important, concept in golf. It involves the plane along which the clubhead moves and the shoulders turn.

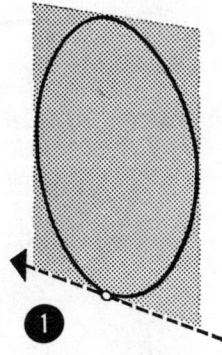

To understand the function of swing plane, imagine that the clubhead moved on a perfectly upright plane (illustration #1). Obviously such a swing plane would have one great advantage—the clubhead would always be on line with the target. However, it would also have one big disadvantage—the clubhead would be at ball level only a short time.

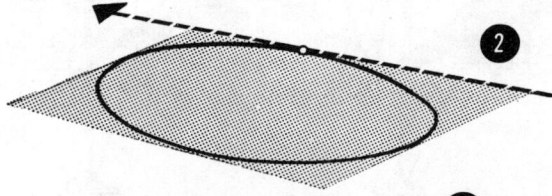

To take the opposite extreme, imagine a perfectly flat swing plane (illustration #2). If swung at ball level, this clubhead would always be at the right height for solid contact. However, it would seldom be moving along the target line.

The ideal swing plane for you is the one that combines these two extremes (illustration 3#) to keep the clubhead at ball level and along the target line as long as possible. Have a professional look at your plane to determine if it meets this ideal.

67

3—THE SWING

A TALK ON TIMING

Timing the golf swing is much like dancing: you must swing to a certain rhythm. The important thing about timing is not whether your tempo is slow or fast; what is important is that your rhythm is uniform in all shots with all clubs, from driver to putter.

Naturally, you'll swing faster on a drive than you will on a pitch, because you take a longer swing with the longer club. But just look at it this way: Rhythm or tempo or timing should never change; speed is determined by the club you happen to be using and by the swing length. Clubhead speed, you see, increases with the longer-shafted clubs.

START YOUR SWING WITH A FORWARD PRESS

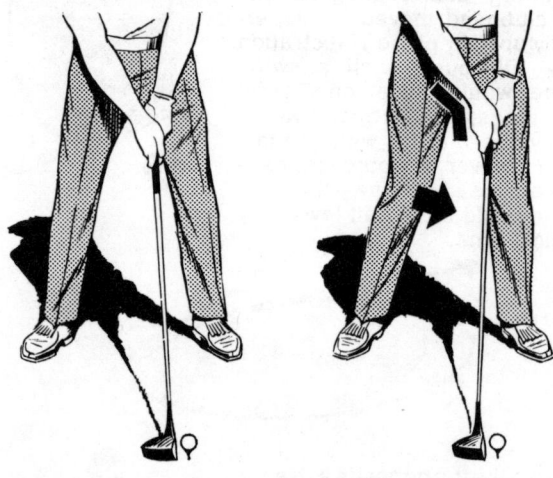

If you have trouble building a rhythm into your swing, check to see if you are making a "forward press" before starting your backswing.

The forward press is merely a very slight movement of the hands and/or the right knee toward the target (see illustration). This action should be followed immediately by the start of the backswing. It is sort of a rocking forward, then back and into the swing.

Such a pressing forward helps free the body from any tension that might have built up during the address period. It activates your actual swing in a manner that will provide a smooth, unified takeaway, rather than one in which one part—say, the hands—move out ahead of everything else.

SWING CLUBHEAD STRAIGHT BACK FROM BALL

At the start of the backswing, I think it is very important for the clubhead to move directly back from the ball (illustration #1). Now, here's a good rule to follow: Swing your clubhead straight back along the target line until it passes your right foot.

By initiating your swing in this manner, you will automatically extend your left arm to the fullest. It is this extension that gives you the wide swing arc and forces the big back muscles into play. Such a takeaway also causes a full shoulder turn; one on a sufficiently upright plane. The end result is more distance and straighter shots.

If you push the clubhead outside the target line during your takeaway (illustration #2), or if you pull it around inside the line too quickly (illustration #3), you will not achieve the desired results. Your swing will move out of the proper plane from the start.

ADDRESS THE BALL WITH HANDS FORWARD

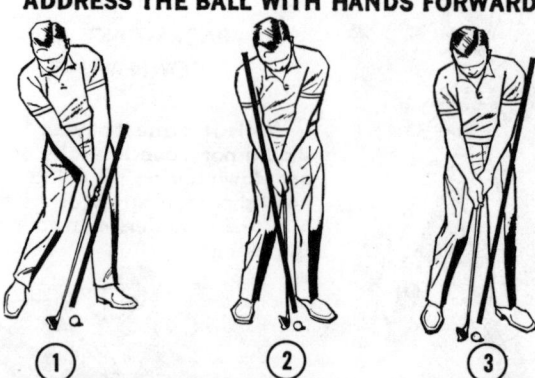

Illustration #1 shows the proper impact position. Note that my hands are leading the clubhead; my left arm is more or less continuous with the clubshaft.

Yet many golfers incorrectly address the ball with the RIGHT arm more or less continuous with the clubshaft (illustration #2).

I suggest positioning the hands just about opposite the ball on wood shots. If you play the ball farther back in your stance on irons shots, be sure your hands are in the same forward position as with the woods. (illustration #3).

3—THE SWING

SWING THE CLUBHEAD

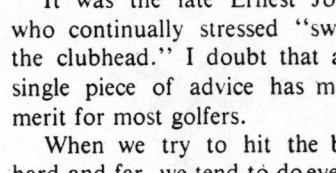

It was the late Ernest Jones who continually stressed "swing the clubhead." I doubt that any single piece of advice has more merit for most golfers.

When we try to hit the ball hard and far, we tend to do everything except SWING the clubhead. We push it, shove it, lift it, throw it—but we don't let it merely swing (Illustration #1). This is why we so often hit shots off to the side instead of forward.

How does one learn to swing the clubhead? I suggest you merely practice hitting balls while swinging solely with your arms (Illustration #2). Put your feet together and try to make solid contact without any body movement. Merely let the clubhead swing back and up and down and forward. You will be amazed how solidly—and how far—you can hit shots in this manner. Eventually, once you have sensed the feel of the moving clubhead, go back to hitting shots with a normal body turn and leg movement.

TURN YOUR BACK TO THE HOLE

The amount of shoulder turn on the backswing will vary with the golfer, depending on his or her suppleness. The best advice I can give is to make as big a shoulder turn as you can, short of losing balance, of course.

This isn't to say that you need a *long* backswing, one in which the club passes horizontal. If anything, the average backswing of top pros has become shorter over the years—shorter and tighter. These players make as big a shoulder turn as ever, but swing shorter because of less "wrist cock."

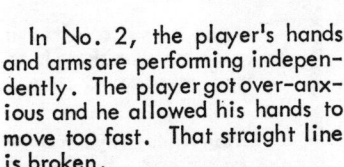

I see many golfers who think they are making a full turn, when really they are simply picking the club up with their arms (Illustration #1). I'd rather see those players simply *swing* the club up to the top while they *turn* their back to the hole (Illustration #2). *Swing* and *turn,* these are the key words to a full, distance-producing backswing.

ONE WAY TO ACHIEVE GROOVED SWING

Avoid any independent rolling of your hands and forearms on the backswing. Such rolling makes it difficult to return the clubface squarely to the ball.

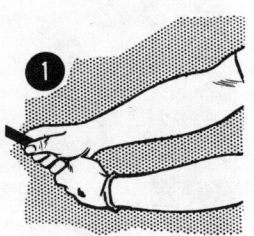

Check the position of your hands when they are hip high on your backswing. If you have taken the club back properly, the back of your left hand should be facing at right angles to the target line -- straight out from your body.

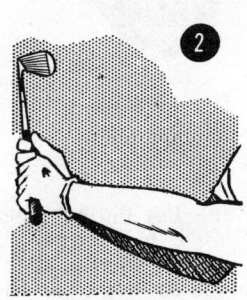

If the back of this hand is turned down or up (No. 1 and No. 2), you will have to compensate on your downswing to produce a square clubface during impact.

SWING IS A MATTER OF COORDINATION

In the swing, your hands, arms, shoulders, hips and legs are all part of the same package. If any one of these "misfires," your swing can easily get out of kilter.

Let's concentrate on the hands and arms.

Ideally, the left arm and clubshaft should form a straight line in the takeaway (see No. 1). All parts of my body are in step.

In No. 2, the player's hands and arms are performing independently. The player got over-anxious and he allowed his hands to move too fast. That straight line is broken.

Only when the swing is well coordinated will the muscles pull together to produce powerful, consistent shots.

69

3—THE SWING

FLAT FINISHES CAN FINISH YOUR GAME

The flat finish in No. 1 indicates an improper shoulder turn on the downswing that can cause everything from a slice to a pull-hook, depending on the position of the clubface at impact. Probably the clubhead has moved into the ball from outside-to-inside the target line.

The proper high finish I demonstrate in No. 2 indicates a proper lowering of my right shoulder and a return of my right elbow to my side on the downswing. My clubhead will have moved into the ball from inside-to-along the target line. If my clubface was facing the target, a straight shot would have resulted.

EXTEND IMPACT ZONE FOR BETTER DIRECTION

A good way to increase accuracy on your shots is to "extend your impact zone."

Often shots stray because the golfer has either rolled his wrists to the left – closing the clubface – during impact, or moved the clubface "across the ball" while striking it.

To eliminate these causes of misdirected shots, I suggest you continue the clubhead along the target line for an instant longer than normal following impact (see illustration). Don't sway your whole body toward the target; merely throw the clubhead out along the target line.

Extending the impact zone will automatically give you a full extension of your right arm on the follow-through and a nice, high finish.

GROUND THAT FLYING RIGHT ELBOW

It is true that Jack Nicklaus and Gay Brewer have had good success despite a flying right elbow. However, both have outstanding coordination and rhythm. They can return their right elbow to their side early in their downswings without adversely affecting their timing. Most golfers, however, will suffer from an improper swing plane and a premature uncocking of their wrists if they let their elbow fly.

Keep your right elbow in fairly tight as I am doing in illustration No. 1 and then return it to the right side (No. 2) at the start of the downswing.

A CRUCIAL STAGE OF THE SWING

I think that one of the most crucial points in the golf swing occurs when the player begins returning the club to the ball. If you will look at the illustrations, which show this stage of the swing from different angles, I will point out key features that will help any golfer.

In No. 1, note that though the downswing has just started, already my left heel is firmly planted and my lower body has uncoiled to my left. This quick shifting of weight to my left foot eventually results in additional clubhead speed.

In No. 2, you will see that my right elbow has returned to my right side. This not only helps insure a delayed uncocking of my wrists, but it also helps keep the clubhead on its proper path.

Illustration No. 3 shows that my right shoulder has started to lower, thus keeping the clubhead well inside the target line, and that my left hand and straight left arm are pulling the club downward to the ball with my wrists still cocked.

3—THE SWING

THE GOLF SWING IS STILL A "SWING"

Ever feel that you'll never learn to play golf well? Does the game seem to be an endless stream of "Do's" and "Don'ts?" Did you ever identify with the golfer in the illustration?

I'm sure that most golfers make the game much more complicated than it really is. We think about so many different checkpoints and key positions and basic moves that we tend to forget that the golf swing is, indeed, still a swing.

Don't let yourself get trapped into "paralysis from analysis." Make it your first and foremost rule to never, absolutely never, think about more than one thing while swinging a golf club. This may be the best, yet most difficult piece of advice I've ever given in this column.

LEARN TO COIL UP ON THE BACKSWING

To find yourself in proper position at the top of the backswing learn to coil on the backswing. Here's an exercise to help you coil, with the hands, arms, shoulders and hips working together:

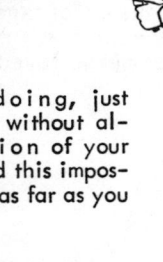

As you see me doing, just practice swinging without altering the position of your heels. If you find this impossible, swing back as far as you can anyway.

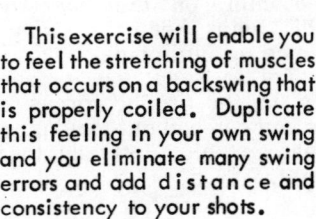

This exercise will enable you to feel the stretching of muscles that occurs on a backswing that is properly coiled. Duplicate this feeling in your own swing and you eliminate many swing errors and add distance and consistency to your shots.

TIP FOR LONGER SHOTS

Look carefully at illustrations No. 1 and No. 2. Note that my head and shoulders remain behind the ball throughout the swing, just as they were at address. Note also that this occurs even though much of my weight has moved off my right foot on the downswing.

The ability to "stay behind the ball" in this manner, while still moving weight from right to left on the downswing, can help assure any golfer of increased distance. This action builds up clubhead speed and unleashes it into the ball with maximum force.

The golfer who lunges or slides his upper body to the left (No. 3) sacrifices distance. He weakens his left side and releases his wrists before the clubhead reaches the ball. Such lateral movement of the head and shoulders also may cause the clubhead to move outside its proper path. This will result in sliced shots to the right or pulled shots to the left, depending on the direction the clubhead faces during impact.

COUNTDOWN FOR LOWER SCORES—4,3,2,1

Successful golfers follow a pattern of behavior when they set up to a shot. You too should follow a "countdown"—checking off key indicators that tell you you're ready to fire. For instance:

4! Put the clubface squarely behind the ball so that it looks at the target.

3! Put your feet in position so that the ball is opposite the desired spot in your stance.

2! Check to see that your stance is square—toes equidistant from the target line.

1! Check to see that your shoulder line is also square—parallel to the target line.

Finally, blast off just like the rockets do—slowly and smoothly, gradually increasing in velocity.

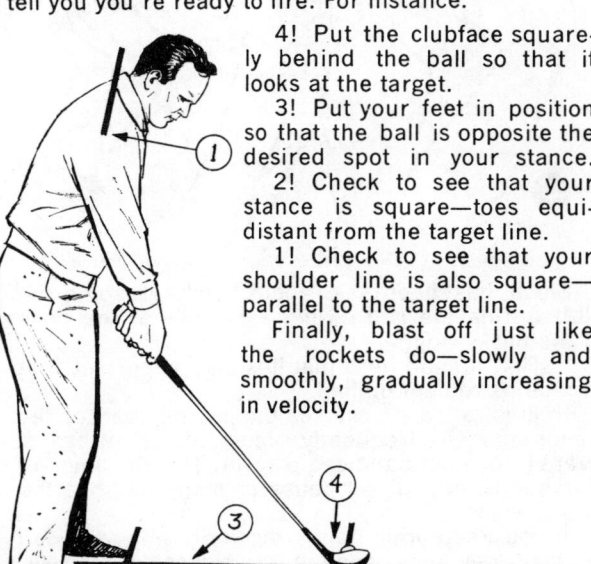

3—THE SWING

Put your hands in the power position

There is a lot of talk about "weak" grip positions and "strong" grip positions that I happen to take issue with.

To me the strongest possible grip is one in which the palms face each other and the right palm looks down the target line (Illustration #1). This grip allows the hands to work together as a unit unto themselves AND in alignment with the clubface.

A weak grip is one in which the palms do not face each other (Illustration #2) nor align with the clubface. It takes a great sense of timing to consistently return the club squarely to the ball using such a grip.

KEEP HANDS UNIFIED AT TOP OF SWING

Much has been said about firmly grasping the club during the golf swing, especially at the peak of the backswing.

I'd like to add here that it is also important that the hands remain unified.

In illustration #1, we see the pulling apart of the hands that so frequently occurs in the swings of average or high handicap players. This dis-union of the hands is a direct cause of many half-hearted shots.

If you keep your hands together, with your left thumb firmly entrenched in your right palm (illustration #2), you just may find your shots, especially the irons, taking off with a great deal more zest.

EVER TRY A 6-WOOD?

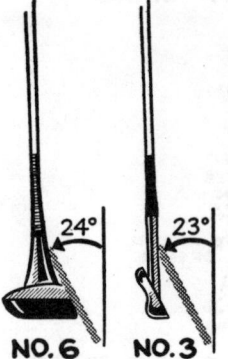

Ladies sometimes do not feel confident with a long iron in their hands. If this is true, the 6-wood may be the answer. It has about the same loft as a 3-iron (see illustration) and most women find it an easier club to swing.

The only thing to remember is that the 6-wood swing is a sweeping action, rather than a down-and-through shot as with the 3-iron. Play it just slightly ahead of your stance-center and plan on a fairly high finish. You should take little or no divot in front of the ball.

TAKE CLUB BACK LOW

The low takeaway, shown in the illustrations, produces several desirable effects in the golf swing.

By starting the club back low, you fully extend the left arm. This assures that your swing will have a nice wide arc.

Also, the low takeaway delays the unhinging of the wrists until later in the backswing. This encourages a later unhinging in the downswing so that power is saved until impact.

Finally, the low takeaway causes the left shoulder to properly lower, around and under the chin, on the backswing. This helps keep the swing on a nice upright plane.

Try to keep your takeaway low to the ground for as long as you can without moving your head or hips laterally to the right.

3—THE SWING

BEND FROM THE WAIST THROUGHOUT YOUR SWING

Many golfers address the ball by bending slightly at the waist. However, some of these same players tend to straighten up during the backswing. This alters the path of the clubhead.

Study the illustrations. Note that my waist-bend remains more or less consistent throughout my swing.

Keeping your waist-bend consistent will prevent lifting up or swaying laterally during the backswing. This allows you to strike the ball solidly more frequently. And your shots will go farther and straighter.

WIDE SWING INCREASES DISTANCE

A wide swing of the clubhead on full shots produces extra distance, not only because the clubhead travels farther in a wide swing, but also because a wide swing forces you to take a full shoulder turn.

The width of your swing is determined early in your backswing.

The club must go back low to the ground with your left arm fully extended, as mine is in No. 1.

Also there must be some shifting of weight to inside your right foot. If your weight remains on your left foot (No. 2), your swing will narrow as the club lifts too abruptly.

Remember to take the club away low and wide, but make certain that your weight shifts only to the inside of your right foot (No. 3). Should it move to outside this foot, your body may sway to the right and you'll lose your balance.

DEFINING SHOULDER 'TILT' and 'TURN'

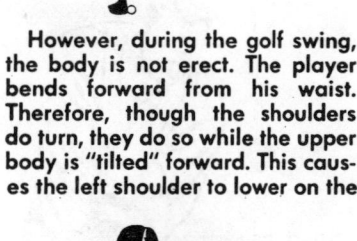

We often hear or read the expression, "Tilt and turn the shoulders." I'm afraid this may be a bit confusing to some golfers and therefore I'll try to explain.

If a person stood perfectly straight, and then turned his upper body to look behind him, he would have "turned" his shoulders on a level or horizontal plane.

However, during the golf swing, the body is not erect. The player bends forward from his waist. Therefore, though the shoulders do turn, they do so while the upper body is "tilted" forward. This causes the left shoulder to lower on the backswing and raise on the down and through stroke.

In the illustrations, you will note that my right shoulder is a bit lower than my left at address. This is because my right hand is lower on the club. On the backswing my shoulders tilt and turn until they are more or less vertical. On the downswing they return to a position similar to that of address as the club enters the hitting area.

PRACTICE BUILDS CONFIDENCE

Practice . . . aside from actually improving your shots . . . bolsters confidence. I know of no better way to eliminate nervousness during play than to thoroughly prepare yourself beforehand.

Once you are confident of making a certain shot, you probably **will** make it. Practice not only makes perfect, but it also frees your mind from doubt. As a result, you can give every shot your best possible swing. Only when doubt creeps in do you start to rush you swing and reduce your shotmaking proficiency.

3—THE SWING

SWEEP LONG IRONS WITH FIRM LEFT-HAND GRIP

I really believe that golfers who have trouble hitting long-iron shots—and there seem to be plenty in this fix—should stress three simple points in their swings.

First, grip the club especially firm with your left hand (illustration #1) on these shots. The left hand, and the left side, must dominate.

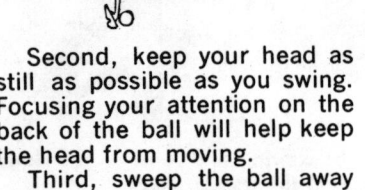

Second, keep your head as still as possible as you swing. Focusing your attention on the back of the ball will help keep the head from moving.

Third, sweep the ball away (illustration #3). Try to contact the ball at the bottom of your swing arc, as it flattens and the club is moving parallel to the ground.

THE BEST WAY TO 'LOOP'

Very few golfers can make their club move along the same path on the downswing that it took on the backswing. Most golfers, including the very best, must "re-route" or "loop" on the downswing.

There are two ways to re-route the swing. In the first illustration the golfer shows the incorrect method. Note how the club moves or loops to

a more vertical position at the top of his swing. Also note how this forces his elbow away from his body. This sort of loop "loosens" the swing and produces off-line shots.

The second method of re-routing the swing is shown in the second illustration. Here I have moved the club to the inside, or to a more horizontal position. See how this forces my right elbow to return to its proper position against my right side just as I start the downswing. This puts me in position to deliver a powerful and solid blow to the ball.

RETAIN KNEE FLEX THROUGHOUT THE DOWNSWING

It is important that golfers swing the clubhead through the ball with their knees still flexed. Stiffening the legs, usually the left (Illustration #1), can cause several problems, such as lifting the body, spinning the hips—and the shoulders—and falling back onto the right foot.

Start with your short shots—your wedges and 9-irons—to see how far past impact you can retain this knee flex. As you work into the longer clubs, you'll find it more and more difficult to maintain, due largely to the fact that your right side tends to take over and throw the club into the ball on these fuller shots. But stick with it. Keep that left knee flexed as I am doing in illustrations 2a and 2b. You'll find yourself striking the ball solidly much more frequently.

PULL CLUBHEAD WITH BACK OF LEFT HAND

At that point in the swing when the clubhead is on the ball, the back of the left hand, ideally, should be facing the target (illustration #1) just as if you were hitting a backhand shot in tennis.

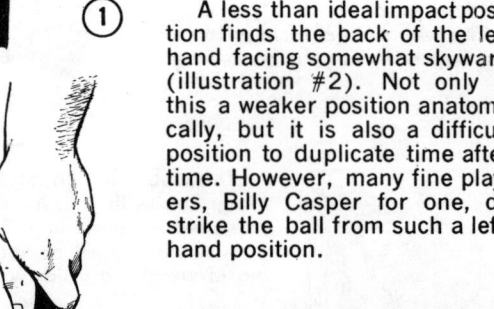

A less than ideal impact position finds the back of the left hand facing somewhat skyward (illustration #2). Not only is this a weaker position anatomically, but it is also a difficult position to duplicate time after time. However, many fine players, Billy Casper for one, do strike the ball from such a left-hand position.

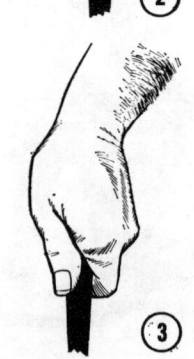

The worst possible impact position is that shown in illustration #3. Notice that the back of the left wrist has collapsed and bent inward. This collapsing of the wrist "turns off" the smooth flow of power down the left arm and to the club. It also closes the clubface and puts it into a hook position. More often, however, such an impact position indicates that the golfer's right hand has taken over control of the swing—an error that can cause both hooking and slicing.

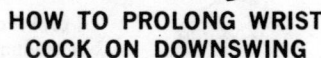

YOUR CLUB CAN POINT THE WAY TO FINE RESULTS

To rid yourself of hooking, try "throwing the clubhead at the target" after impact.

I don't mean that literally, of course. But, by thinking about continuing the swing toward the target, you can cut down the tendency to close the clubface at impact and to finish with a flat follow-through.

Strike the ball with a firm left wrist, with the back of the left hand facing your target (No. 1).

Then continue "swinging toward the target" (No. 2) with that wrist still firm. The clubface will "look" at the target for a longer time, thus minimizing the hook.

Just be sure to keep your head behind the ball throughout the swing. Don't let it sway toward the target.

THE "INSIDE" FEELING PAYS OFF

Promote an "inside-out" swing pattern for best results. As soon as you bring the clubhead back to the ball from the top of the backswing (see illustration #1), get that "inside" feeling and let it continue through impact and for a couple of feet past the original ball position.

The fact that I believe my left hand guides the downswing (see illustration #2) helps that inside movement. My left arm is close to my body, assuring a hit from inside the intended line of flight.

Still staying inside after impact, I swing so that the back of my left hand faces the target for as long as possible, or until the force of the swing brings the hands up and out.

Result? A slight draw or hook, the ball curving from right to left, for maximum distance.

HOW TO PROLONG WRIST COCK ON DOWNSWING

As I have often pointed out, the extra distance that results from good timing of a golf swing will only occur if the wrists remain cocked until late in the downswing, when the hands are about hip high.

The easiest way to insure against premature uncocking of the wrists is to make certain that they are still cocked at

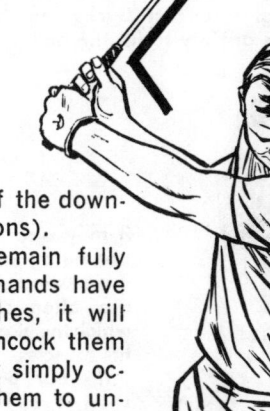

the earliest stage of the downswing (see illustrations).

If your wrists remain fully cocked after your hands have lowered a few inches, it will be impossible to uncock them too early; the swing simply occurs too fast for them to unhinge prematurely thereafter.

SPEAKING OF STANCE

At address, your feet should be spread far enough apart to provide a firm foundation for your swing. Too wide a stance will restrict leg action and body turn.

I personally like to feel that my feet are spread to the extent that the distance between my inner soles equals the spread between the outer edges of my shoulders (see illustration). I think this might be a good guide for most players.

However, if you seem to have trouble making a full turn, try a narrower stance. If you have trouble maintaining balance during your swing, try a wider stance.

3—THE SWING

HOW FAST SHOULD YOU SWING BACK?

I feel that the speed of a golfer's backswing is determined largely by his temperament. A somewhat laconic person, such as Julius Boros, often has a slow backswing; mine is quite fast.

Basically the speed of the backswing is optional, so long as the golfer makes a full turn, retains a firm grip on the club and remains in balance.

If the backswing is too fast, the golfer may expend unnecessary energy that he should save for the downswing. If a fast backswing stems from anxiety to hit the ball,

it may also produce a premature unhinging of the wrists on the downswing. Also, fast backswings are often short backswings, in which the player fails to fully stretch his muscles.

If your backswing seems too short, if you loosen your grip at the top, or if you have a problem maintaining balance, I'd suggest you try a slower backswing.

BEND SLIGHTLY AT KNEES AND HIPS

Most golfers have heard or read that they should bend slightly at their knees and hips as they address the ball (see illustration No. 1). This bending is necessary to produce a smooth, fluid swing and good balance during your swing.

However, many golfers who correctly bend at address tend to straighten their legs or body as they move to the top of their backswing. This not only minimizes chances for a smooth swing, but also alters the plane of your swing. Thus altered, it becomes difficult to return the clubhead squarely to the ball.

Remember to retain the same flex in your knees and hips during your swing that you originally had at address (see illustrations Nos. 2 and 3).

HOW BALL POSITION AFFECTS HEIGHT OF SHOT

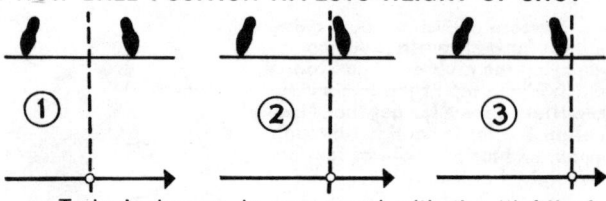

Today's lesson is concerned with the "loft" of the ball. In golf, there are two types of "loft." The first is of the normal variety...the angle of tilt the manufacturer has built into the club's face. The second is known as "effective loft." This is related to the amount of loft the clubface carries when it actually strikes the ball.

Generally speaking, positioning the ball far back into the stance reduces the "effective loft" the club will be carrying at impact. At this point in the swing as you see, the club is still moving downward.

As the clubhead moves parallel to the ground, its "effective loft" is equal to its "normal loft." Then, as the club begins moving upward, the "effective loft" is greater.

Thus, it becomes obvious...the farther back in your stance you play the ball; the less will be the "effective loft" at impact. The result is a lower shot. Therefore, to hit low shots, play the ball back. But to hit high shots, play it forward, allowing the club's "effective loft" to be greater at impact.

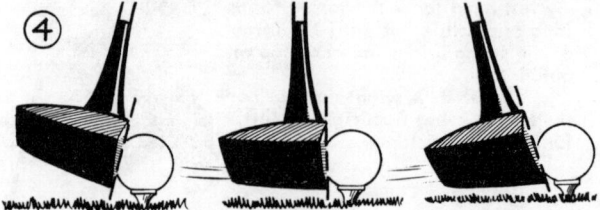

VARDON OVERLAP HAS GREAT EFFECTIVENESS

I feel the best way to combine the hands on the clubshaft is to use the Vardon, or overlap, grip. This grip fits the hands together snugly and occupies less space on the club than any other orthodox grip. The thumb of the left hand fits snugly into the palm of the

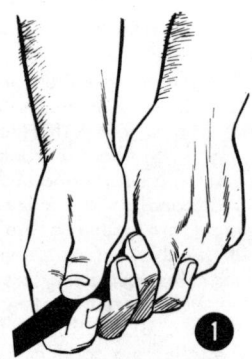

right hand because of the unique locking of the fingers (see illustrations).

When this grip is combined, you should feel most pressure in the last three fingers of your left hand and the middle two fingers of your right (see shadowed areas in illustration #2).

3—THE SWING

PLAY BALL OFF CENTER OF CLUBFACE

It may seem too obvious to mention, but the ball should be just in front of the center of the clubface when you address the ball. It is truly amazing how many golfers fall into the habit of positioning the ball carelessly, and thus suffer from miss-hit shots.

You will find that if you start with proper ball positioning, and then concentrate during your swing on striking the ball squarely, several other swing fundamentals will fall into place. Not the least of these is that such a procedure will practically force you to keep your head relatively still on both your backswing and downswing.

LOOK AT TARGET 'OVER' YOUR LEFT SHOULDER

You will note from the illustration that I have set myself up a perfectly square address position. The lines across my hips, shoulders and toes all are parallel to the line from ball to target. This is the ideal position, I feel, for hitting straight shots.

The difficulty, however, lies in arriving at this square address position. It is especially difficult, for instance, for many golfers to align their shoulders squarely. They are often turned left of target in an "open" position. A sliced shot is likely to result from such positioning of the shoulders.

If you slice shots, try positioning your upper body so that you feel you are looking "over" your left shoulder when you sight the target. You will feel you are aiming to the right of target. But see what happens. If the shot flies straight and you hit the ball solidly, chances are you have been mis-aligning your upper body.

PUSH OFF RIGHT FOOT TO AID IN WEIGHT SHIFTING

One very important move in every full golf swing is the shifting of weight from the right side to the left side at the start of the downswing. Yet, this apparently simple shifting seems to puzzle and frustrate so many golfers.

It may help you shift your weight to the left if you start your downswing with a "pushing off" of your right instep (see illustrations).

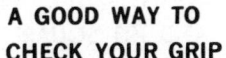

If this feels uncomfortable to you, I suggest you concentrate on your right knee. Think about moving it towards the ball at the start of your downswing, as illustrated. This, too, is an excellent way to start your weight shift to the left.

A GOOD WAY TO CHECK YOUR GRIP

Regardless of how you hold your golf club, remember that the position of the hands is a key to proper gripping. The hands should essentially face each other. Only with such placement can the hands function as a unit... securely controlling the club so that it returns squarely to the ball.

To insure that the hands are properly unified, first assume your normal grip. Next, open the hands so that the palms are facing each other (illustration #1). If they do not, reposition them and repeat the process until they do. The second illustration shows the hands when the palms are situated correctly. Try to emulate this grip.

3—THE SWING

RETURN RIGHT ELBOW TO RIGHT HIP

A very crucial downswing move is the return of the right elbow to the right hip. This movement should begin at the very start of the downswing so that the elbow is snug against the hip by the time the clubhead moves into the hitting area (illustration #1).

If the elbow has moved towards the hip in this manner, you will automatically achieve a proper lowering of your right shoulder. This is vital in keeping your clubhead "inside" the line to the target.

If your elbow fails to return to your right side, your right shoulder may not lower properly (illustration #2). This will cause you to swing "over the ball."

Your clubhead will move into the ball from "outside" the target line, causing you to either pull the shot to the left or to cut it and slice it to the right.

TRY LEFT-ARM SWING TO IMPROVE TIMING

Golfers who fall into the habit of rushing the downswing should practice hitting shots while holding onto the club with only the left hand.

If you will try this with a short iron—say a 9-iron—you'll find it impossible to hit the ball solidly unless you pause dramatically at the top of your backswing.

This gives your hips and legs time to start moving and lead the downswing.

If you start down too soon, you'll drive the clubhead into the ground behind the ball.

It's vital in golf that you give your swing time to change directions. Swinging with only the left hand on the club forces you to do just that.

LEARN TO HIT HARD AND HIT SQUARELY

Somewhere, in the course of their playing, golfers find that they can hit the ball squarely with greater consistency if they do not swing hard. This attitude leads to losing the will to hit the ball hard, and an easy swing gets to be a difficult habit to break.

As soon as an easy hitter tries to add power, he often begins missing shots and he soon gives up trying for distance.

I maintain that almost any golfer can learn to hit the ball hard AND squarely.

Learning to hit the ball hard requires a whole new mental outlook, along with considerable practice and instruction. But I think the serious golfer should make plenty of effort in this direction.

TORQUE ACTION INCREASES CLUBHEAD SPEED

When your hands move below your belt line on the downswing, you are moving into the all-important hitting area. This is the area in which your clubhead speed should be greatest. Your buildup of clubhead speed in this area should be gradual; it doesn't help to lunge or jump at the ball.

The increasing clubhead speed is derived from what engineers call torque action, as the body and arms and hands move to the left ahead of the clubhead. Clubhead speed will increase only so long as the hands lead it. Note in the accompanying illustrations how my hands remain ahead of the clubhead until after impact.

Remember that the hands lead the clubhead into the ball, but that they must move smoothly without any hint of sudden thrust.

3—THE SWING

LEFT KNEE CONTROLS HIP TURN

It is essential to a well-timed golf swing that the backswing be free of restriction. A common form of backswing restriction occurs when the player "points" his left knee at the ball. Sticking the knee forward in this manner (No. 1) makes it impossible to turn the hips fully to the right.

Instead, this knee should point to behind the ball, as I demonstrate in

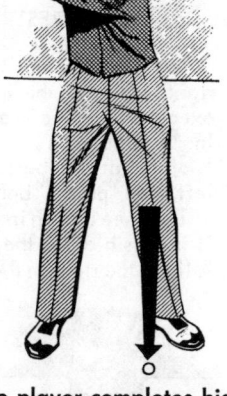

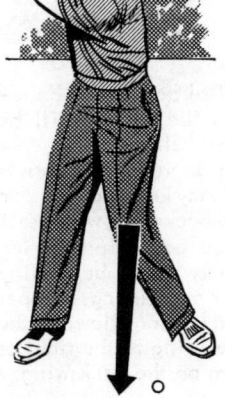

No. 2, as the player completes his backswing turn. You will note the greater degree of turn that this correct knee position permits.

Much of the swing's power generates from the golfer's legs. This power – and a great deal of timing – is wasted unless the player employs proper leg and footwork. A key to proper footwork is to let the left knee swing to the right as the hips turn on the backswing.

RETAIN KNEE FLEX DURING SWING

If you want to get all the distance possible, you must be certain that your legs never stiffen until the ball is well on its way. Always maintain an element of flex in your knees.

Be particularly careful that your right knee isn't stiff on the backswing. Keep some bend in your leg (illustration #1). Maintaining this flex during your backswing is important. It will help prevent your weight from shifting onto the outside of your right foot. This shifting causes

a loss of balance. The bent right leg also reduces the hip turn as you make a full shoulder turn. Consequently, the back and leg muscles are not utilized.

During the downswing, you must not allow your left leg to stiffen. This, however, will occur eventually with most golfers after the ball is struck. Should this leg stiffen during your downswing, your hips will start to swivel or spin to the left. This forces your shoulders to start turning on a too-level plane. This level turn will throw your clubhead outside the target line, causing you to pull or slice your shots.

POSITION FEET FOR A POWERFUL SWING

Don't overlook the fact that the position of the feet directly affects the swing.

Most of today's better golfers point their right feet straight out, but they "tee out" slightly with their left foot (illustration #1).

Pointing the right foot straight out gives you resistance against swaying laterally to the right during the backswing. It keeps you "over the ball" as I am in illustration #2.

Teeing out with the left foot facilitates driving your legs forward to your left at the start of the downswing (illustration #3). Not toeing out restricts this movement and "blocks out" your swing.

In short, these foot positions provide full coiling on the backswing and free-wheeling lower-body movement on the downswing. The end result is better balance and more distance.

MAKE BIG TURN, SHORT BACKSWING

The backswing should produce a full coiling of your big muscles and maximum control of the club. In other words, you should seek a big shoulder turn and a short backswing (see main illustration).

Never feel that you must make a long backswing. This only leads to loose wrists and loss of club control (smaller illustration). The modern professional usually makes a full 90° shoulder turn, yet seldom reaches a horizontal clubshaft position during his backswing.

At the top you should feel tension across your back and down your left side. Your hands and wrists should feel "frozen" to the club itself.

3—THE SWING

SWING THE CLUBHEAD

A most common error among novice golfers is the mistake of picking up the clubhead at the beginning of the backswing.

This premature cocking of the wrist takes the body right out of the shot, for a person swinging in this manner will not be able to pivot correctly. They'll use only the hands and arms.

For as long as possible, the left arm and club shaft should form a straight line, as illustrated.

By keeping the wrists passive, or unbroken, the golfer will be able to use his body and all of its power in the shot. Don't worry about your wrist-break. If you start out this way, they'll break at the right time.

THE BACKSWING MUST BE UNRESTRICTED

Today's drawings illustrate the right way and the wrong way to execute an effective backswing. In #1, the player's left knee "points" at the ball. In #2, my left knee "points" behind the ball.

The knee action in #1 will make it impossible for the hips to turn fully to the right in the backswing.

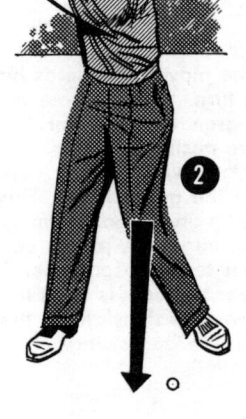

Thus, the vital action will be restricted and the swing will be anything but well-timed.

A greater degree of hip turn is permitted by my knee position; an unrestricted backswing will result.

Unless you employ proper leg and footwork, you'll be wasting swing power and timing. Proper footwork calls for allowing the left knee to swing to the right as the hips turn on the backswing.

KEEP HANDS "HIGH" AT ADDRESS

The next time you watch a top amateur or professional golfer, notice how he positions his hands at address. I'm sure you will find that his hands ride "high." That is, the top of his forearms and his thumbs form more or less a straight line (see illustration).

This positioning of the hands indicates that the player is holding the club more in his fingers than in his hands. This will give him more "feel" for the club than if he were gripping largely with his palms. After all, when we want to feel something, we touch it with our fingers—not our palms.

I guarantee you that if you see a golfer who allows his wrists to sag at address, he will not be a low handicap player.

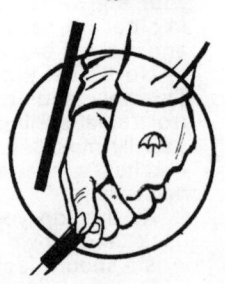

IT PAYS TO CHECK AND RECHECK YOUR GRIP

Illustration #1 is a picture of correct grip: The pinkie of the right hand is wrapped around the left-hand index finger; the club handle rests on the third joint of the index, middle and third fingers; the left thumb fits in the groove at the base of the right hand.

In a close-up of the standard grip (see illustration #2), the right thumb points downshaft and a little to the left of center.

At address, the forefingers and thumbs of both hands form "V's" which point in imaginary parallel lines to my chin.

3—THE SWING

'STRAIGHT' LEFT ARM DOESN'T MEAN 'RIGID'

It's almost impossible to have a solid swing if your left arm isn't straight. If the left arm collapses at any point, the flow of body power to the club is broken.

So make sure this arm is straight (not rigid) at address, on the take-

away, at downswing start, and during impact. In this way, you will have a wide swing arc and will maintain a firm left side.

Whatever you do, don't feel that the arm must be rigid, or even completely straight throughout every second of the swing. It may bend slightly at the top of the backswing, but be sure it straightens out again on the downswing.

IT'S ALL IN YOUR HANDS

Whether or not your clubface is properly aligned, and whether your shots will fly straight, can be determined by your hand position.

Make this experiment: Place an iron club down so that the leading

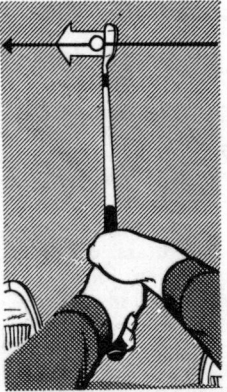

edge of its clubface points toward, say, a doorknob across the room (see No. 1).

What happens when you move your hands toward the knob? The

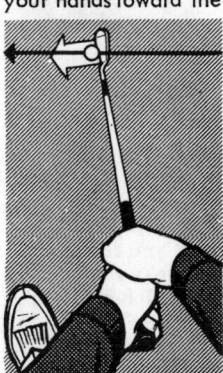

clubface opens and faces to the right of the knob, as in No. 2. It closes and faces left when your hands move back (see No. 3).

All this is by way of illustrating the importance of hand positioning. At impact, try to have your hands in their original address position.

KICK LEFT KNEE IN DURING BACKSWING

One of the key moves of the backswing involves proper foot and leg action. The left knee should gradually turn to the right so that it points behind the ball, as I am demonstrating in the illustrations.

This simple action will help insure that your backswing turn is correct. It will help you move the club smoothly back, around and up, instead of jerking it abruptly upwards.

This latter problem occurs when golfers merely point their knee forward and go up on their left toe during the backswing.

If you cannot keep your left foot planted during your backswing, at least try to keep your instep on the ground. Proper left knee action will automatically cause the instep to stay grounded.

SHOULDER TURN HELPS SHOT ACCURACY

Your shoulder turn on the backswing can give you a good indication of how straight your shot has been.

If your turn has been proper and the left shoulder has moved under your chin, at the top of the swing,

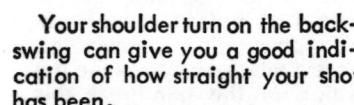

the club should be pointing along the target line (see #1). From this position, it's easy to return the clubface squarely to the ball.

Illustrations 2 and 3 show you the results of an excessive and incomplete shoulder turn respectively. From either of these positions, it's possible to hook, slice, pull or push, depending upon the clubhead's return path.

3—THE SWING

TAKE YOUR RIGHT HAND OUT OF YOUR BACKSWING

The golfer in illustration #1 is obviously a victim of a right-hand dominated backswing. His left arm has collapsed and he's lifted the club to the top of his swing with practically no coiling of his shoulders and back muscles. He's going to hit a weak shot; probably a slice.

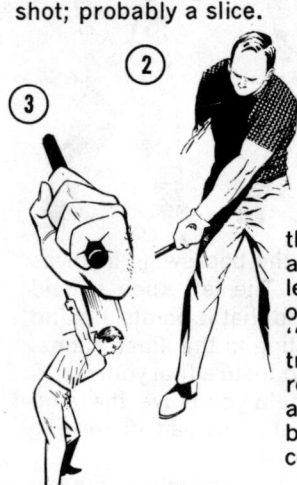

To make a full backswing that will produce a forceful and accurate blow to the ball, your left hand must dominate control of the club. Take your right hand "out" of the backswing (illustrations #2 and #3). This may require exercising your left hand and arm. But I can't think of a better way to add distance and control to your shots.

LOOK BACK AT HANDS WHEN ADDRESSING BALL

Too many golfers "reach" for the ball at the address position. Their hands on full shots are either below their eyes or even farther out from their bodies (illustration #1).

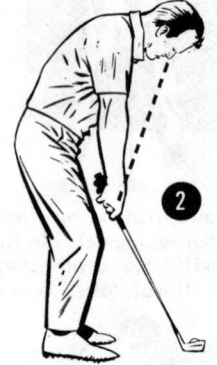

I like to feel that I can "look back" at my hands when I address the ball. This means that the hands must be hanging fairly close to my body (illustration #2).

With your hands close to your body—about 3 or 4 inches away

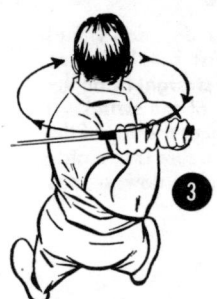

on full shots—your torso will extend out toward the ball. You will be bent from the waist with your back fairly straight. Bending in this way encourages a nice full tilt of the shoulders (illustration #3) and minimizes the hip turn. A full coiling of back and shoulder muscles will result.

PROPER HAND POSITION SETS STAGE FOR PROPER DOWNSWING

One of the key swing checkpoints is the position of the hands just before they begin their downswing movement. This is a vital point because the position of the hands at this stage determine the path along which they will direct the club during the downswing. Since the

downswing occurs so fast, the hands really "commit" you to success or failure before they even begin to swing downward.

Check for two things in your grip on the club at the top of your swing.

First, your fingers should be more or less around the top of the clubshaft and your palms more or less beneath the shaft (illustration #1). Second, the back of your left hand should form a continuous line with the back of your left arm (illustration #2).

If you have a proper grip and if these two points check out at the top of your swing, your downswing should automatically assume a reasonably proper clubhead path.

FULL SHOULDER TURN INCREASES DISTANCE

Modern golf teaching stresses a full coiling of the shoulder and upper body muscles. There must be something to this, for it seems that long-hitters, regardless of their over-all size, make very full shoulder turns (See illustrations of Sam Snead, Ben Hogan and myself).

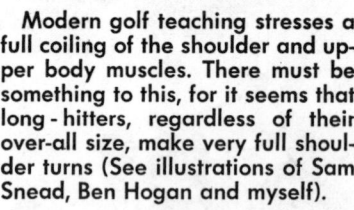

I feel that many amateur golfers could be hitting the ball farther if they would work to develop a fuller coiling of their shoulders. And I think almost every golfer can in-

crease his or her turn. I suggest that every morning, upon arising, you merely simulate your normal backswing (you don't need a club in your hands) then increase your shoulder turn until you feel a definite tightening across your upper back and down your left side. Hold this position for about 10 seconds.

Also stress this fuller shoulder turn when you hit practice shots. In play, longer shots will soon result.

3—THE SWING

SWING 'WIDE' TO HIT FAR

A swing characteristic that is common to all long-ball hitters is their very wide backswing. Note the illustrations here of Jack Nicklaus on his backswing and you will see what I mean by a wide swing. See the full extension of his left arm as he seems to push the clubhead as far away from his body as possible.

The wide swing actually increases the distance the clubhead travels. This, in itself, will usually produce extra yardage. But more important, the wide swing insures a full stretching of the golfer's muscles—a full wind-up on his backswing. It is this muscular action that really builds up the power.

Try to make as wide a swing as you can. But make sure you don't sway laterally to the right in your efforts to widen your arc. Don't let your weight move outside your right foot.

HOLD 'IMPACT POSITION' THROUGH TO YOUR FINISH

Sooner or later most golf swings break down and the back of the left wrist collapses inward. It "cups" as a result of the more powerful right hand and side taking over.

This doesn't happen, however, in the case of a strong golfer who can maintain left-side dominance.

During impact, the back of your left hand, wrist and lower forearm should be straight and more or less facing down the target line. You should "backhand" the shot. If you really have strong left-side dominance, you'll retain this straight left wrist until the finish of the swing.

Not many golfers can do this, but it is a worthwhile goal for any golfer to seek. If you succeed, you'll hit the ball much straighter, much more frequently.

STAY DOWN WITH YOUR SHOTS

If your left leg stiffens before or during impact (see illustration #1), you are prone to lifting your left shoulder. This, in turn, causes your clubhead to come up too quickly, resulting in a topped shot.

The good players have the knack of swinging through the ball with the clubhead traveling at ball level for a relatively long time. This helps insure that the club strikes squarely into the back of the ball.

These players make this happen by "staying down" with the shot. They swing through the ball with both knees still slightly flexed (illustration #2) and their head still well behind the ball. Their knees slide forward, but the head stays back. The left leg does not straighten until near the finish of the follow-through.

GOLF IS A 'BACKHANDED' GAME

Hitting a golf ball is a "backhanded" motion. You should feel that you are striking the ball with the back of your left hand, as opposed to the butt end of this hand.

In illustration #1, I show the incorrect technique. My hands have failed to return to their original position. The clubface is still "open," looking to the

right of target. Obviously the shot will slice in that direction.

In illustration #2, I have squared my hands to the target line. I am backhanding the ball, which will fly straight.

If you consistently slice shots, you may be failing to "backhand" your shots. Try to hit the shot with the back of your left hand. To help achieve this, do not roll or turn your hands to your right at the start of your backswing.

83

3—THE SWING

POINT CHIN BEHIND BALL FOR FREER SHOULDER TURN

It is vital on full shots that you execute as complete a shoulder turn as possible without straining. Yet, some golfers have difficulty making a full turn because their chin blocks the route of their left shoulder. This problem is most prevalent among players who are stocky and short-necked. Too often these players tend to sway their heads to the right on their backswings to allow space for the left shoulder to move into.

Rather than sway the head to the right, I suggest that golfers who have cramped backswings point their chin behind the ball at address (as I am doing in the illustration).

By pre-turning the head before actually swinging, the golfer eliminates the trouble that might result from excessive head movement. Yet, this pre-turning still allows more freedom for the shoulder turn.

KEEP YOUR HANDS "QUIET" AT TOP OF BACKSWING

Many golfers ruin their swings by cocking the wrists too much at the top of the backswing (illustration #1). Their hands get too "flippy" as a result of trying to make a big, full backswing. When the wrists cock too much at the top of the swing, they uncock too soon on the downswing.

I suggest trying consciously to curtail ANY cocking of your wrists at the top of your backswing. Don't worry if this shortens your swing. Make certain that the back of your left wrist never cups inward so that wrinkles appear at the base of the back of your hand. (I'm in the proper position in illustration #2).

Give this a try during one or two practice sessession. Stress controlling the club with your left hand. If it doesn't work, merely go back to your old swing.

WIDEN SWING ARC FOR EXTRA DISTANCE

I think that everyone who ever owned a bicycle understands the principle that the rim of a large wheel turns faster than the rim of a small wheel if both wheels make the same number of revolutions per minute. The same principle applies to the golf swing.

If you swing in a wide arc, your clubhead will move faster than if you swing in a small arc. Since the distance of golf shots is determined largely by clubhead speed, it should be obvious that a wide swing arc will produce more distance than will a small or shorter arc.

To increase the width of your swing—and, thus, your distance —you must stress a straight left arm throughout your backswing and downswing (see illustrations #1 and #2) and a straight right arm on your follow-through (illustration #3).

As you swing in a wide arc, make certain your head remains near the center of your "wheel"; don't let it move out towards the "rim."

HERE'S CORRECT GOLF SWING WRIST ACTION

Let there be no independent action of hands and wrists in the golf swing.

Halfway through the backswing (see illustration #1), the palms of both my hands face on a line exactly parallel to the ground. Because they are in this position, I know I haven't twisted my wrists on the backswing.

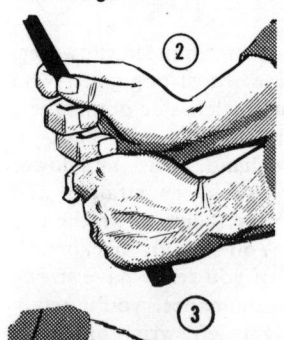

Just before impact, my wrists are fully cocked, but they haven't turned over. The butt end of the shaft, as you can see from illustration #2, points down toward the general vicinity of the ball, which helps keep the wrists cocked until impact.

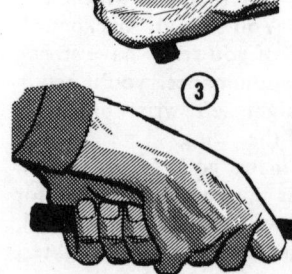

Halfway through the follow-through, if I were to open my palms, my hands would be perpendicular to the ground -- another way of saying that my wrists haven't turned over (see illustration #3).

By aiming for this position, I make sure the clubhead "follows" the ball after impact for as long as possible, thus giving me accuracy.

3—THE SWING

CHECKPOINTS FOR PROPER POSTURE

Your posture at address will expressly determine the direction that your body, arms and club move when you swing. Check my positioning in illustration #1 and then compare your own posture—(look at yourself in a mirror)—with the drawing. Is your back straight and with the knees slightly bent? If so, your buttocks should protrude.

You should feel that your upper body is separated from your lower body. If your arms are hanging normally, you should be able to look straight down or slightly back to see your hands.

By over-reaching for the ball you will be forced to "look out" to see your hands (illustration #2). By bending your back too far or standing too stiff-kneed (illustration #3) you will not feel sufficiently "separated" at the waist.

THE MODERN BACKSWING

The modern backswing features fewer "moving parts" than did any previous swing technique. It also emphasizes a maximum shoulder turn and a minimum hip turn. Reducing the moving parts lessens the need for loose hand action that can make square contact difficult to achieve consistently. The full shoulder wind-up adds power by emphasizing the big muscles of the back.

To execute the modern backswing you should: (1) swing the clubhead straight back from the ball with the left arm fully extended and with firmly locked wrists, (2) work your left shoulder down and under your chin, and (3) keep your right knee slightly flexed throughout, in order to minimize your hip turn.

Study the illustrations and you will learn how to practice these three fundamentals of the modern backswing.

How Much Practice?

1. HOW LONG SHOULD YOU GOLFERS PRACTICE? HOW MANY SHOTS? WELL, LET'S CONFINE THIS TO THE SHORT GAME, FOR THAT'S WHERE QUICKEST IMPROVEMENT CAN BE SEEN.

TAKE YOUR WEDGE TO THE PRACTICE GREEN, OR TO THE DRIVING RANGE WITH THE SAME, AND HIT 50-YARD SHOTS UNTIL YOU CAN PUT 10 OF THEM STRAIGHT ON THE GREEN, AND THEN FIVE OUT OF 10 WITHIN 10 FEET OF THE PIN.

2. BY THIS TIME, YOU MAY BE TIRED OF HITTING THOSE WEDGES, ANYHOW, SO MOVE TO A SHORTER CLUB. TAKE UP A POSITION ABOUT 20 FEET FROM THE GREEN AND START TO CHIP. USE WHATEVER CLUB IS BEST TO LAND THE BALL ON THE GREEN – IT WOULD MOST LIKELY BE THE 8-IRON IN THIS CASE. THEN HIT IN LOTS OF 10, UNTIL YOU CAN PUT 8 OUT OF 10 SHOTS WITHIN THREE FEET OF THE PIN.

'PLANE' FACTS

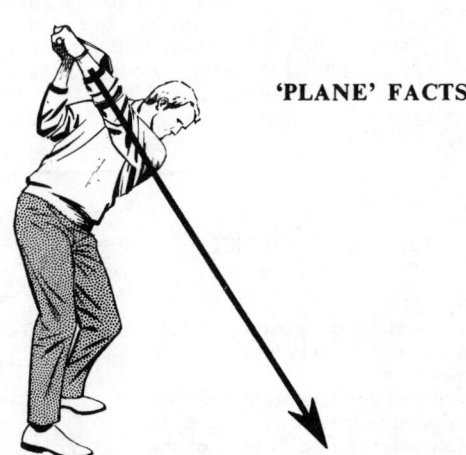

Study the illustration and note the line across my left arm. This line indicates the "plane" of my swing. If this line extends more or less to the ball, my swing is "on plane." This means that I am in position at the top of my backswing to return the club squarely to the ball.

Check yourself in the mirror to see if your left arm is on plane. Does the line across it extend approximately to where the ball would be? Or does it extend inside or out beyond that spot?

Also check to see that you have worked your hands up into position by turning your shoulders as I have. Merely lifting your hands and arms doesn't do the job, even if it does appear that you are on plane.

If you are not on, I'd advise against your changing your swing plane without professional guidance. Being on plane is important, but changing your swing to reach that goal will be much simpler if you have help.

85

3—THE SWING

STAY "OVER THE BALL" DURING BACKSWING

The golfer in illustration #1 has made the common mistake of "moving off the ball" during his backswing. As a result, his upper body has swayed to the right.

Now the problem is this: To compensate for the swaying motion during the backswing, a reverse sway must be applied during the downswing. This back and forth lateral movement makes it very difficult to consistently return the clubhead

squarely to the ball. It is, likewise, difficult to fully utilize the large muscles of the body.

The ideal situation is shown in illustration #2. You see me staying "over the ball" during the backswing.

The best method of accomplishing this is to place most of your weight on the left foot at address. At the same time, you should feel a slight downward pressure on the inner portion of your right foot.

During the backswing, be certain that any movement of weight does not go beyond the inside of your right foot.

THREE GRIP CHOICES; TAKE ONE

Depending on your hand size and strength, you have three grip choices.

Strong-handed golfers should consider the interlocking grip, in which only three fingers of the left hand rest on the club (see #1).

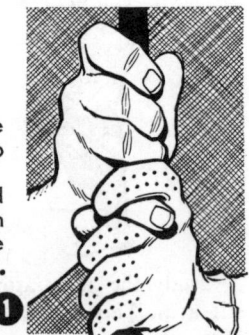

Then there is the "10-finger" grip. Here, both thumbs and all fingers provide a firm hold on the club (see #2).

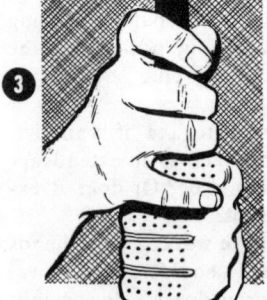
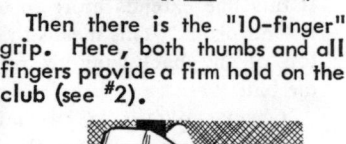

The third grip is my personal choice -- the Vardon or overlapping grip (see #3). The thumb and four fingers of the left hand are placed on the club, and this serves to unify the hands effectively.

SETTING UP TO THE BALL

Sooner or later golf must become a habit if you want to succeed. As you become proficient, you find yourself doing the same thing the same way time after time.

One area in which it is especially important to have a set pattern is in setting up to the ball.

I have a 3-step pattern that brings me up to the point where I'm ready to start waggling the club. First, I size up the shot from behind and to the side of the ball, as you see me doing in No. 1. At this time I check the best line to the target and consider the proposed flight of the ball. Next (No. 2), I place the clubhead squarely behind the ball so that the clubface looks down the target line. Finally, I assume my stance (No.3).

It is important that step 3 not precede step 2. If you take your stance before aligning the clubface, you might force yourself to "reach" for, or "crowd," the ball.

TWO BALL POSITIONING SYSTEMS

There are two schools of thought about where the ball should be placed in relation to the feet on various shots. One school (illustration #1) holds that all shots should be played opposite the left heel and that the right foot should move left—narrowing the stance as the club's loft increases.

The second school holds that the ball should be played progressively farther back in the stance, as the club's loft increases (illustration #2).

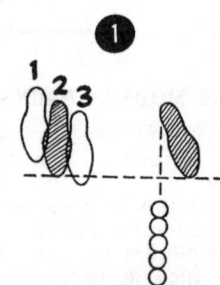

1. DRIVER
2. MIDDLE IRONS
3. SHORT IRONS

The advantages of the first method include having the hands above the ball on all shots so that each swing is similar in that respect. This method might be best for novice players who are not yet ready to improvise and finesse shots.

The second method, which most skilled players use, also finds the hands in the same position relative to the body, but because the ball is played farther back on short iron shots, the club's effective loft is decreased. This allows the player to hit low approach shots—especially valuable on windy days—and also increases his ability to hit down and through the ball.

3—THE SWING

3 FINGERS THAT CONTROL YOUR SWING

If you are not already doing so, I suggest that you try hitting some full shots using the following advice on grip pressure.

Hold your club with both thumbs and fingers relaxed, with the exception of the last three of the left hand. Actually squeeze the clubshaft until you feel that you are gripping almost solely with these fingers. (illustration #1)

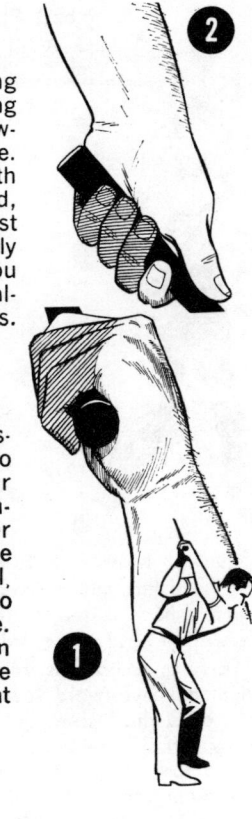

This distribution of grip pressure will aid your swing in two ways. First, it will relax your right hand, as well as your entire right arm and shoulder area. Consequently you will be able to make a smooth, full, unrestricted backswing with no blocking by your right side. Second, it will put pressure in those three fingers that are most susceptible to slippage at the top of your swing.

SET UP TO BALL "AT ATTENTION"

The golfer who is setting up to the ball properly may feel like he's in the army—back straight, shoulders back, stomach in. He is "at attention."

If you assume such a posture, your buttocks will protrude as you bend your knees slightly (illustration at left). You should actually feel as if there is a bending inward of your back at the base of your spine.

From this posture it becomes almost automatic to swing on a proper plane and fully coil the big muscles of your body.

Such is not the case, however, if you stand too straight (middle figure) or if you squat at the knees while your back is rounded (figure at right).

Check your address position in front of a full-length mirror to see that you are "at attention."

HOW YOUR GRIP AFFECTS YOUR SHOTS

ADDRESS POSITIONS
PROPER   STRONG   WEAK

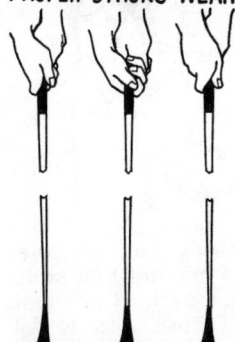

The proper grip is the most important fundamental of good golfing. The reasoning is simple ... the grip directly affects the facing of your clubhead as it strikes the ball.

The top illustration shows three possible positions. The first is the proper grip. It is followed by the "strong" grip, wherein the hands are well turned to the golfer's right. Finally, you see the so called "weak" grip; or one characterized by the hands being turned to the extreme left.

As a means of checking your grip for infractions, I suggest using a mirror.

Note that the gripping position at address is closely related to proper placement of the hands at impact (lower grip illustrations).

Remember, if your grip is too strong or too weak, you will probably close or open the clubface (lower clubhead illustrations) in order to reach the correct impact position with the hands.

IMPACT POSITIONS
PROPER   STRONG   WEAK

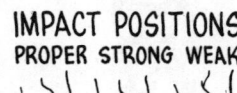

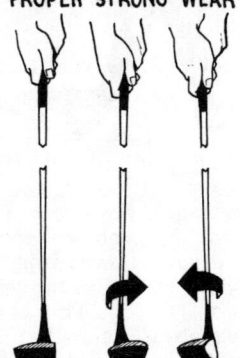

RIGHT GRIP WITH RIGHT HAND

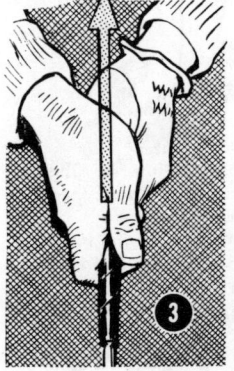

In No. 1 we see a common grip fault that can only lead to inconsistent shot-making. The golfer has gripped the club too much in the palm of his right hand, much like a baseball player would hold the bat.

In a proper grip the club should pass across the top of all four fingers of the right hand (No. 2). It shouldn't lay against the palm.

When the right hand is closed around the club (No. 3), the "V" between the right thumb and forefinger should point approximately at your chin.

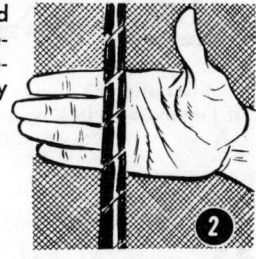

In other words, the right hand grips the club almost entirely in the fingers. Such a grip gives you maximum "feel" and control of the club. It also places the right palm in a position that more or less parallels the face of the club. This enables you to return the clubface squarely to the ball time after time.

87

3—THE SWING

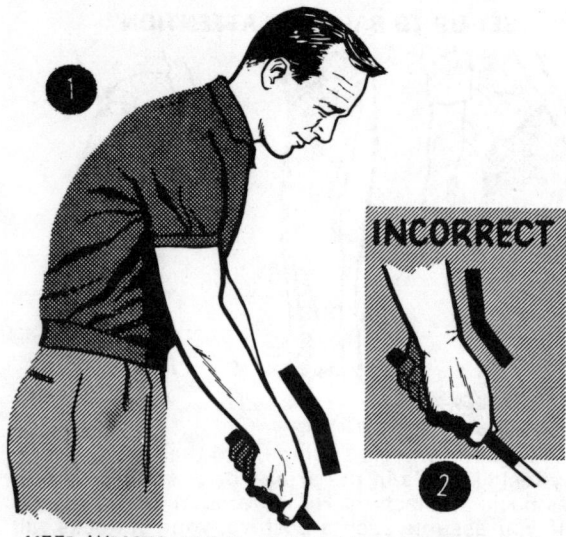

KEEP WRISTS HIGH AND READY FOR ACTION

Does your wrist positioning resemble that shown in No. 1? Congratulations, low handicapper. You're learning fast. The wrists at address should be high, alert, ready for action. No sag (as in No. 2), no wrinkles visible on the tops of the wrists.

The major function of any full swing is to return the clubface squarely to the ball -- to return it to the same position it was in at address. Conversely, a player's address position should closely approximate the position he will be in at impact. Since the wrists must be high at impact, you would be better off if they are high at address.

YOU NEED PLENTY OF LEG ACTION IN BACKSWING

In No. 1, note that, at the top of my backswing, my left knee has moved inward so that it points behind the ball. I have rolled my left foot to its instep. Much of my weight has transferred to the inside of my right foot.

Early in the downswing (illustration No. 2), my right knee moves forward toward the ball and my right foot rolls onto the instep. My weight has transferred largely to my left side -- but my head remains behind the ball.

The faster your legs can reverse their direction of movement from right to left at the start of your downswing, the more power you will generate for added distance.

LADY GOLFERS HAVE KNEE TROUBLES

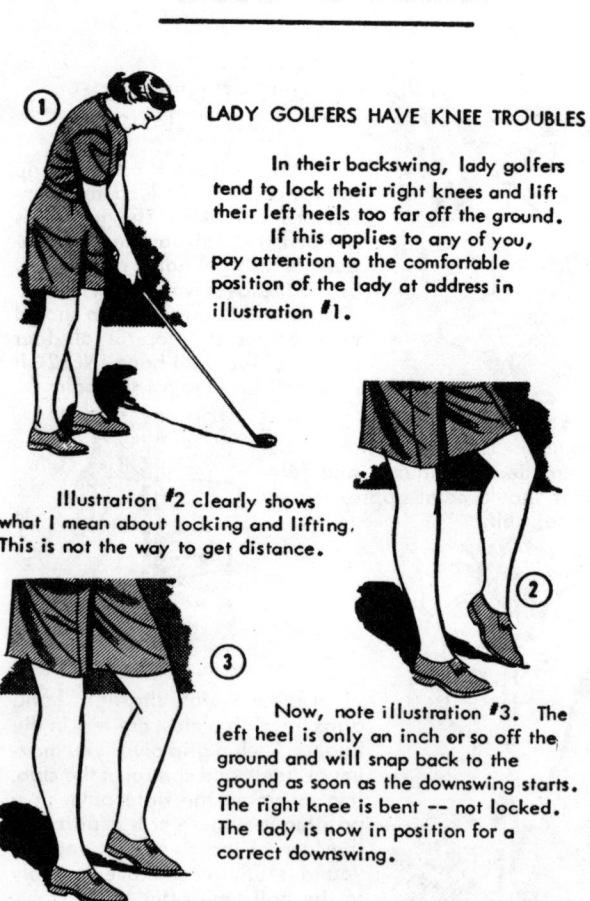

In their backswing, lady golfers tend to lock their right knees and lift their left heels too far off the ground.

If this applies to any of you, pay attention to the comfortable position of the lady at address in illustration #1.

Illustration #2 clearly shows what I mean about locking and lifting. This is not the way to get distance.

Now, note illustration #3. The left heel is only an inch or so off the ground and will snap back to the ground as soon as the downswing starts. The right knee is bent -- not locked. The lady is now in position for a correct downswing.

ROLL INSIDE ON LEFT FOOT

The manner in which you lift your left foot during your backswing influences the success of your over-all swing.

If you go up on the toe of this foot, as the golfer in illustration No. 1 is doing, you react in a reverse manner on

your downswing. You will lower the heel in a manner that shifts weight to the back of this foot. This could cause you to fall back on your heels.

If you roll onto the inside of your left foot during your backswing, however (illustration No. 2), you will tend to react on your downswing by shifting your weight to the left (illustration No. 3). This is the proper weight transfer that is so necessary for consistent shot-making.

3—THE SWING

PULL WITH YOUR LEFT SIDE ON DOWNSWING

We have heard advice to "kick" the right knee toward the target at the start of the downswing (illustration #1). This advice might be helpful to golfers who have trouble shifting their weight onto their left side. However, such advice might cause the right side to dominate the downswing—and this is bad.

I prefer to feel that my downswing begins with a pulling with my lower left side. My left knee bends toward the target as that side pulls forward. Meanwhile, my right leg remains fairly straight. The result is a fairly awkward looking position with knees spread wide apart at the start of the downswing.

However awkward this may look, it is the correct position and indicates that you are pulling with your left side, rather than pushing with your right.

FOR A WELL-TIMED SWING

Think of the upper body "cocking" the gun on the backswing, and the lower body "pulling the trigger" on the downswing.

In other words, make a full shoulder turn on your backswing (as I'm doing in illustration #1). This fully stretches the big back muscles.

On the downswing, start things moving to the left by shifting your feet, legs and hips in that direction (illustration #2).

By starting the downswing with your lower body, you will hold back the release of that power you have built up in your back and shoulders until your clubhead is in the hitting area.

Tip for white collar golfers

The white collar golfer is one whose business responsibilities do not allow him much time for playing or practicing on the course. Instead he merely sheds his suitcoat and drives balls into an indoor net during his lunch hour.

In some ways this sort of practice can be even more beneficial than outdoor practice. The inability to see the results of shots, for instance, reduces the tendency that many of us have to swing from our heels on the practice range.

The thing to work on indoors is your feel for a properly timed shot. Concentrate merely on making a smooth, rhythmical swing in which your clubhead returns squarely to the ball. The more times you swing in proper rhythm, the easier it will be to duplicate that rhythm on the course.

BODY TURN OPENS AND CLOSES CLUBFACE

In golf, pronation is the act which moves either hand toward a position in which the palm faces the ground. Rotating the hand so that the palm faces upward is supination. In moving a golf club, one hand pronates while the other supinates.

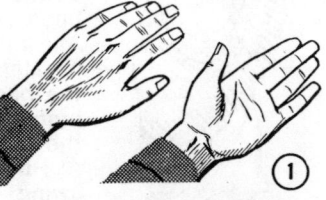

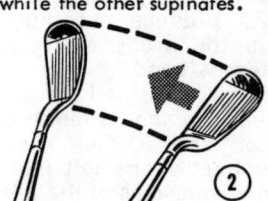

Some golfers pronate the left hand on the backswing in an effort to open the clubface, but all they produce is a flat swing, in which the clubhead is swung "around the knees." Then, too, the left shoulder rides too high on the backswing.

A correct golf swing involves no independent twisting of the hands on the backswing or downswing. Body turn, or pivot, will do all the necessary opening and closing of the clubface.

Use your body to originate the backswing and downswing (see illustration #3) -- and forget about pronation.

3—THE SWING

PROPER SHOULDER ACTION CAN KEEP BALL ON TARGET

How is your shoulder action in the downswing? Do your shoulders turn on too level a plane? If so, this may be the cause of those pulled shots or those sharp hooks.

When the shoulder plane is too level, your club may move into the hitting area from outside the target line.

Remedy this by working the shoulders on more of an up-down pattern in your downswing. As your club moves toward impact, concentrate either on lowering your right shoulder or raising your left, as illustrated.

This proper shoulder action will keep the clubhead moving well inside the target line on the downswing and along the target line in the hitting area. The clubface will drive the ball forward, instead of to the left.

HOW BACKSWING TENSION PRODUCES DOWNSWING POWER

The main purpose of the backswing is to create tension in the golfer's muscles. When this tension is released on the downswing, it produces clubhead speed and shot distance. All things being equal, the greater the tension created on the backswing, the greater the amount of force released into the shot.

However, only a proper backswing will produce maximum tension in the areas where it will do the most good.

If you have performed a proper wind-up, you should feel two ribbons of tension. One runs from the heel of the left foot, up the inner muscles of the left leg, and up the left side and left arm. The other tension ribbon runs up the inside of the right leg, across the back and to the left armpit area, where it joins the other ribbon (see illustration).

If you coil, rather than sway, your body, and if you keep your head fairly steady, you should feel tension in these areas at the top of your swing.

RHYTHM NEVER CHANGES

SHAFT AND SWING LENGTH DETERMINE SPEED!

Very little is written about timing the golf swing. Yet, good timing is a key factor in all successful swings, and the subject certainly merits attention.

Learning to time your golf swing is much like learning to dance. You must swing to a certain rhythm. I happen to have a very fast tempo when swinging. Others, such as Julius Boros, swing to a slower beat. The important thing about timing is not whether you swing slow or fast, but rather that you swing in the same rhythm on all shots with all clubs, from driver to putter.

Naturally, you will swing faster on a drive than you will on a pitch shot, because you take a longer swing with the longer club. The thing to remember is that though the SPEED of the clubhead increases with the longer-shafted clubs, the TEMPO or TIMING of the swing remains the same on all normal shots.

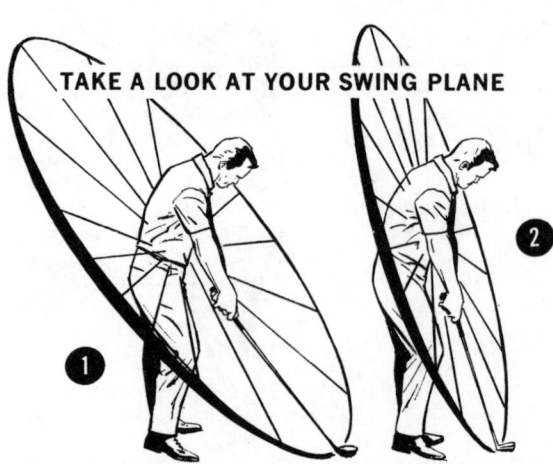

TAKE A LOOK AT YOUR SWING PLANE

Today's illustrations show my concept of just what the swing plane is. To me, swing plane is the "wheel" of the swing, with the clubhead passing along the "rim" and your body being the "hub."

Now, this swing plane may be fairly upright, or it may be fairly level, or it may be in between. This would be the angle of your swing plane, or the amount of tilt of your plane.

Note in the illustrations that the plane of the swing with a wood club (illustration #1) is less upright than the plane on an iron swing (illustration #2). This is so because you stand farther from the ball on wood shots. The farther you stand from the ball, the more level your swing plane becomes.

If you are having trouble with your shots, ask your professional to check your swing plane.

3—THE SWING

"AIM AND FIRE"

One purpose of the backswing is to put the club in a position to solidy "smack" the ball. I sometimes think of the backswing as "aim" and the downswing as "fire."

A properly aimed club is parallel to the target line at the top of the backswing (illustration #1). This is the best position to return the clubhead **along** the target line during impact.

The clubshaft is aimed to the left of target in illustration #2 and to the right in illustration #3.

In both cases, the clubhead will tend to move **across** the target line during impact. This will cause mis-hit shots that fly offline.

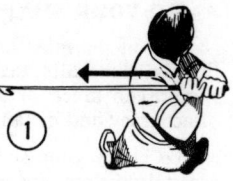
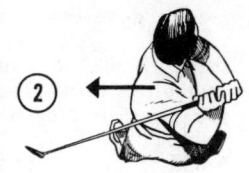
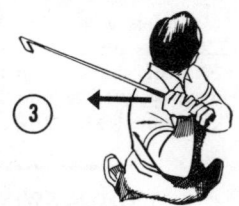

ADDRESS THE BALL WITH ELBOWS IN CLOSE

The inward positioning of the elbows in Illustration #1 is much preferred to the sagging, outward-bending position in Illustration #2.

I believe it was Ben Hogan who first stressed this inward position for the elbows, and he's so right. Keeping the elbows in close at address forces you to make a backswing in which you use your shoulders, hips, legs and arms as a unit. Everything moves together.

If you position your elbows away from your body, the tendency is to lift the club solely with your hands and arms. This is a relatively powerless movement that costs you distance and accuracy.

The pause that refreshes

You should make it a habit to pause for a few seconds before you place the clubhead behind the ball. During this brief interval, decide what your one key thought will be as you actually swing the club. I feel that one positive thought is better than none. It occupies your mind so that a negative thought can't creep in.

Also use this time to take a deep breath—inhale then exhale. Taking fresh oxygen into your body produces a relaxation that will help you make a smooth, unhurried backswing.

ALIGN BOTTOM EDGE OF CLUBFACE

It may seem like a minor point, but I'd like to stress the importance of properly placing the clubhead behind the ball.

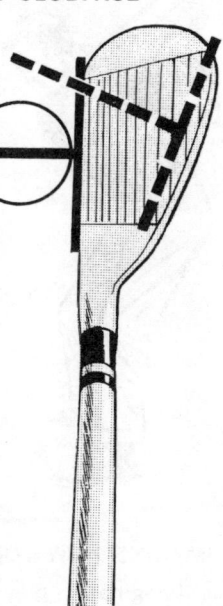

Because the top edge of the clubhead is cut at an angle facing to the right of the target (see illustration), it is relatively simple to mis-align the clubface.

Make sure that your alignment is based on the bottom edge—not the top—of the face. Make sure that this leading edge is squared at exact right angles to the target line.

If you have any doubt about the alignment of your clubface—if you consistently hit off-line in the same direction—I suggest you have a friend look at your positioning to make sure you are on target.

SWING ARMS FREELY

One thing that all good golfers have is a free-swinging arm movement, as opposed to a pushing, shoving or jerking of the club.

This free-swinging stems largely from swinging THROUGH the ball rather than AT it. We all make smooth practice swings because we are not swinging AT an object. Only when the ball gets in the way do we fail to make our arms SWING.

It is difficult to swing the arms freely if your shoulders uncoil too soon in your downswing. Note in the illustration how the distance from my right shoulder to my left hand rapidly increases during my downswing. This indicates that I swing my arms freely while restraining the uncoiling of my shoulders.

FREE YOUR MIND OF THEORY

I'm sure that all of you have hit a ball from a "close" or "tight" lie. In that situation you probably reacted by striking the ball squarely.

It's easy to get bogged down in **too** much golf theory. And it is impossible to make a full, free swing when you are consciously directing yourself toward a certain type of move.

Sometimes it is better to forget theory and just concentrate on swinging the clubhead squarely into the back of the ball (see illustration).

3—THE SWING

BOW-AND-ARROW PRINCIPLE ADDS TO FORCE

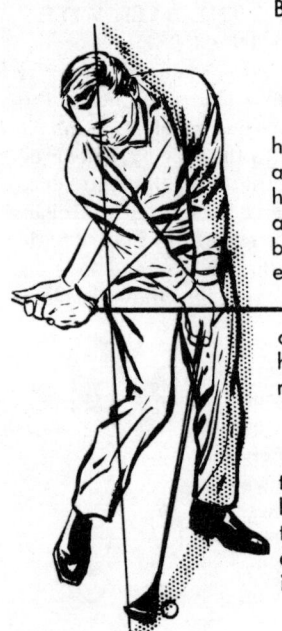

In today's illustration, notice how the body is bowed, much like an archer's implement, as my hands move through the hitting area. If you will imagine your body forming a similar bowing effect, you will have a better chance of keeping your head behind the ball. You will produce more forceful shots as a result.

If you wish to go one step further, you might also imagine your hands as being the arrow. Let them zip through the hitting area and out toward the target, just as if the arrow had been released.

STRAIGHT DOWN THE LINE

At the top of your swing, your fingers should be around the top of the clubshaft and your palms beneath the shaft. Also, the back of your left hand should form a continuous line with the back of your left arm.

If you have a proper grip and if these two points check out at the top of your swing, your downswing should automatically assume a straight clubhead path.

IMAGINE HOW YOU WANT TO FEEL AT IMPACT

Imagination plays a great role in the game of the successful golfer. Many, if not most great players have developed the ability to visualize the flight pattern of an intended shot. They subsequently produce a shot of a similar trajectory.

This really isn't as complicated as it may appear. Simply imagine the type of shot you wish to hit... high, low, draw, fade, whatever. Then, as you address the ball, try to create in your hands and legs the feeling you'll want at impact.

Continue to imagine this desired feeling as you swing. Surprisingly your mind will direct your body to perform the moves that are needed for your returning to the impact position mentally "requested."

DO YOUR SHAFTS MATCH YOUR SWING?

One of the most important aspects of good golf is finding clubshafts that match your particular swing speed. Too much or too little shaft flex can rob you of accuracy and distance.

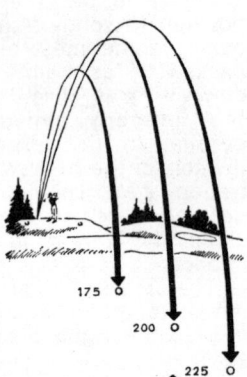

To check your shafts, merely ascertain the amount of carry you get on your normal drives. If your average drive carries under 175 yards, I suggest you use "A" shafts (flexible) in your clubs. If your drives carry 175-200 yards, you are generating a bit more clubhead speed. The "A" shafts would be too difficult to control. You need "R" shafts (regular).

Golfers who carry drives 200-225 yards on average should use "S" (stiff) shafts, or, if they usually carry well beyond 225 yards, "X" shafts (extra stiff).

LADIES, SWING YOUR ARMS — FAST

Women golfers, especially, need to generate maximum clubhead speed. One way to do this is to increase the speed with which you swing your arms. Note: I said "arms", not "hands." Your hands and wrists will work correctly automatically once you develop sufficient centrifugal force with your arms.

To get the feeling of swinging your arms freely, first hit practice shots with your feet together. Once you are making solid contact, gradually widen your stance and start swinging your arms faster through the ball.

This may disturb your balance at first. If so, try hitting shots in your bare feet. This will force you to adjust your timing subconsciously so as to maintain balance.

In short, practice swinging your arms as fast as you can — in your bare feet.

THINGS TO LOOK FOR IN THE MIRROR
(front view)

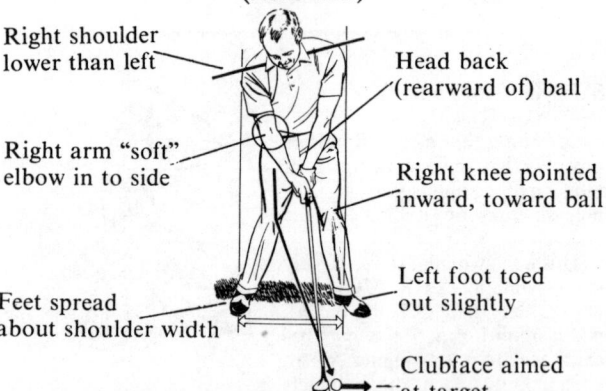

No two golfers are identical in the way they set up to the ball, but there are certain characteristics that all proper address positions include. The front-view features that your set-up should include are shown here. Merely set up in front of a mirror and check yourself. My next column will show the fundamentals of proper set-up as seen from the golfer's right side.

3—THE SWING

POINT YOUR KNEES FOR PROPER FOOTWORK

An easy way to get the feeling of proper footwork in the golf swing is to make sure your knees point in the right place at the right time.

In illustration #1, we see the top of the backswing position. The knee has turned to the right and now points behind the ball.

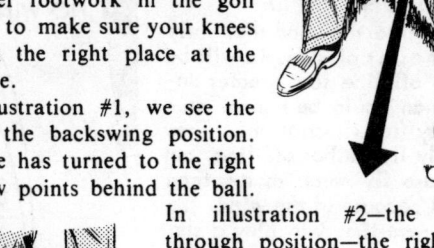

In illustration #2—the follow-through position—the right knee has turned so that it points in front of the ball.

If you learn to move your legs into these positions, your weight will automatically shift properly during your swing. This proper weight shift will improve your balance and your timing; you'll hit the ball farther and straighter.

SWING CLUB TARGET-TO-TARGET

You'll strike the ball much more solidly and with more consistency if you think "target-to-target."

By this I mean that you should swing the club back and up so that the shaft points to the target at the top of your backswing (illustration #1).

Then swing back through the ball so that the club points to the target once again after you have hit the shot (illustration #2).

Think "target-to-target" and you will automatically swing your clubhead in a proper groove.

EXTEND LEFT ARM FOR WIDE BACKSWING ARC

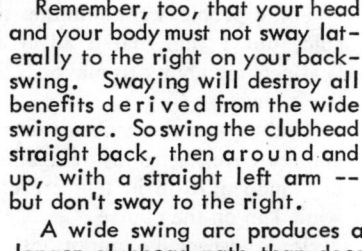
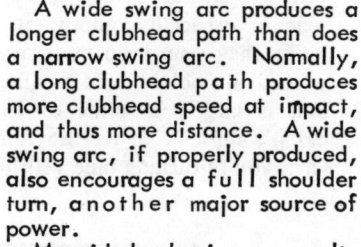

Remember, too, that your head and your body must not sway laterally to the right on your backswing. Swaying will destroy all benefits derived from the wide swing arc. So swing the clubhead straight back, then around and up, with a straight left arm -- but don't sway to the right.

A wide swing arc produces a longer clubhead path than does a narrow swing arc. Normally, a long clubhead path produces more clubhead speed at impact, and thus more distance. A wide swing arc, if properly produced, also encourages a full shoulder turn, another major source of power.

My wide backswing arc results from maintaining a fully extended left arm throughout. Also, I take the clubhead straight back from the ball.

A KEY TO TIMING AND DISTANCE

The order of movement on the downswing finds the arms following the lead of the lower body, the hands following the arms, and the clubhead following the hands.

To achieve a proper sequence of movement in your downswing,

imagine that you are swinging a chain and ball. To keep the chain taut, you will have to lead with your lower body, then come your arms, and finally the ball. It's the same sequence you should adopt in your golf swing.

EXTEND YOUR "FLIGHT PATH"

Golf scores would improve greatly if the "flight path" and the movement of the clubhead along the target line (at ball-level) could be maintained for a longer time.

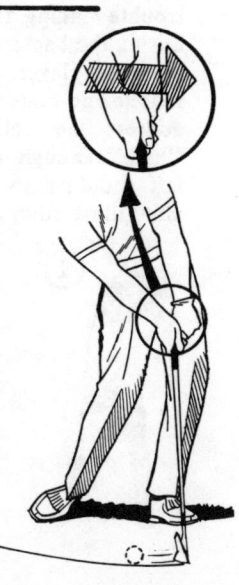

One way to do this... and thus increase your chances for solid contact... is to extend your hands forward toward the target well through impact. Make sure that you hit the ball with the back of your left hand facing down the target line. Then keep it facing that direction for a split second beyond.

UNCOCK WRISTS IN HITTING AREA

Today's illustrated downswing position shows that my wrists have not uncocked, although my hands have already moved to hip level. I won't unhinge them until my hands have begun to enter the hitting area.

This is known as the "delayed hit," a major source of swing power. A golfer who can reach this "L" position and still square up the clubface by impact will certainly hit a long ball.

To reach this position (1) shift your weight to your left at the start of your downswing, (2) lower your right shoulder and return your right elbow to your right side, and (3) avoid forcing the downswing with your hands or swaying your head to your left.

3—THE SWING

START DOWNSWING WITH PULLING ACTION

To start your downswing properly, you should feel that you are pulling your left hand more or less straight down towards the ground (see illustration).

Actually the path your hands take on the downswing (see dotted line) should be within the arc they took on the backswing (solid line).

Pulling down with the left hand at this point in your swing will help you shift your weight back to the left side and will also help insure that your wrists do not release from their hinged position prematurely. Longer, straighter shots will result.

HERE'S TO A HIGH FINISH

A high finish, as illustrated in No. 1, is no guarantee of a great shot. But your chances for one improve if you plan from the start to finish in this manner. In order to finish this way, you must move the shoulder down and under -- a proper move.

With such a right shoulder move, the clubhead will move toward impact from inside to along the target line (see No. 2). This gives you full shot power and minimizes slicing or pulling, which occurs when the clubhead moves into the ball from outside the target line.

LADIES, MORE POWER TO YOU

The lady golfer who hits the ball farthest is usually low lady on the scoring totem pole.

Lady, if you want to add distance, see that your drive flies in a right-to-left draw pattern, so that more roll is added to it. To realize this pattern, let the "V" formed by the left thumb and forefinger point toward your right shoulder (#1) rather than to your chin. This "strong" grip will force the clubhead to strike the ball in such a way that produces this right-to-left draw.

DON'T PRESS FOR EXTRA YARDAGE INTO STRONG WIND

Shots into the wind that carry any amount of sidespin will be pushed off-line to a greater degree than would be normal on a still day (see illustration). They not only fly farther off-line, but they also fly much shorter than normal because of the wind.

The next time you play a shot into the wind, forget about distance. Just give the shot your best swing, one that will strike the ball as squarely as possible. Stress control, rather than length. By striking the ball squarely -- even if it means shortening your swing -- you will not only achieve a shot of decent length, but, more important, you will keep the ball in play.

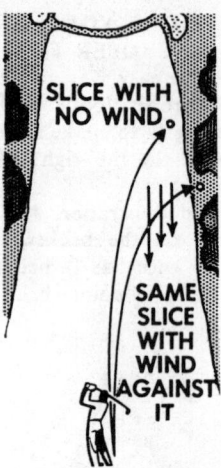

IN GOLF, IT'S 'COOL' TO KEEP WARM

Some people seem immune to cold, but I find that it adversely affects my ability to make a full, free swing.

I always make sure to carry enough covering to insure against any sudden drop in temperature while I'm on the course.

It is especially important, I think, that you keep your arms covered in cool or cold weather. Golf is largely a game of feel, and it's difficult to feel anything when you're turning blue with the cold.

HOLD HEAD HIGH TO LENGTHEN BACKSWING

Golfers with broad shoulders and short necks face a special problem. Often these players have trouble making a full shoulder turn during the backswing.

Every player, regardless of his muscle and bone structure, should address the ball with his head "high" enough to allow for his left shoulder to move under his chin (illustration #1).

If the shoulder can't clear the chin (illustration #2), the player will be forced to make an incomplete upper-body turn. He'll find it necessary to pick the club up and lift it into position with his arms and hands.

It will help those with especially short necks to not only hold their head high, but also pull their shoulders back slightly at address, rather than hunch forward.

SECTION FOUR

THE SHORT GAME

How to Hit Those Pitch & Chip Shots Close to the Hole.

ACCURACY: PRIME GOAL ON SHORT SHOTS TO GREEN

In the illustrations I am demonstrating how to execute a full shot with the pitching wedge. Pay special attention to my left heel.

Note that this heel remains firmly planted throughout the

swing, though my legs move and my hips and shoulders tilt and turn.

By keeping this heel on the ground, I eliminate one more moving part from my entire swing.

It may be necessary for some golfers to raise their left heel on longer shots in order to make a full backswing, but since a long backswing is not necessary -- or even desirable -- on short shots, you will get better accuracy by keeping the left heel firmly planted throughout.

HOW TO PINPOINT SHORT-IRON SHOTS

Accuracy is the key requisite on short iron shots and every golfer can improve his scores by concentrating on this aspect of his or her game.

I can't think of a better way to insure accuracy on short shots than to stress the importance of keeping the left arm

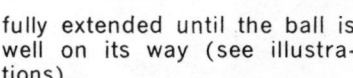

fully extended until the ball is well on its way (see illustrations).

The extended left arm forms the radius of the swing arc. If it remains extended, the swing arc becomes consistent. If it bends, the arc alters and the clubhead moves out of its proper path. Crooked shots result.

Extending the left arm also helps create a firmness in the wrists that keeps those shots on line. A sloppy, loose swing produces miss-hit shots.

95

4—THE SHORT GAME

PROPER BACKSWING FOR SHORT SHOTS

The golfer in illustrations #1 and #2 shows us two very common errors that golfers make on short shots. In illustration #1, the golfer has abruptly lifted the club on his backswing. In the second illustration, he has

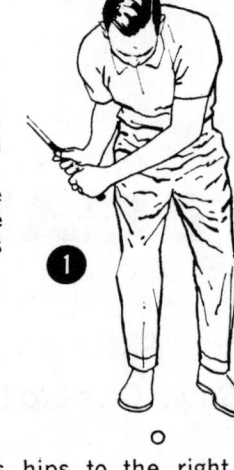

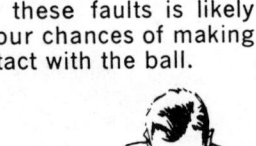

swayed his hips to the right. Either of these faults is likely to spoil your chances of making solid contact with the ball.

Proper technique on short shots finds the head steady and the left arm straight during the stroke (as I show in illustration #3). Keep your right elbow fairly close to your body. The swing itself should be crisp and forceful. Make certain that your clubhead accelerates into the ball.

FINISH SHORT SHOTS WITH CLUBFACE SKYWARD

One reason so many golfers muff shots around the green is because they get too wristy on these short shots. Another reason is because they fail to finish their stroke.

Both of these problems can easily be solved. Look at the illustration of me at the finish of a short shot. Note that the clubface is looking upward. It would not be in this position if I had not extended my through-swing out toward the target.

I'm sure you will hit crisper chip and pitch shots if you'll merely work on finishing with your clubface looking skyward and your left wrist still firm.

FOR SHORT-IRON IMPROVEMENT

Here's a short cut to short-iron accuracy. Line up three balls in a row, then try to make all three fly on the same shot.

To get the full advantage of this routine, you must strike the first ball just before the clubhead reaches the bottom of its swing arc.

This is the same technique all good golfers employ on short iron shots. They always "hit down" on the ball, contacting the ball first and then the turf.

If you practice this trick shot until you have it mastered, I'm sure your short-iron game will improve immensely.

HIGH-LOFTED PITCH TO GREEN HAS UNDESIRABLE EFFECT

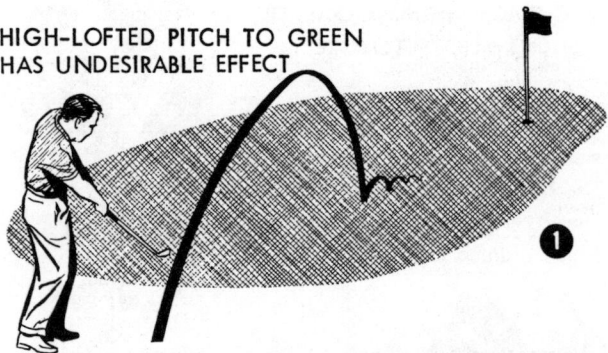

Whenever you're a few yards from the edge of a green and the terrain between your ball and the hole is fairly normal, don't take a chance on trying to pitch with a highly lofted club.

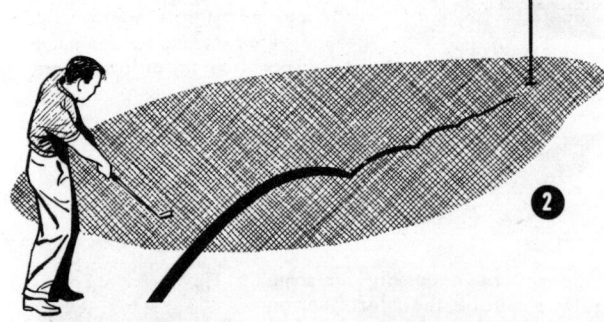

On such a short shot, a wedge or 9-iron will cause the ball to fly high with a lot of backspin. When it hits the green, it "grabs" far short of the hole (see #1).

Far better to chip with a middle iron, such as a 5 or 6. Such a chip will bounce and roll to the hole, even if it isn't struck perfectly square. Pick the spot on the green from which your ball will bounce and roll to the hole, then try to land your chip near that spot.

4—THE SHORT GAME

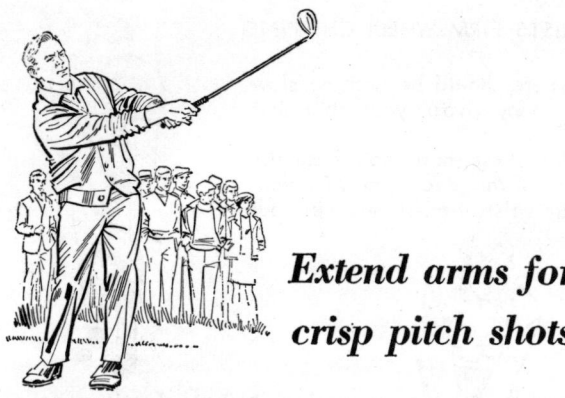

Extend arms for crisp pitch shots

Generally, short shots should be struck crisply, with no looseness in the arms or wrists. The left hand and arm should assume majority control of the club, but both arms should *swing* freely—no shoving or pushing.

If you are striking these shots crisply, you should find that your follow-through does not take your hands into the high finish position that you achieve on your wood shots. Instead, you should finish with your arms well extended toward the target as I have in the illustration.

KNOW-HOW NEEDED ON SHORT APPROACH SHOTS

Short approach shots call for accurate planning, especially when you are playing to a bi-level green on which the pin has been placed on the upper level.

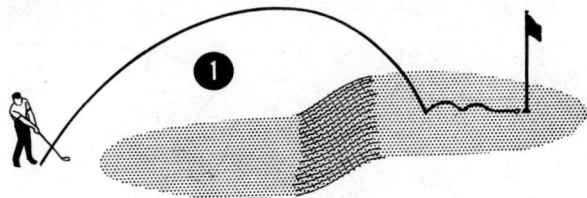

To play this shot--if you have sufficient landing space --pitch the ball to land on the upper level (No. 1).

If sufficient landing space is not available, use a less-lofted club and play short of the bank (No. 2).

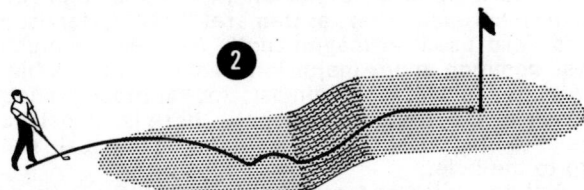

Avoid playing into the back (No. 3). The shot might land on the sidehill and stop short, or even roll back down the hill. If you carry the bank with a low-flying shot, the ball will probably roll over the green.

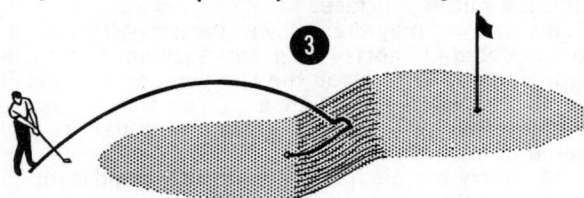

PLAY YOUR CHIP SHOTS AS IF THEY WERE LONG PUTTS

Many golfers who have a sensitive putting touch on the greens suffer from lack of finesse on chip shots from off the green. If this is your situation, merely imagine you are stroking a long putt whenever you have a chip shot from off the edge.

You might even wish to try using your putting grip on these chip shots.

Imagine how firmly you would need to stroke the ball if you were putting it. Then merely give your chip shot the same force, using any clubhead from a 2- to a 5-iron.

Keep your head and body still on these chip shots, just as you would if you were putting. Sweep the ball off the grass so that it runs forward, low to the ground, with very little backspin.

If it makes you feel more comfortable and gives you more club control, don't hesitate to choke down on the clubshaft on these chip shots. Again, this will make the shot seem similar to a long putt.

AIM APPROACH SHOTS AT TOP OF FLAGSTICK

I'll bet that if anyone ever studied the subject they would find that most greens have more sand and water in front than in back.

Yet, most golfers invariably fall short of the green more often than they go over. If they are not short of the green itself, they usually are short of the flagstick.

To counteract this tendency to fall short, I suggest that, instead of aiming for the hole, golfers should aim for the top of the flagstick. This will automatically cause approach shots to carry deeper into the green and, more often than not, closer to the hole.

4—THE SHORT GAME

SHORTER CLUBS NEED SHORTER SWING

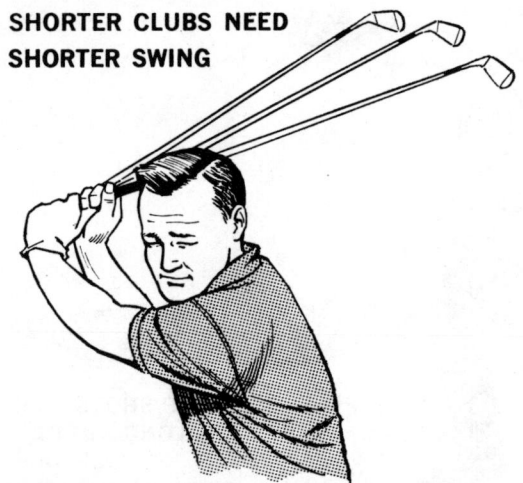

Don't make the mistake of trying to take as full a swing with your short irons as you do with your long irons. Clubs are of different lengths for a specific reason, and you should let them do the job for which they were designed.

The short irons, used on relatively close-in approach shots, are built for maximum control and accuracy. Because they are shorter in length, they require a shorter backswing. This will happen automatically. Don't force yourself into a long swing with these "accuracy" clubs.

The longer irons, though still designed to produce straight shots, must also provide more distance. Therefore they are necessarily longer—and they require a longer swing. You may run into trouble if you don't make a full backswing, say, with a 2-iron.

Let the length of your clubs determine the length of your backswing. That's the way to get top results from whichever club you select to use.

Putt when you can

Let's face it, most of us are better putters than we are chippers. And why not; we all use the putter much more frequently than we do a chipping club.

Therefore, I suggest you continue to use your putter on shots from just off the green. Only when the grass is extremely high or patchy—when you might not get a true roll—should you chip a shot from within, say, three feet of the green.

When putting from the fringe, be sure to put a good roll on the ball. Try to strike it squarely, and follow through toward the hole with your putterhead.

WRISTS FIRM WHEN CHIPPING

There should be nothing slow or sloppy about your chip shot style.

On these short shots from the edge of the green, you will want your wrists firm throughout your

stroke. Note in the illustrations that my hands remain forward of the clubhead until the ball is well on its way to the hole. The wrists are firm throughout, especially the left wrist which never collapses.

Chipping with firm wrists will give you clean contact with the ball, so important on these shots.

THE PITCH-AND-RUN—A HANDY SHOT TO KNOW

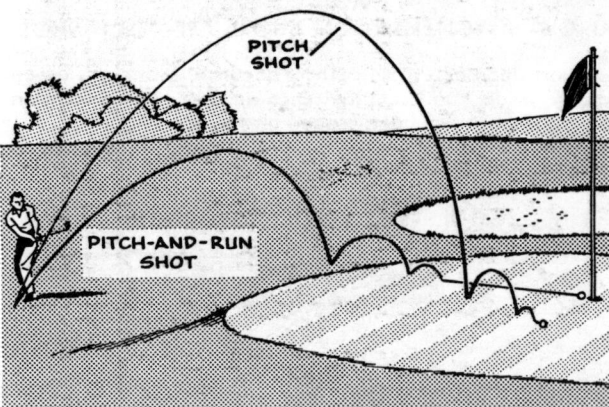

With the advent of the huge greens that most modern golf architects design, and with the coming of modern watering systems, the old pitch-and-run shot which such golfers as Demaret, Nelson, Harrison and Ford used so magnificently has become much less common in our major tournamets. Today's big, soft greens will hold almost any approach shot, practically in a matter of inches. There is almost no need to play short of the green and let the ball run up to the hole.

Yet, this pitch-and-run shot is still useful on most daily fee courses and at many private clubs around the country.

The object is to make the ball stop by the hole at times when you don't have enough green to pitch onto the putting surface.

Instead you play the ball well back in your stance, to make it land short of the green. Playing it back in your stance will give you the run you need to get it up to the hole—even with an 8- or 9-iron. Use a highly lofted club, but hit down on the ball as you would on a chip shot.

Never try the pitch-and-run if the ground is rough in front of the green.

4—THE SHORT GAME

ADVANCE HANDS ON CHIP SHOTS

Many golfers make the mistake of setting their hands behind the ball on chip shots (Illustration 1a). This often produces a flippy wrist movement during the swing (Illustration 1b) which alters the alignment of the clubface. This may also cause hitting behind the ball.

I suggest you set up to these short approach shots with your hands slightly forward of the ball, as I am doing in Illustration 2a. Then merely pull the clubhead through the ball on your downswing (Illustration 2b). With your hands leading the way, you will greatly increase your chances for solid contact and straight shots.

THE HIGH FADE APPROACH SHOT

There is much to be said in favor of a high fade approach shot. This shot curves slightly from left to right, floats down onto the green and settles very quickly. When the greens are hard or when the putting surface is raised or if there is a wind at your back, the high fade approach, which Ben Hogan executes so masterfully, is well worth having in your arsenal.

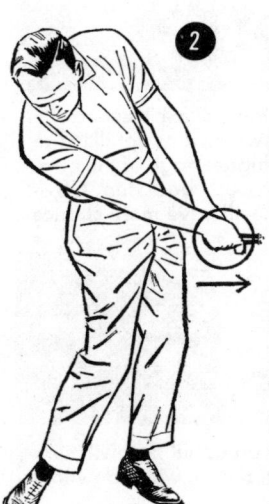

To hit this shot, address the ball with your feet, hips and shoulders all turned slightly to the left -- but with your clubface still looking at the target. This address position causes your club to cut across the ball slightly, producing the fade.

Also, play the ball forward farther than normal in your stance (illustration #1), up near your left heel. This will give your shot extra height.

Finally, be sure that your right hand does not cross your left during or shortly after impact (illustration #2). Such crossing over would close the clubface and cause a low pull-hook to the left.

ON SHORT SHOTS, WEIGHT STAYS TO LEFT

On chip shots from around the edge of a green, we must make certain that the club does not strike the ground before it meets the ball.

The best way to avoid such scuffed shots is to address the ball with your hands slightly ahead of the ball and with most of your weight on your left foot (No. 1).

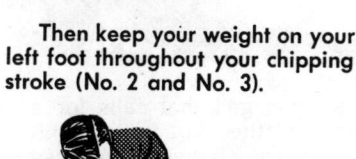

Then keep your weight on your left foot throughout your chipping stroke (No. 2 and No. 3).

Keeping your weight to the left will cause your club to brush the grass and sweep the ball into the air. Only when your hands move behind the ball or your weight shifts to the right will you be in danger of scuffing the shot.

CHIP WITH APPROPRIATE CLUB

I have always advocated chipping with the club that best fits the situation.

By following my technique you can land the ball in the same landing area on any type of chip shot -- the normal landing area being on the green just past the

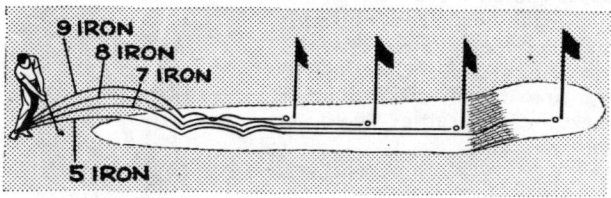

fringe. The club to be used depends on the distance from the landing area to the flagstick and the terrain of the intervening portion of the putting surface.

If the flagstick is far away, or if it's atop a rise in the green, you will probably run the shot up with a less-lofted club (see illustration). If the pin is near the edge of the green, you will loft the ball higher and it will settle more readily on the green.

4—THE SHORT GAME

SHOTS TO PLAY SLOW BUT FIRM

There is a special shot in golf that calls for a special technique. I speak of the shot from rough grass, close-in to the green. The challenge on these shots is to strike the ball firmly enough to move the clubhead through the deep grass, yet delicately enough so as not to fly the ball over the green.

I like to think "slow but firm" on these shots. I swing a bit slower, or more methodically, than normal, yet with an especially firm grip. The firm grip keeps the club from wavering in the grass and the slower swing keeps the ball from flying too far.

The over-all feel on these short shots from rough should be that you are swinging a bucket of water. You must hold it firmly, yet swing it slowly.

LEARNING THE 'CUT' SHOT

If you don't own a sand wedge and if the greens at your club are usually hard, learn the "cut" shot. Even if you are using a 9-iron or a pitching wedge, the "cut" moves the clubhead through the sand readily and doesn't allow it to cut too deeply. From the fairway, the cut shot pitches the ball high into the air with a lot of backspin, so it settles quickly on hard greens.

Today, I illustrate the things to do to produce a cut shot. Play the ball forward, opposite the left heel. Use the open stance. Let the left hand remain firm on the downswing and don't let the clubface close at impact. If anything, the clubface should be facing to the right of target on this shot.

PITCHING WEDGE -- A STROKE SAVER

The average golfer, generally speaking, misses the green as many times on shots from 100 yards or less during a single round as the number of handicap strokes he carries. If, for instance, your handicap is 15, you'll probably miss the green 15 times on shots from less than 100 yards out.

To lower your scores quickly, master the pitching wedge, which can be used from 100 yards out to within a few yards of the green.

With this club, use a "swinging" stroke instead of a "slopping" one. Execute it the way you would toss a ball underhand.

Minimize body and leg movement and be sure the clubhead contacts the ball before the turf.

THE IMPORTANCE OF PLANNED APPROACH SHOTS

No doubt you have often been told that you should play approach shots to finish below the hole (No. 1) so that you leave yourself an uphill putt.

I think that No. 2 shows why this advice is especially sound. You will note that the ball which runs uphill to the hole has a built-in backstop—the higher edge of the hole. The downhill putt has little, if any, such backstop. Obviously, a putt, struck a bit too hard, will have more chance of falling on an uphill putt.

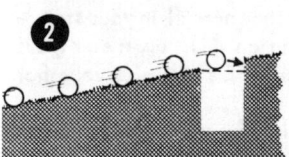 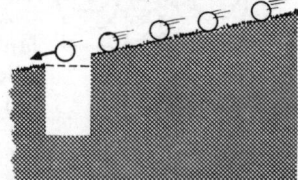

Also, we must remember that an uphill putt will stop closer to the hole if it misses the cup than will a downhill putt that rolls on and on.

I hope this explanation of why uphill putts are preferable will encourage you to plan your approach shots accordingly next time you play.

4—THE SHORT GAME

AVOID HIGH LOFT ON SHORT SHOTS

Do you hit short shots from just off the green with a highly lofted club, such as the wedge or 9-iron?

This can be dangerous. Such shots will fly high and settle quickly -- often too quickly -- well short of the

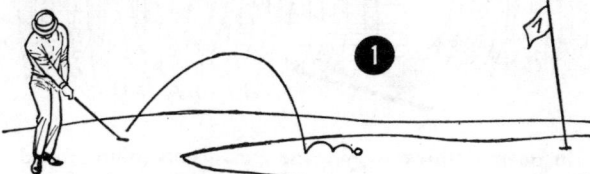

hole (No. 1). Also, there is a greater chance of missing a shot with such a club than there is with a less-lofted iron, such as a 5- or 6-iron.

I suggest that you always chip with the least-lofted club that will allow the ball to land on the green and stop near the hole (No. 2).

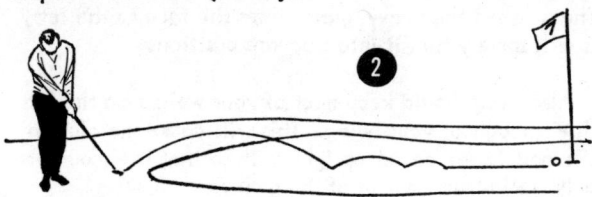

LOB SHOT FOR QUICK STOPS

When you are within, say, 50 yards of the green and you need a shot that will stop quickly, I suggest you try the "lob" shot.

Play the ball well forward in your stance (illustration #1) with a fairway wedge or 9-iron. Break your wrists early on your backswing (illustration #2),

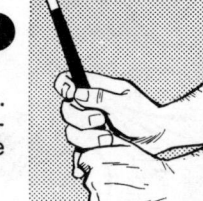

which should be slow and full. Then complete your swing, slowly but firmly sliding the blade

into and under the bottom half of the ball.

This shot will fly higher than normal because you have played it far forward in your stance. It will float through the air because of your slow swing. It will settle quickly on the green, hopefully near the flagstick (illustration #3).

LAND THE BALL ON THE GREEN

Though practice may be second nature to the experienced golfer, many novice players fail to play their approach shots to land on the green. Instead they usually play the ball to land short and run onto the putting surface.

Whenever possible, plan to land your ball on the green. The odds are such that you can expect a much truer bounce from a shot that lands on the manicured putting surface than you can from one that lands in the fairway.

Also, the grass around the edges of most greens is unusually thick because of the heavy watering it receives. This lush turf frequently will slow the progress of your ball so that it finishes far short of the hole.

Practice pitching all the way to the green from various distances (see illustration). Soon you will learn how the ball reacts on various shots so that you can properly pre-plan your future approaches.

SWING ARMS FREELY AND SMOOTHLY

The secret to success on short pitch shots—say from 50 yards on in—is to simply swing the clubhead. The key word is SWING. Not shove. Not push. Not thrust. Just SWING.

You'll be most likely to swing the clubhead smoothly and rhythmically if you hold the club lightly in your hands—not too loose, not too tight—and maintain this same light grip pressure throughout your stroke.

Let your arms hang as you address the ball. Swing the club back and through with your arms. Never hurry the shot. You'll find that the ball floats softly through the air and settles gently on the green.

101

4—THE SHORT GAME

PLAY RUN-UP SHOT TO A BANKED GREEN

A good shot to have in your bag of tricks is the run-up approach. This is especially useful on shots up a bank to an elevated green, as shown in the illustration.

The run-up shot is less likely to drop onto the side of the bank and die than is the normal, highly-lofted pitch shot.

You'll need less loft than normal for the run-up shot. The more you can reduce the influence of the bank on the movement of the ball the better. I suggest you choke down on a 3- or 4-iron, and then merely play the shot as you would a normal chip.

STRIKE BALL FIRST ON IRON SHOTS

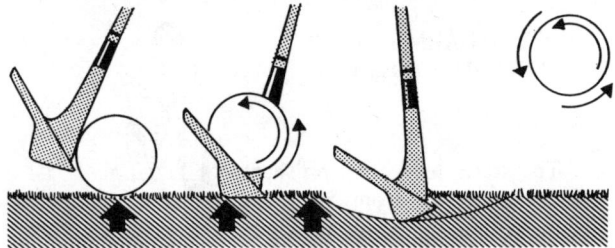

The next time you watch the pros play golf, either on TV or in person, notice how they hit their iron shots. Invariably their clubhead strikes the ball first, and then cuts into the turf. The divot mark is always ahead of the ball's original position.

Striking the ball first in the manner shown in the illustration helps put backspin on the ball. (Vertical arrows in the drawings indicate the ball's original position.) The clubhead moves downward into the ball; the ball rolls up the clubface, taking on backspin, and it finally jumps off the face as the clubhead continues downward into the turf.

The backspin enables the ball to fly at the height expected from the club you have used. It also helps the ball to fly straight, instead of spinning to the side.

Always catch the ball first on iron shots—especially on the shorter irons which you play a bit farther back in your stance.

HINTS FOR SHOOTING FROM THICK ROUGH

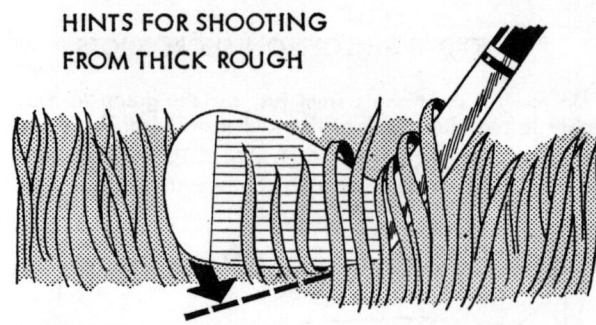

In deep or thick rough, the grass, entwining around the neck of the club as it moves into the ball, often causes the clubface to turn to the left and forces shots to take off in that direction.

Avoid this by grasping the club with an especially firm left hand. Address the ball on these shots with an "open" clubface. That is, place the club behind the ball with the face looking to the right of your intended target. Then, when the heavy grass closes the face to the left, it will merely turn it into a square position.

Also, you should keep most of your weight on the left side throughout your swing. This will cause the club to lift and lower on an upright path so that it encounters only a minimum amount of the grass.

A QUICK WAY TO LOWER YOUR SCORES

Stop and think for a minute just how much you could lower your golf scores if you had a guarantee of hitting every green on shots from 100 yards or less. Generally speaking the average golfer misses the green as many times on such shots during a single round as the number of handicap strokes he carries. If you carry a handicap of 15, you will probably miss the green 15 times on shots from less than 100 yards out.

To avoid this needless waste of strokes, perfect your skill with the pitching wedge, which can be used from 100 yards out to within a few yards of the green.

To pitch with this club, I suggest you use a "swinging" stroke as opposed to a slapping hit. Think of executing the shot in the same manner you would toss a baseball underhand (see illustrations). Keep your body and leg movement to a minimum and always contact the ball before your clubhead cuts into the turf.

4—THE SHORT GAME

FOR BETTER CHIP SHOTS

There is really no reason to move your body on short chip shots from around the edge of a green.

For accuracy, follow the same advice I give in putting: keep your head and body still. Let your arms and hands do the work.

The golfer who shifts his body laterally to the rear on short shots (#1) is liable to strike the turf behind the ball and "poop" the shot.

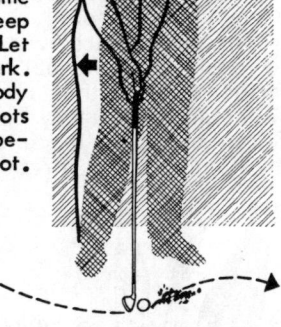

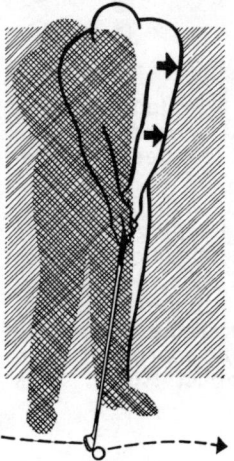

If a player moves his body forward with the club on such shots (#2), he may strike too high on the ball. This is called "blading the shot."

If you keep your body steady, your chances of returning the iron to its original position, under the ball, will be improved. Just brush the turf with your iron and sweep the ball away.

HANDY SHOT ON PAR-5 HOLES

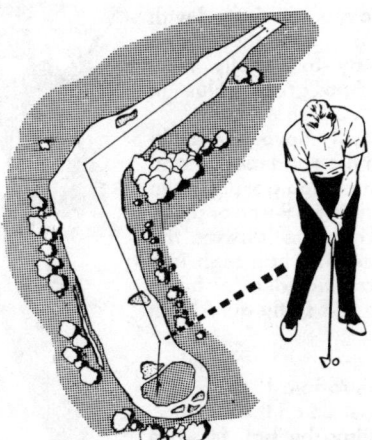

Most par-5 holes have greens that are guarded by sand or water. The golf architect reasons that a good player will be hitting a short approach shot into these greens and, therefore, should face additional challenges.

Often the flagstick will be positioned behind the hazard, leaving little landing area between the fringe and the hole. The shot required is a high, soft pitch that settles gently and stops quickly on the putting surface.

I suggest you make this shot with a sand wedge. Play the ball far forward in your stance. This gives you maximum loft for a high shot. Swing the clubhead under the ball with a "lazy" stroke, but keep your left arm and wrist firm to avoid scuffing behind the ball.

HOW TO MAKE A TOUGH SHOT LOOK EASY

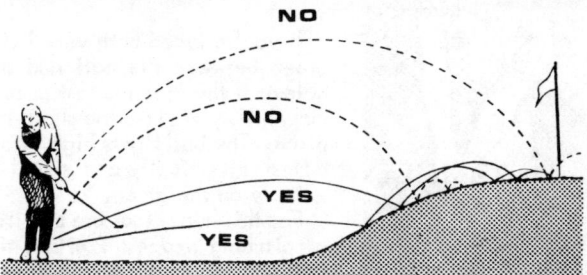

I'm sure that you've run into shots like this: you're just off the green and there is a slope between you and the flagstick, which sits on a plateau just past the top of the rise.

This may look like a tough shot, but it really isn't —if you plan it properly.

You don't want to try to pitch the ball over the rise to the hole because you may either leave it short— into the slope—or carry it too far.

What you should do is use a club with less loft— say a 6 or 7 iron—to land the ball just short of the slope and let it run up to the hole.

Or, use the same club and land into the bank. The slope will take some of the forward momentum from the ball, but this will be offset by the fact that you've carried it closer to the hole.

Actually, you have a suitable landing area of several feet—from the base of the slope to any where along it. This really makes such a shot easier than it would be if the ground were level all the way to the hole.

WEDGE-SHOOTING CALLS FOR SLOW, SMOOTH SWING

The soft, floating wedge shot that settles quickly on the green requires a smooth, even tempo, as opposed to the sharper blow you might employ on a normal wedge shot.

To produce a slow, smooth swing, I emphasize my shoulder turn and minimize hand action.

In short, I swing with the feeling that my club is moving solely as a result of my shoulder turn. I keep my left arm and wrist firm and extended as if they formed the spoke of a wheel that is turning around my shoulders.

103

4—THE SHORT GAME

EMPLOY THE HANDY 'LOB PITCH' SHOT

If you're faced with very little green between the ball and the hole or if the green is fast or runs downhill, employ the short lob pitch. The ball floats high, drops almost vertically and settles quickly on the green.

For this handy lob, use a 9-iron or pitching wedge. Position the ball well forward in your stance (#1) and let the clubhead slide un-

der the ball. The normal pitch, however, requires a downward blow and the ball flies lower than the lob and has more backspin.

The backswing should be longer on the lob than for a normal pitch of the same length.

Maintain a smooth and easy swing throughout and wind up as I have in #2.

HOW TO PLAY SHOT TO ELEVATED GREEN

Often, when shooting to an elevated green, a golfer would like to have more height than normal on his shot.

This can be achieved simply by positioning the ball slightly farther forward than normal in your stance. Normally I play my 5-iron about in the middle of my stance (see illustration #1).

On shots to elevated greens, I may move it forward almost to opposite my left heel (illustration #2).

Playing the ball farther forward—while keeping the hands in their normal position—causes the clubface to strike the ball later than normal in the swing. This means that the club will be carrying a bit more loft than normal at impact. Higher shots result.

PLAN APPROACH SHOTS TO ALLOW SIMPLE PUTTS

There is a slight advantage in putting up to, rather than down to, the hole. On uphill putts the back edge of the hole is higher than the front. Firmly struck putts will hit the higher back edge and still drop. A downhill putt struck too firmly will not only fail to hold the cup, but also will run past.

I suggest you plan your approach shots to finish below the hole whenever possible. If you really want to cut it fine, plan to finish below the hole and in a spot offering a straight-in putt...not a side-hiller.

A USEFUL SHOT TO KNOW

Golfers who are not blessed with a sand wedge, and those who frequently play to usually hard greens, will find great value in learning the "cut" shot.

This shot will move the clubhead through the sand readily and not allow it to cut too deeply, even if you are swinging a 9-iron or pitching wedge. From the fairway, the cut shot pitches the ball high into the air with a great deal of backspin so that it will settle quickly on hard greens.

In the illustration I show the things you must do on the cut shot. Note that I play the ball forward in my stance, about opposite the left heel. My stance is open, with my left foot pulled back farther from the target line than my right. I make sure that my left hand re-

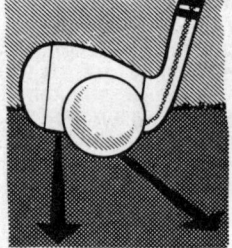

mains firm on the downswing and does not allow the clubface to close in the hitting area. If anything, the clubface should be slightly opened – facing to the right of target – on this shot.

4—THE SHORT GAME

INCREASING SHORT-IRON ACCURACY

Applying backspin to the ball is one key to golfing accuracy. This is especially necessary for the short-iron shots which place a premium on direction.

To hit accurate irons with plenty of backspin, you must strike the ball just before the clubhead cuts into the turf. Therefore, your divot should appear just ahead of the ball's original position.

To assure striking the ball first, these short irons should be played well back in your stance (No. 1). The exact position depends on your normal short-iron stance and your swing. Just make certain that you play the ball back far enough so that your divot appears forward of the original ball position as in No. 2.

HOW TO APPROACH APPROACHING

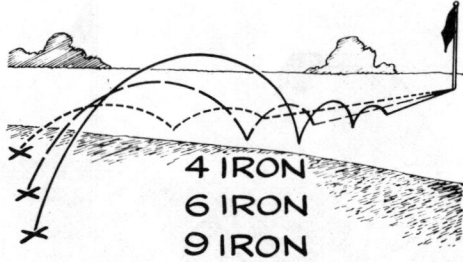

There are two ways to plan your short approach shots around the green. Select the one that works best.

The first is to play all normal short shots with the same club. This sounds logical, since it seems easier to master one club than several. The problem is that only a highly-lofted club—a 9-iron or wedge—gives you the wide variety of shots needed around the green. And these clubs must be swung harder than others to achieve the necessary distance and the harder the swing, the greater the chance for error.

The second method is to use a different club for each situation. Most of the time this allows you to make a shorter, easier swing with less-lofted clubs, thus decreasing your chances of mis-hitting the shot. But obviously, it does require mastering several different clubs.

Whatever technique you choose, always take advantage of the green's smoothness and land the ball on the green whenever you can (see illustration).

BANK ON THE 'BANK SHOT'

Occasionally you will find yourself facing a short shot to a raised green with very little putting surface between you and the hole. A shot into the bank might not make it onto the green. A shot over the top might not hold the putting surface. The only chance you have is to putt.

First make sure that all debris is removed from the line of this "putt." "Read" the line just as you would if you were on the green. You might even wish to use your putting grip.

The key to the shot is to sweep the ball on its way, just like you would a putt. This will make it roll, rather than hop. A rolling ball will be more likely to readily scoot up and over the bank, and it will be less likely to kick off line.

CHIP SHOT LANDING

It is common practice among better golfers to select a landing spot for chip shots.

This is sound technique, to be sure. However, I suggest that less-skilled golfers choose a "landing area" rather than a "landing spot" (as I have done in the illustration).

I feel it is too much to ask of a middle or high handicap golfer to expect him to land a ball on a given spot.

You should select an area large enough to give you confidence that you can land a ball upon it. You will be surprised at how many of your chip shots actually land near the center of your landing area and thus finish very close to the flagstick.

4—THE SHORT GAME

THE SHORT AND SOFT WEDGE SHOT

When you are just off the edge of a green, but you can't chip with a 6- or 7-iron because the pin is too close, then you must hit the soft chip shot with your wedge. You want a shot that will land on the green and stop quickly before the ball goes way past the hole.

The way to make this shot is to use the wedge but to swing as though you were chipping. You will get a higher shot that will settle even more quickly if you lay back the blade at address, thus increasing the club's loft.

Strike the ball with a slightly downward blow, and keep your hands ahead of the ball and your left wrist firm.

SHORT IRONS AND BACKSPIN -- YOUR GOLFING TEAMMATES

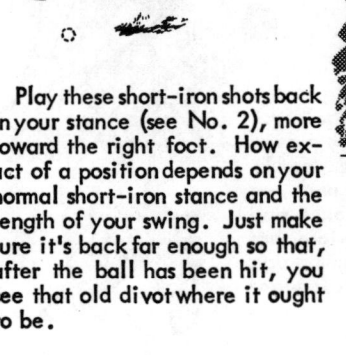

Short-iron shots and backspin go hand-in-hand most of the time, since such shots depend on backspin for direction-hitting.

To get backspin on these shots, the ball must be struck just before the short iron digs into the turf. Thus, the divot will appear just in front of the original position of the ball (No 1).

Play these short-iron shots back in your stance (see No. 2), more toward the right foot. How exact of a position depends on your normal short-iron stance and the length of your swing. Just make sure it's back far enough so that, after the ball has been hit, you see that old divot where it ought to be.

CHIPPING PRACTICE CAN BE FUN

Golfers do not spend nearly enough time perfecting their shots for the greens. It's so much more fun to get out and bang away with the driver.

Yet, chipping practice is the quickest way to cut strokes from your score—assuming your putting is in good shape. Most golfers miss several greens in each round. Chipping then becomes a major factor in scoring.

If you now chip up for one putt on 50 per cent of your shots, practice until you can do so 75 per cent of the time. Chip a batch of balls to the hole and keep track of what percentage you can put within a putter-length of the cup. Most golfers could cut at least two strokes per round from their scores if they could get down in a chip and one putt on 50 per cent more of their shots from just off the the green.

BACK-UP TO LOWER SCORES

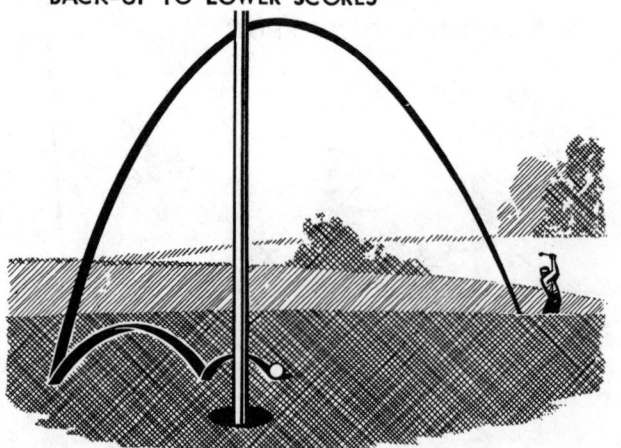

The handy back-up shot, illustrated today, must be of about 90 or 100 yards in length, so that it enables you to take a full swing with a highly lofted club, such as a fairway wedge.

Also, the ball should be lying on firm ground in order to make the back-up a successful shot.

Position the ball well back in your stance and keep as much of your body weight on your left foot as possible throughout the swing. Lift the club abruptly on the backswing and return it to the ball with a sharp downward movement. The club will lend backspin to the ball as it slides up the face of the club.

Since the club must cut down and through the turf, keep a firm left-hand grip.

SECTION FIVE

PUTTING

How to Make a Solid Putting Stroke and Become a Good Putter.

CHECK THE GRASS ON SIDEHILL PUTTS

The characteristics of the grass on the green largely determine the amount of sidehill roll a putt will take.

For instance, sidehill putts on greens that have long thick grass will break less to the side than will putts on greens with short sparse grass (illustration #1). The thicker texture of the grass

resists the ball's roll to the side. Also, on greens that are thick and long, you will strike the ball quite hard. It will travel fast for a large distance and then slow down rapidly. Because it is traveling fast for a long distance, it is less susceptible to sidehill roll.

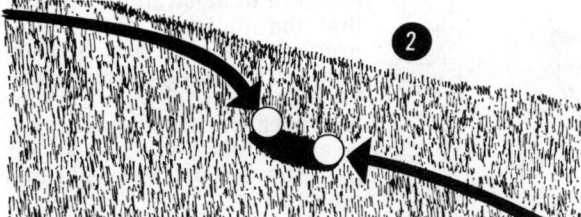

The same principle holds true for putts that are going uphill (illustration #2) and over wet greens (illustration #3). In both cases the balls will take little sidehill roll because they must be so firmly struck. Naturally the sidehill roll is increased

on downhill putts and putts on dry greens wherein the ball rolls slow for a greater portion of the putt.

Simply remember to play for less break on putts you must strike firmly; play for more break on putts that require a gentle stroke.

SYSTEMATIZE YOUR PRE-SWING MOVES

There is much to be said for building a system of moves that you can repeat each time before swinging at the ball. Most good players have such a system. It stands to reason, I think, that you will be more likely to swing the same way each time if your pre-swing moves are also consistent.

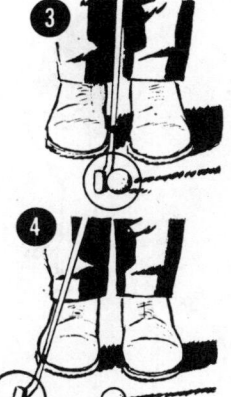

You should systematize your pre-swing moves on all shots, including putts. Consistency on the putting green is certainly just as important as elsewhere on the course.

Julius Boros is one player who makes the same moves on every shot. Watch him in a tournament or on television and you will see how smoothly he repeats his pre-swing actions and lets them lead into his swing. The illustrations show how he moves his putter first in front of, then in back of, the ball. He does it so smoothly that there is hardly any hesitation between his putting the blade behind the ball and actually taking it away on the backstroke.

107

5—PUTTING

WATCH PUTTER STRIKE THE BALL

I think that more putts are missed (especially the short ones) because the player moves his head during the stroke than for any other single reason. I have fallen into this habit myself. In fact, I won the 1962 British Open only after my wife,

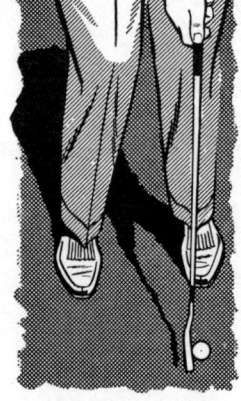

Winnie, pointed out this failing to me during a practice round prior to the tournament.

When you move your head during your putting stroke, not only is the rhythm of your stroke destroyed, but also the putter's alignment to the target line is adversely affected.

The best advice I can give to preserve a steady head is to actually watch the putter strike the ball. This, in itself, requires a certain amount of concentration, and this forced attention helps eliminate any anxiety that might cause you to lift your head prematurely.

PLAY SHARP SIDE-HILLERS AS 'SPEED' PUTTS

How many times have you missed a side-hill putt, finished far past and below the hole, and then failed to make your "comebacker?"

Unless you absolutely must sink your first putt to stay alive in a match, I suggest exercising extreme caution on sharp side-hillers.

Instead of stroking the ball firmly, and thereby minimizing the amount of break it will take, I suggest that playing the ball to roll well above the hole. Then trickle down slowly to the cup. The slower-moving ball will come to rest sooner if you should miss. You'll save yourself a lot of mental anguish on your next stroke.

LEFT WRIST FIRM FOR ACCURATE PUTTING

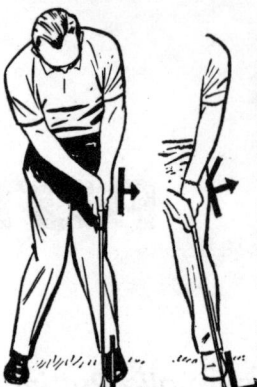

Many golfers fail to stroke their putts on line because they allow their left wrist to start collapsing before the ball is on its way (see illustration). Unless your left wrist remains firm, the clubface will be turned to your left when it meets the ball. This will cause you to pull your putts. It may, over a period of time, cause you to start compensating by pushing them to the right.

Grip your putter so that the back of your left hand faces down the target line.

CORRECT   INCORRECT

Keep it facing down this line both on your back and on your through stroke. If the back of this hand moves through the ball along the line, your putter will face down the same line.

STROKE OUT TOWARDS TARGET

Illustrations #1 and #2 show two common putting faults. The putter, in each case, is moving off-line. The problems that cause such putter movements are many—head movement, collapse of the left wrist, decelerating clubhead, etc.

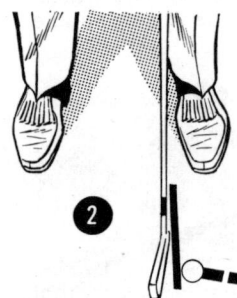

However, one cure can eliminate many of these errors. This is shown in illustration #3. Note that the putter is facing the proper direction and moving straight out towards the target. This is the key. Move the putter out towards the target, consciously, for at least six inches past the ball's original position on all putts.

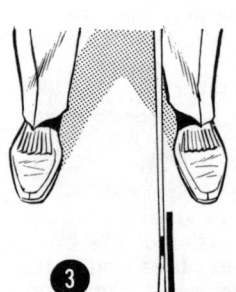

Such movement of the putterhead will force you to maintain a firm left wrist. It will cause you to accelerate the putterhead into the ball. It will make you concentrate so that your head will automatically stop moving. In short, this one simple movement of the putterhead out past the ball for six inches will force you to become a better putter.

108

5—PUTTING

"TOPPLE" YOUR PUTTS TO THE BOTTOM OF THE CUP

On several occasions I've pointed out the importance of planning putts to topple just over the edge of the hole and into the cup. Obviously, the putt that "dies" at the hole is likely to fall, even if the ball catches only the side edge.

Here's a good way to help yourself stroke the ball with the exact amount of force you need. Visualize the ball toppling just over the edge of the hole and falling to the bottom of the cup...without touching the far side of the hole.

If you imagine this happening before you putt, your reflexes will transmit the proper force to your actual stroke.

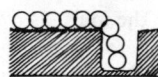

DEVELOPING A SENSE OF DISTANCE FOR LONG PUTTS

Leaving long putts short of, or well past, the hole is caused by a player's inability to properly judge the amount of force required to move the ball a certain distance on the putting surface.

There are several ways to increase your ability to judge proper putting force. One of the best, I feel, is to imagine that you are rolling the ball towards the hole, as I am doing in illustration #1. In fact, you might actually practice doing this.

The same amount of force required to toss the ball up to the hole is needed to stroke it there with a putter (illustration #2). Thus, if you can imagine how much force you need to toss the ball to the hole, you can readily transfer this image to your actual putting stroke. Then when you stroke a long putt during actual play, you need only imagine tossing the ball to the hole.

HOW GRAIN AFFECTS DIRECTION OF PUTTS

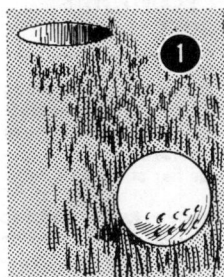

Flat-lying grass on the greens, commonly referred to as "grain," can have a dramatic effect on the direction of a putt. The illustrations show just how grain will alter the course of your putts. Check these and then apply your knowledge by reading "grain" when you play.

In illustration #1, we see the ideal putting situation—no grain. The ball will break only as a result of any sidehill terrain that might be present.

In illustration #2, we note that the grain runs into the putt head-on. Such a putt will fall short of the cup unless you give it an extra bit of force.

Illustration #3 shows just the opposite—the grain runs with the putt. This will help it roll forward farther than normal.

Finally, in illustration #4, we have the common cross-grain situation. The ball will roll to the side in which the grain lies—unless offset by sidehill terrain running to the opposite side.

Check slope from side of line

Occasionally you will run into putts that appear to run both uphill and downhill depending on whether you look at the line from behind the ball or from behind the hole.

In such instances, I like to check the slope from the side of the line. This is the only way to get a true reading on whether a putt will run up or down the slope. Naturally, what you see tells you how firmly to stroke.

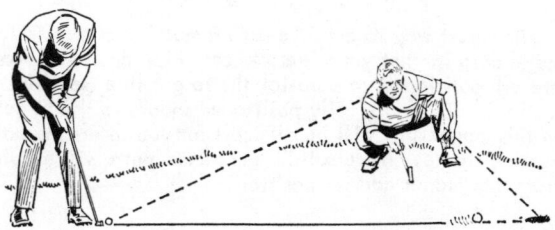

5—PUTTING

TWO SCHOOLS OF THOUGHT ON PUTTING

There are two popular methods of taking the putter back from the ball. The first (illustration #1) has the putter moving straight back with the putterface always looking at right angles to the putting line. The second method has the putter moving back "inside" the line and the putterface looking at right angles to the path on which it is moving (illustration #2).

The first method involves a slight counterclockwise rotation of the hands on the backstroke

in order to keep the putterface looking down the line. Naturally, this turning of the hands must be reversed on the through stroke to return the clubface squarely to the ball.

The second method, which seems more natural to me, involves no rotation. The putterface merely opens and shuts like the opening and closing of a door.

I suggest you try both methods and use that which gives you the best results. I further suggest you also apply whichever method you choose to your short shots from around the green.

BE A 'SQUARE'

To become a consistently good putter, you must stroke your putts so that the clubface is moving along the target line as you strike the ball.

The surest way to achieve such a putting stroke is to make certain that your feet, knees, hips and shoulders are all positioned to parallel the target line (see illustration). If you are fully positioned square to the target in this manner, it will be difficult for you to err in your putting stroke. More solidly stroked putts will result from this proper address position.

'SEE' YOUR PUTTS BEFORE YOU STROKE

All good players visualize the pattern of their shots before setting up to the ball and swinging.

This is especially worthwhile on putts. Try to actually see the ball rolling toward, and into, the hole. Try to feel in your hands just how much effort you'll need to make such a putt.

Then set up to the ball and make the putt as you've planned it, preferably without too much delay. Don't give your muscles a chance to stiffen and your mind a chance to second-guess your original decision.

WHEN YOUR PUTTING GOES SOUR

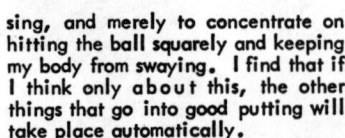

Perhaps no part of golf is more of a "here today, gone tomorrow" thing than is putting. Therefore I think it is important that every golfer have one particular course of action to follow when his or her putting starts to sour.

When this happens to me, I like to forget about the many putting fundamentals, to quit worrying about mis-

sing, and merely to concentrate on hitting the ball squarely and keeping my body from swaying. I find that if I think only about this, the other things that go into good putting will take place automatically.

If I think about hitting the ball squarely, I will naturally keep my eye

on the ball and my head steady (#1) throughout the stroke. I will naturally take the club back smoothly and low to the ground (#2). Finally, and most importantly, I will continue my follow-through, low and along the target line (#3), until the putt is well on its way.

5—PUTTING

DON'T USE SAME STROKE LENGTH ON ALL PUTTS

If you use a short stroke on long putts, you will have to increase the force of your stroke to get the ball to the hole. When you increase the force or speed of your stroke, it often becomes rushed or jerky.

Try to stroke all of your putts with the same rhythm. When you have a long putt, merely make a longer stroke as I am doing in the illustration. If the rhythm of your putting stroke remains consistent on all putts, your pattern of putting results also should become more consistent.

NOTE GENERAL SLOPE WHEN APPROACHING THE GREEN

I'm sure it's happened to you many times. You read a putt, stroke it properly along the line you have chosen, and then the ball breaks off in the opposite direction.

When this happens, it is probably because you have failed to note the green's over-all tilt. It is very possible to read a specific sidehill roll correctly, yet miss the putt because the green has a general slope in the opposite direction. Greens on courses that have high hills or mountains nearby seem to be especially susceptible to such tilting—usually away from the higher terrain.

Make it a habit to note any green as you approach it from a distance. This will give you the perspective you need to detect a general slope. Then take any over-all tilting into account when planning your specific putt.

GET THE MOST OUT OF PRE-ROUND PUTTING PRACTICE

Before you begin your round of golf, after you have hit your full shots on the practice fairway, it is always wise to sharpen up those delicate putts.

Pre-round practice putting should serve not only to build a sense of touch in your hands, but it also should inform you of the character of the greens you will encounter during the round.

With these two goals in mind, I suggest you begin your pre-round practice putting by putting "around" the hole from about a four-foot distance, as shown in the illustration.

Putt around the hole in this manner until you feel your stroke is on the beam, and that you have a definite idea of how fast the green is and how much break those side-hillers will take.

If you miss a putt, don't go back and try it again. Go on to the next ball and try to sink it. There will be no second chances out on the course.

DO YOUR OWN PLANNING ON PUTTS

I see many golfers, even some who are on the professional tour, seeking advice on putts from their caddies. I have done this myself on occasion, if the putt really has me puzzled.

Generally, however, I will ask the caddie only for a general line on the putt. I won't ask him for a specific amount of "break" to play, and I don't think that the average amateur player should either.

It stands to reason that some caddies will have a better idea of the direction a green slopes than you will, especially if you are playing a strange course. However, the caddie can have no idea how firmly you plan to stroke the putt. Therefore, he cannot, and should not, advise specifically on where you should aim.

Having confidence in your chosen line is important in successful putting. I doubt that you can be fully confident if your caddie has chosen the line.

111

5—PUTTING

DON'T OVER-ALLOW ON LONG PUTT ROLLS

In sidehill putting, you can hit it lightly for maximum break or hit it hard for little or no break, as illustrated in #1.

Now suppose you have a sidehill putt of 10 feet and a similar putt from 20 feet. Would you allow for twice as much roll on the 20-footer because the ball must travel twice as far?

Of course not. Since the 20-footer must be stroked harder, it will travel faster at first. Thus, it will be less susceptible to roll until it nears the hole (#2).

This all may seem like mere common sense, but many golfers overlook the fact and allow for too much roll on long putts.

Improve putting with smaller target

A good way to develop a strong putting game is to practice putting to a small coin on the green, rather than to a 4½-inch cup.

Try to make your ball roll over the coin and finish 6-to-8 inches beyond. This distance gives your putts every chance of reaching the hole without leaving you a difficult "come-backer."

Ten or 15 minutes of such practice before a round will not only sensitize you to the speed of the greens, but it will also make those normal-sized cups on the course look huge.

ONE HAND FACES OTHER IN PROPER PUTTING GRIP

The putterface must look down the target line when it meets the ball. To accomplish this, grip so that each hand faces the other.

In the illustrations, the back of the left hand and the palm of the

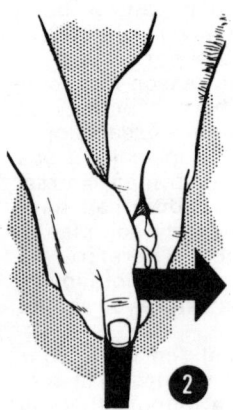

right face down the target line at address. The palms face each other. Both thumbs point down the top of the clubshaft.

In short, I have prescribed an almost perfectly balanced grip, one that minimizes any tendency to open or close the putterface during your stroke.

A CURE FOR PUSHED PUTTS

One of the prime requirements for consistently successful putting is that the golfer's body remain still during the stroke. Once his body moves, he loses control of the clubface position.

A common body movement in putting is the sliding of the hips toward the hole as the putter moves into the ball (No. 1). Such movement usually opens the clubface so

that the putt is pushed out to the right of the intended line.

To eliminate any such movement during my putting stroke, I stand over the ball with my knees firmly locked together (No. 2). By pre-locking myself in this position before I putt, I find it easier to stroke the ball solely through hand and arm movement.

Again, the fewer moving parts you must control, the better your chances for consistent accuracy — and on no shot is accuracy more important than on the putt.

5—PUTTING

WHEN THE PRESSURE BUILDS

We all get a little edgy just before we try to sink a putt that we know is crucial. And, believe me, I have faced plenty of those "sink-or-die" putts.

At such times it's best to force yourself to concentrate on meeting the ball squarely. Focus down on the back of the ball and think of giving it a firm rap. Such focusing serves a double purpose -- it eases some of the tension, and it causes you to keep your head still throughout the stroke.

If you aren't taking the putter back smoothly, loosen up that grip! You might be trying to strangle the life out of it! Then ease into the stroke and connect squarely with the ball.

STRESS DISTANCE ON LONG PUTTS

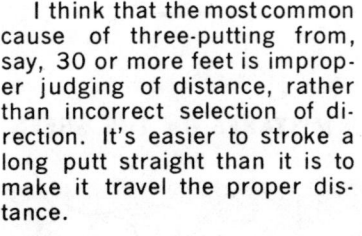

I think that the most common cause of three-putting from, say, 30 or more feet is improper judging of distance, rather than incorrect selection of direction. It's easier to stroke a long putt straight than it is to make it travel the proper distance.

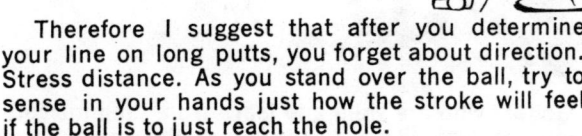

Therefore I suggest that after you determine your line on long putts, you forget about direction. Stress distance. As you stand over the ball, try to sense in your hands just how the stroke will feel if the ball is to just reach the hole.

CONSIDER YOUR FELLOW GOLFERS

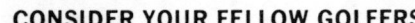
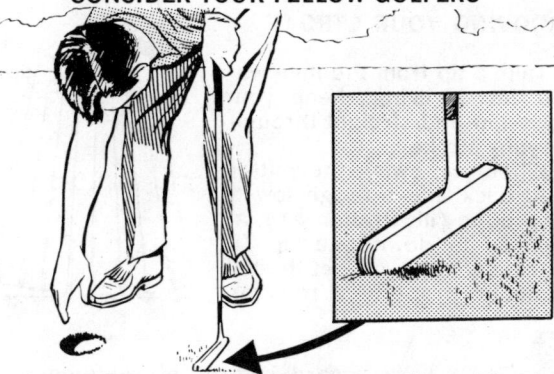

How often have you seen a golfer with whom you are playing use his putter as a "crutch" when retrieving his ball from the hole?

This practice is quite common, yet seems to be a little-discussed point of etiquette.

When a golfer puts most of his weight on the nose of his putter, he not only dents the putting surface, but also runs the risk of snapping his puttershaft.

If you violate the etiquette of the game in this manner, I urge you to think of the players that follow who must putt over your indentation. And remember: the next such mark you must putt over may be your own.

ACCELERATE STROKE ON SHORT PUTTS

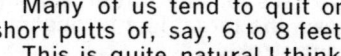

Many of us tend to quit on short putts of, say, 6 to 8 feet.

This is quite natural, I think. A soft stroke, we reason, will prevent any chance of going too far past the cup and leaving a long "comebacker." Also, we seem to think that such a short putt will hold its line within the width of the hole.

Not so! The golfer who eases up on short putts won't get many birdies, and he'll miss a lot of chances of successfully scrambling for pars.

These short putts, like all others, require a firm acceleration of clubhead into the ball (see illustration). Only by rhythmical acceleration will we keep the clubface properly square to our intended line. A firm stroke also will keep the putt on line. Condition yourself to a firm stroke by practicing these short putts.

BACKSTROKE TECHNIQUE IN PUTTING

A proper backstroke on putts should find the putterhead moving either straight back or slightly to inside the target line. This backstroke gives you the best chance for square contact and straight-rolling putts.

Check your backstroke by laying a ruler flat on the floor. If your putter moves parallel to the ruler and touches it at any point, try to correct your backstroke.

Correct such an improper backstroke by keeping your right elbow tight to your right side during your stroke, as mine is in the illustration. This eliminates the possibility of moving the putterhead to the outside.

113

5—PUTTING

GROOVING YOUR STROKE

Take a tip from the men who putt for a living: keep your blade low and straight throughout your stroke.

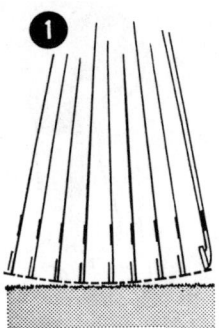

When you swing the putterhead back and through low to the ground (illustration #1), as opposed to down and up (illustration #2), you set the ball in motion properly. It rolls for-

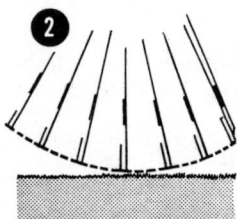

ward instead of skidding and hopping. This forward roll with a minimum of bouncing is especially vital on bumpy greens.

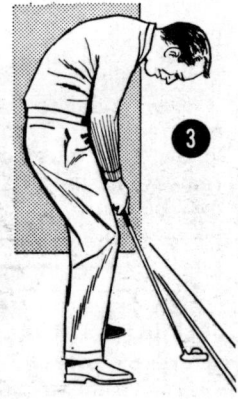

To keep your blade straight on your backstroke and throughstroke, practice moving the blade back and forth along the base of a wall (illustration #3). This movement will help you develop the proper arm and hand motion you need to keep the face of the putter looking down the target line throughout your stroke.

HERE'S TO ACCURATE PUTTER ALIGNMENT

I feel that your putter's face should be positioned directly under your dominant eye. Putting alignment should ideally be a 90-degree angle between your dominant eye, the putterface, and the line to the cup.

To determine your dominant eye, merely cut a small hole in a piece of paper. Put the paper in front of you and look through the hole at an object, such as a light switch on the wall. Close first one eye and then the other. The eye with which you can still see the light switch is your dominant eye.

Then try positioning your putterface directly under this eye. I think you will achieve better putterface alignment on your putts.

A PUTTING-PRACTICE TECHNIQUE

Are you trying to regain your normal putting stroke? Try this technique:

For 10 or 15 minutes, try stroking putts with the right hand only; repeat for the same length of time with your left hand. Then grip with both hands and see if your stroke isn't improved.

Putting this way -- using only one hand at a time, then both together -- will force you to concentrate on stroking squarely and precisely.

Don't get discouraged. Even big-time putters, like Jerry Barber and Billy Casper, go through periods when their putting strokes go haywire.

LEARN FROM YOUR MISTAKES ON THE GREEN

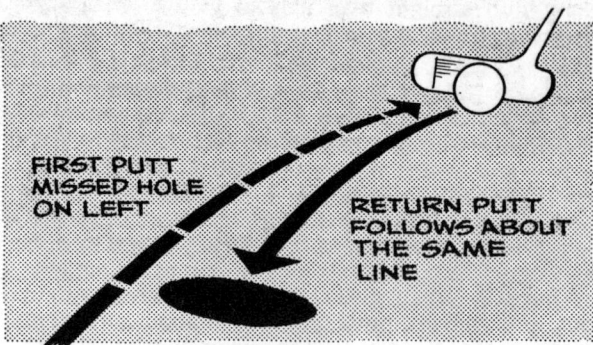

Golfers who are willing to learn from their missed putts are less likely to three-putt than are those players who go into a fit of despair when their first putt slides past the hole.

Let's assume that you had a 25-foot putt for your birdie on a slightly rolling green. Your putt missed the cup and rolled about four feet past. Did you moan about your bad luck and turn away from the putt, or did you learn from your mistake?

If you learned from your mistake, you probably watched your ball roll past the hole and mentally noted how it behaved on the putting surface. I can think of no better way to assure making a comeback putt for a par than to watch how the birdie putt curves after it has passed the hole.

Next time you putt past the cup, watch which way the ball curves. You will thus prepare yourself to properly judge the amount and direction of break on the comeback putt for your par.

5—PUTTING

A USEFUL TIP FOR BETTER PUTTING

Two of the most damaging faults that can thwart good putting are (1) moving the head while stroking and (2) taking the putter back outside the line.

Both of these problems can be eliminated through one simple putting practice technique. Merely putt along the base of a wall, as I am doing in the illustration. Make sure that the toe of your putter almost touches the wall when you address the putt. Also, lightly rest your head against the wall.

By practicing in this manner you will quickly learn to avoid "cutting" putts. The wall obviously prohibits moving the putterhead outside the line. Also, with your head against the wall, you will readily note any head movement during your stroke.

SIGHT PUTTS FROM OVER THE BALL

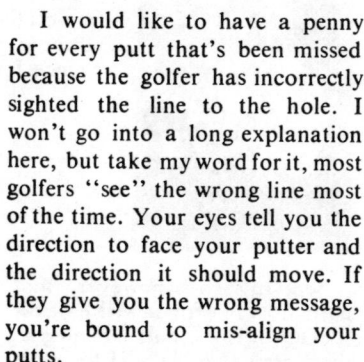

I would like to have a penny for every putt that's been missed because the golfer has incorrectly sighted the line to the hole. I won't go into a long explanation here, but take my word for it, most golfers "see" the wrong line most of the time. Your eyes tell you the direction to face your putter and the direction it should move. If they give you the wrong message, you're bound to mis-align your putts.

I can't line up your putts for you, but I can tell you one way to help make sure that when you are over the ball, you do correctly sight the line that you have chosen.

Your eyes should be over the ball as mine are in the illustrations. Also be certain that the line across your eyes is parallel to the path you wish your putterhead to make through the ball (illustration #1).

THERE'S A 'SWEET SPOT'; FIND IT

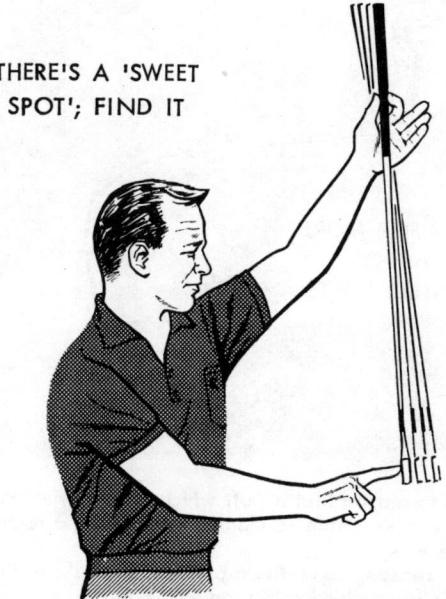

In order to strike a putt as squarely as possible, the ball must meet the club on what we call the "sweet spot."

Hold the grip end of your putter very lightly between the thumb and forefinger of one hand. Just let the club hang in front of you. Now, with the forefinger of your other hand, tap the putterface. You will note that usually when you tap the putterface, the blade will turn as it is tapped. However, if you tap one certain spot on the face, the putter moves straight back with no turning of the blade. You have found the "sweet spot."

FEEL "INWARD" WHEN PUTTING

I've always felt that the most important thing about putting is to remain absolutely motionless. Only your hands and arms should move during the stroke. If you allow your head or body to move, you will never consistently strike the ball with your putterface square to the line.

I find that I can eliminate body movement if I feel "inward" when I set up over the ball. I like to feel that my elbows and my knees are close-in toward an imaginary axis that runs up the center of my body. This feeling tends to keep my weight centered during my stroke.

Whenever my putting goes awry, the first thing I do is check that I am "quiet" with my body during my stroke. As a result, I often save myself a great deal of searching for the cause of the problem.

5—PUTTING

ALLOW FOR MORE BREAK ON DOWNHILL PUTTS

It stands to reason that a putt which is rolling slowly will be more susceptible to sidehill break than a faster moving putt will.

For this reason, as I have pointed out before, the smart golfer pays close attention to the terrain around the cup. It is in this area that the slowly rolling ball will be most affected by any sidehill break.

For the same reason, it is also important to realize that a downhill putt will take more sidehill roll than will an uphill putt on similar terrain. Golfers cannot charge a downhill putt like they can an uphill putt. Since they must "lag" downhill putts to the hole, the slowly rolling ball will be more likely to roll to the side (see illustration).

STRIKE PUTTS AT BOTTOM OF ARC

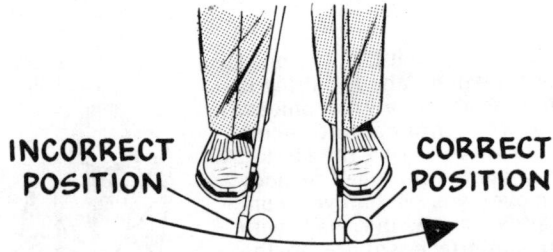

INCORRECT POSITION   CORRECT POSITION

Golfers who play the ball too far back in their putting stance will seldom achieve consistently excellent results.

When the clubhead strikes the ball before reaching the lowest point of its arc, it applies a slight amount of backspin. The ball skids—often slightly sideways—instead of rolling smoothly forward. If the greens are slightly rough, striking down on putts will accentuate the ball's rough roll.

Most golfers find that the lowest part of their putter's arc occurs at a point about opposite their left—or forward—foot (see illustration). Determine where you must play your putts to achieve solid contact. Then consciously see that you position the ball in the same relative spot within your stance on all putts.

STROKE FIRMLY ON RETURN PUTT

Many golfers who overshoot the hole on their first putt have a tendency to "baby" their return try. This may be psychologically logical, but it certainly makes for many three-putt greens.

Actually, a golfer should have some advantage on the return putt. If he has observed the break of his first putt, he should have a pretty good idea how much break his second putt will take (see illustration).

With this knowledge, he should give the second putt a firm, smooth and accelerating stroke. There should be no hesitation or jerkiness about it.

I know it takes nerve to putt boldly on that second try, but I also know from experience that "faint heart ne'er won fair maiden" on the putting surface.

WHEN TO PUTT FROM OFF THE GREEN

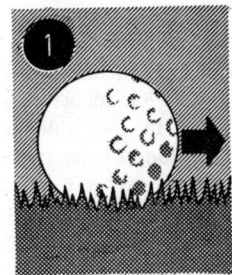

Never feel guilty about putting from off the green, if you feel the putter will give you the best chance for a successful shot.

Bear in mind, however, that putts from the fringe will be most successful if the ball is resting on short grass (No. 1) or if the grass

lays toward the hole (No. 2). If the grass lays away from the green (No. 3) or if your ball is nestled into the grass (No. 4), you will

probably be better off if you chip it out and onto the green with a 5-iron or 6-iron.

5—PUTTING

SLOPING PUTTS ARE TRICKY

If you miss putts to the low side of the hole when the cup is set into a slope on the green, you're failing to realize that a putt will take more sidehill break when it nears the cup than it will in its early stages. The slower the ball is rolling, the more it will be affected by the sidehill slant.

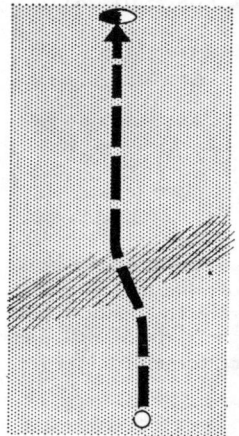
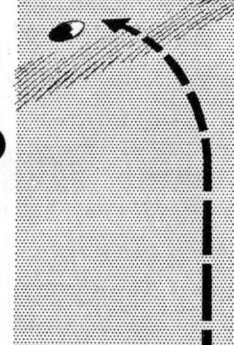

In No. 1, we see a putt that must roll on sidehill in its early stages, but on level ground near the hole. In illustration No. 2, we see the opposite. Note that the putt cuts more to the side in illustration No. 2 because the ball encounters the slope when it's rolling slowly.

PUTTS SHOULD ROLL, NOT DRIBBLE

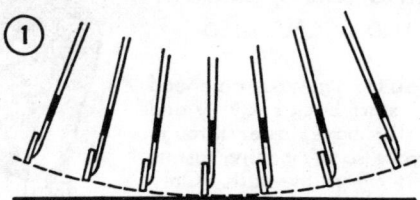

Very seldom will you see a putt drop in the hole if, during the first few feet, it has bounced along the green. Such bouncing almost always makes the ball jump slightly offline.

Ideally, your putts should roll smoothly along the putting surface from start to finish.

One reason that putts dribble instead of roll is because the putterface is looking slightly downward or upward when it meets the ball.

You'll find it easier to avoid such a putterface position, and thus make the ball roll true, if you "flatten" your stroke. Try to produce the pattern of stroke shown in illustration #1, rather than the more up-down pattern in illustration #2.

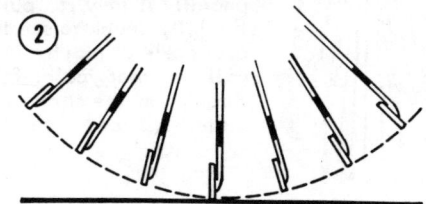

Go to school on the greens

You can learn a great deal about your next putt if you pay close attention to those of others putting before you. This is true even if no one else has a putt similar to yours.

You can learn how fast the green is over-all. You can learn of any general tilting of the over-all green (if other putts come up shorter, or roll farther, than you'd expected they would, it's a good bet that there is such tilting). Most important, you can learn which way the ball will curl near the cup.

Occasionally your playing partner may push or pull a putt, and thus the roll of the ball will give you a distorted impression. Watch his or her stroke. If it looks sound, then match the ball roll. Thus you'll go up to your putt with a positive impression of how it will react.

'GRAIN' CAN OFFSET 'BREAK' ON PUTTS

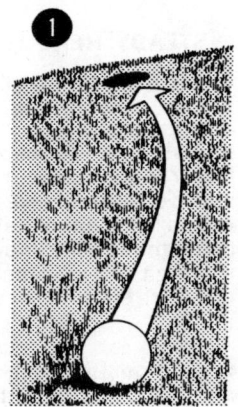

Grain is the direction in which the grass on the green grows. You can detect the grain of a green if you look closely at the grass.

Grain will cause putts to roll in the direction it lies. If it lies with the putt, the ball will roll farther than normal. Grain will slow up a putt if it lies against the direction the ball is to roll.

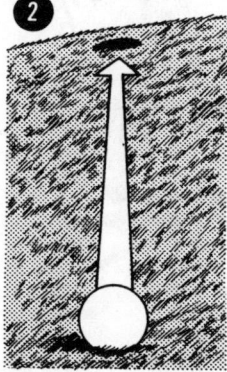

Grain also can offset the slope of a green. In illustration #1, we see how a putt on grass that grows upright will take the break to the left. However, if the grain lies across the putt's line to the right (illustration #2), it will keep the putt straight. The golfer would miss the putt on the right if he played for any "break."

117

5—PUTTING

PUTTING TEMPO, SMOOTH AND ACCELERATED

In putting, your clubhead should start back slowly and gradually move faster through the stroke so it's moving fastest when it meets the ball. Only with acceleration at contact will the putter blade remain

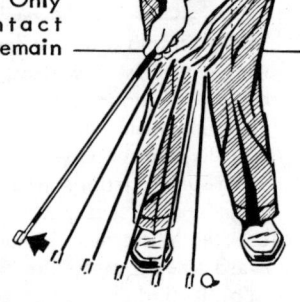

square to the target line during the time that it is moving the ball.

If your putts are erratic, especially if they're "pulled" to the left, check to see that you are accelerating through the ball and that you're following through on the stroke with the putterhead toward the target.

PUTTING CALLS FOR SWEEPING STROKE

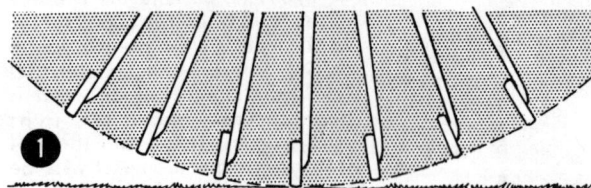

A descending clubhead that strikes down on the ball, then continues through the turf, is not advisable for putts.

If your putterhead descends sharply to the ball (see No. 1), the putt will hop before it starts to roll and may bounce off-line. Also, the putterhead might top the ball.

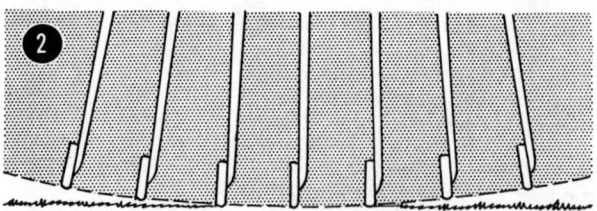

Try to keep your putting stroke low to the ground, both on the backstroke and the throughstroke (see No. 2). Sweep the ball to the hole. With such a stroke your putts will roll, rather than hop or skip, toward the cup.

STEADY HEAD IS KEY TO SOUND PUTTING

Nothing will ruin your putting faster than head movement during the stroke. The head must remain absolutely steady throughout. Any movement will misalign the clubface so that it faces off the line when it strikes the ball.

I suggest you focus your attention on the back of the ball and think about nothing except hitting the ball squarely. This will force your head into a steady position and practically guarantee solid contact between club and ball.

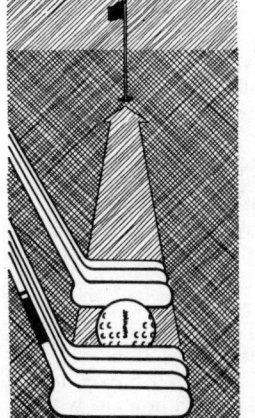

I am convinced that the average golfer misses more putts because of mis-striking the ball than for any other reason. Keep your head steady for solid striking.

A QUICK WAY TO GUIDE PUTTING STROKE

If you have ever wondered why professional golfers seem so meticulous about how they replace a ball on the putting green, this may answer your question.

Naturally, we always try to replace the ball in exactly the same spot it occupied before we marked it. However, some players go a step further. They not only place the ball on exactly the same spot, but they also place it in a manner so that the

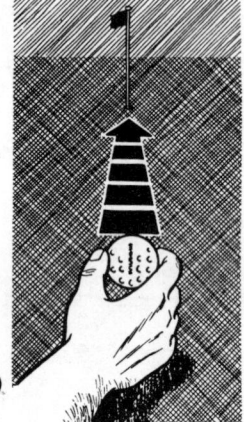

name on the ball points directly along the desired line to the hole (#1).

The reason for positioning the ball in this manner should be obvious. If the lettering on the ball points the way to the target, then all the player must do is to make his back and through stroke follow an imaginary extension of this lettering (#2).

If the stroke is so executed, the ball will roll along the desired line and will have an excellent chance of dropping.

5—PUTTING

THE POWER OF POSITIVE PUTTING

Successful putting--lining up the shot, sighting and finally stroking the ball--depends primarily on your attitude. Positive thinking on the greens can make a technically poor putter successful. Negative thinking-- "If I miss this one, I'll never break 90 today"--will destroy good putting style because you cannot stroke a putt properly if anxiety has made you tense.

I suggest you try picturing the ball following a proper line into the hole. Do this when you sight the putt (#1) and then retain this image when you are over the ball, riveting your eyes to the back of the ball. Merely hit the ball along the line you have in your mind's eye.

It will take some practice to develop this power of visualization, but I guarantee that once you master the technique your putting will improve.

3 WAYS TO EFFECTIVE PUTTING GRIP

Whatever putting grip you decide on, it should include three elements:

The palms should face each other and be parallel with the face of the putter. In this way, both thumbs will face down the handle of the shaft.

Secondly, there should be a

slight pressure between the thumb and forefinger of your right hand (see #1). The other fingers merely feel the shaft and provide control.

Finally, the hands should grip as a unit. I let the forefinger of my top hand overlap the fingers of my bottom hand, as illustrated in #2.

PUTTING RIGHT ON TARGET

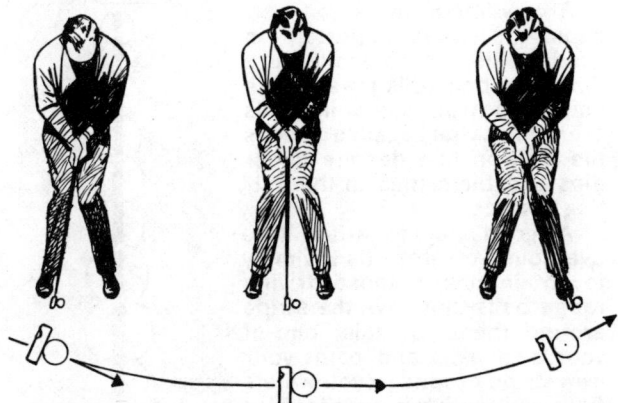

Today's three illustrations show how ball positioning in your stance can affect putt direction.

At left the ball is back in the stance. The putter contacts the ball before its face is square to the target line, causing the ball to go to the right.

The center illustration shows my normal positioning of the ball. The putterface is looking down the line when it meets the ball and the putts roll straight.

If your ball is positioned too far forward, as in the illustration at right, the clubface may have moved past square and be closed, facing left, when it reaches the ball. Obviously the ball will then roll left of target.

PUTTING PROBLEMS? TRY AN ARM STROKE

Sooner or later every golfer tenses up on a putt. It's nothing to be ashamed of; it's just that everyone has a nervous system and sometimes it runs out of control.

Many golfers have more or less solved the problem of putting nerves by going to an "arm stroke." Instead of combining wrist and arm action (illustration #1) they employ only arm movement. The arms move from the shoulders just like a clock's pendulum (illustration #2).

The arms seem to be less susceptible to nervous tension than are the smaller muscles of the wrists and hands. By taking these smaller muscles out of the stroke, you may find that you jerk or jab fewer putts.

5—PUTTING

STRIKE ALL PUTTS IN SAME SPOT ON PUTTERFACE

I cannot over-stress the importance of the words in the headline on today's tip. No one can hope to be a consistently good putter if they become careless about where on the putterface they strike the ball.

It has been proven that the distance putts travel varies by several inches . . . sometimes feet . . . depending upon where the ball contacts the putterface. And I'm talking about putts struck with exactly the same degree of force.

Let's say you are putting on the first green. You hit the ball near the heel or tee of your putter. Because you hit it off-center, it falls far short of the cup. You assume that the greens are slow.

On the next green you make a firmer stroke. But you catch this one on the "sweet spot," so it goes several feet past the hole.

I think you can see what this could do to your putting for that day. Play all putts from the spot. If your putter doesn't already have a guideline on top, I suggest you make one. Then align with it each time.

HAVE CONFIDENCE IN YOUR PUTTING LINE

I am convinced that more putts are missed because of indecision about the line than are missed because of failure to detect the proper line. In other words, I believe that determining the correct putting line is relatively simple; it's making yourself believe in your decision that becomes tough. Any doubt about the line will thwart a smooth, square putting stroke.

Maybe you will find it easier to believe in your choice of putting line if you follow this tip: Eliminate all other potential putting paths except one. Then concentrate on the one that remains. Don't let yourself think there is any other possible route to the hole than the one you have chosen.

IMPROVE YOUR CHANCES FOR SINKING PUTTS

Don't let the diagrams for today's article scare you. I'm not presenting an exercise in advanced geometry. However, I will show you how to increase the size of your putting target.

We've all heard the saying, "Never up, never in." Someone usually says it after you fall short on a putt. These diagrams will help me show why I disagree with this philosophy.

In #1, we see the chances a player has when he bangs away at the hole. Only when the ball squarely hits the

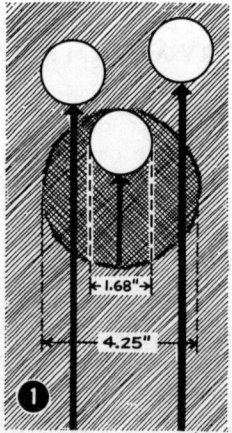

back of the cup will it drop. In effect this player has reduced his hole from one of 4.25" in diameter to one no wider than the ball itself, or 1.68".

In #2 we see the target for a golfer who hits his putts just the correct speed to reach the center of the hole. Since putts that nick even the sides of the hole will drop if over one-half the ball hangs over the lip, it becomes apparent that the target is no longer merely 4.25 inches wide but rather about 5.75" in diameter.

Correct putting speed does widen your margin for error.

A SIMPLE AID TO BETTER PUTTING

A very important factor—perhaps the most important—in good putting is to make sure that your ball rolls towards the hole with true overspin. This overspin is vital because it keeps the ball on line despite minor dips and blemishes in the putting surface.

A good way to attain true overspin on your putts is simply to obtain one of those driving range balls that have the stripe around them. Or take one of your own balls and paint your own stripe around it (your wife's fingernail polish is excellent for this purpose).

Make sure that the stripe runs parallel to the target line as you address the putt. Then stroke the ball and note if the stripe wavers from side to side as the ball rolls. If it does, you need to work on your putting stroke to achieve a more perfect overspin. Practice putting until you achieve such spin on your putt almost every time.

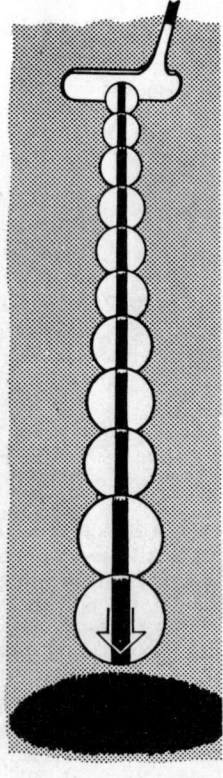

5—PUTTING

THE 'PLUMB LINE' METHOD OF JUDGING PUTTS

Though I don't personally use the "plumb line" method of judging putts, many good putters do.

To plumb line putts, you must first determine which eye is dominant. Put your thumb out at arm's length so that it "covers" some distant object, like a doorknob. Then close each eye alternately. The eye which sights the thumb still over the knob is dominant. This is the eye you keep open when you plumb line your putts.

On the green, stand a few feet behind your ball. Raise your putter in one hand, covering the ball with the putter shaft. Just let the putter dangle. Then look at the top part of the shaft. If it passes to the left of the hole, the ball breaks right. If it passes to the right, the ball breaks left.

In the illustration, the putt shown will break to the right, so the player must aim to the left.

DON'T MOVE OUTSIDE PUTTING TARGET LINE

A proper backstroke on putts should find the putterhead moving either straight back or slightly to inside the target line. This backstroke gives you the best chance for square contact and straight-rolling putts.

Check your backstroke by laying a ruler flat on the floor. If your putter moves parallel to the ruler and touches it at any point, try to correct your backstroke.

Correct such an improper backstroke by keeping your right elbow tight to your right side during your stroke, as mine is in the illustration. This eliminates the possibility of moving the putterhead to the outside.

PRACTICE STRAIGHT-IN PUTTS

I know of very few golfers, even among the pros, who can putt successfully without practicing this phase of the game regularly. Everyone has a basic rhythm to his or her stroke, and it takes some effort to maintain it from week to week.

When you practice your putting, you should try to re-capture this basic rhythm. And the best way to do this is to practice straight-in putts.

If you practice breaking putts, you'll tend to become too conscious of your line and the force of your stroke. You'll overlook the fundamental need to merely re-instate your basic rhythm. Move on to longer, more difficult putts, only after you have regained the proper pace of your stroke.

PUTTING STROKE TAKES PRACTICE AND FINESSE

Golfers frequently three-putt because they have applied improper speed to their first putt. In most cases the line of a long putt is only a secondary cause of three-putting. Seldom do golfers miss by much on either side.

It's important to play long putts to "die" at the hole and the illustration shows why. Such a putt uses all four sides of the hole. A putt that is stroked too firmly uses only one side--the front. The putt that falls short, of course, doesn't use any side.

Strive for direction when you practice your putting--but don't neglect practicing for distance too. There is no shortcut in developing this sense of distance. But nothing will cut strokes from your score faster than the development of a sensitive putting touch.

EFFECTIVE PUTTING, UPHILL AND DOWNHILL

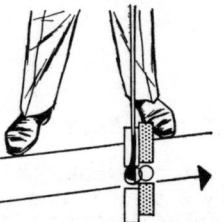
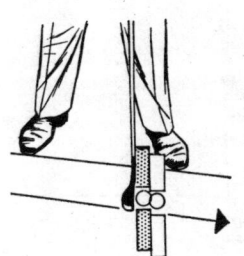

Whenever you must address a shot with one foot higher than the other, the arc of your swing will change. You will not strike the ball squarely unless you position it in a manner to compensate for the change in arc.

I normally address my putts with my nose aligned over the ball. However, I find I achieve a more solid putt if, on uphill putts, I play the ball a shade farther forward (illustration No. 1). Downhill putts I play slightly back in my stance (illustration No. 2).

I think you will feel more comfortable on hilly putts if you follow this procedure. You should enjoy better club-ball contact as as result.

ACCURATE FOCUSING CUTS DOWN RISK OF PUSHED AND PULLED SHOTS

When putting, you might want to focus your eyes in front of or behind the ball, just as long as you don't focus outside or inside your putting line. Always be able to look from your ball to the target, merely by rotating your head.

If your eyes are not over the putting line, it is all too easy to mis-read the line to the hole, and to mis-align your putterface before you start your stroke. This leads to pushed putts to the right or pulled putts to the left.

SECTION SIX

SAND SHOTS

How to Make Those Tough Sand Shots Easier.

PROPER CLUB MAKES SAND SHOTS EASY

One of the best investments you can make to improve your golf scores is to buy a sand wedge. The illustrations in this lesson show why this is true.

In illustration #1 we see how a 9-iron or a fairway wedge cuts into the sand. Note that it cuts much more deeply than does the sand wedge in #2. This deeper cut will cause most players to leave too many shots in the sand. The shallow cut is much more desireable when shooting from sand.

The sand wedge makes a shallower cut because of the configuration of the bottom, the sole, of the blade. You will note that the sand wedge's back edge hangs a bit lower than its leading edge (see shaded area on clubs in illustration #2). This raised leading edge doesn't occur on the fairway irons. Thus they cut deeper into the sand.

The sand wedge also is slightly shorter and heavier than the fairway wedge, thus aiding its ability to make a shallow cut with less difficulty through the sand.

SPLASH—DON'T BLAST—FROM SAND

I think that the term "blast" is an unfortunate choice of words to describe the average sand shot. When the ball is buried, obviously you must "blast." But when the lie is normal, the proper sand shot is more of a "splash." Too often those who try to blast from sand will cut too deeply and leave the ball short.

Before splashing, be sure that your sand wedge is laid back and opened slightly so that it looks a bit to the right of target (illustration #1). If you set the blade squarely behind the ball and facing down the target line (illustration #2), it will tend to cut too deeply.

Also, position your feet in the sand so that a line across your toes will point to the left of target. This is the so-called "open" stance. This placement will cause your clubhead to slice across the target line, from outside to inside (illustration #3), as you swing. The result of all this is that the clubhead makes a relatively shallow cut under the ball. The ball pops up high and sort of floats to the green where it settles quickly.

122

6—SAND SHOTS

LET YOUR LIE DETERMINE WHERE CLUB ENTERS SAND

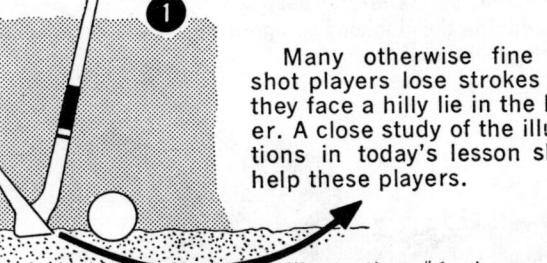

Many otherwise fine sand shot players lose strokes when they face a hilly lie in the bunker. A close study of the illustrations in today's lesson should help these players.

Illustration #1 shows a side view of the clubhead's path on a sand shot from a level lie. The point of entry of the club into the sand may vary with individual taste. If you are in doubt about this, I suggest you consider 1½ to 2 inches behind the ball as being normal.

In illustration #2, we see an uphill lie. Note that the clubhead will have to pass through much more sand depth

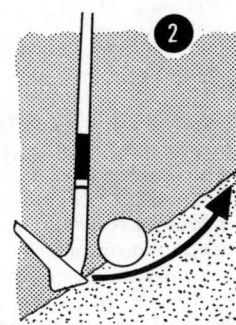

in cutting under the ball than it would from a level lie. If we enter the sand at the normal point, the club will not make it through all that sand with much speed. Therefore, on uphill lies, we must enter the sand closer to the ball.

On downhill lies (illustration #3), the reverse is true—less sand to impede the club. The point of entry must be farther behind the ball than normal.

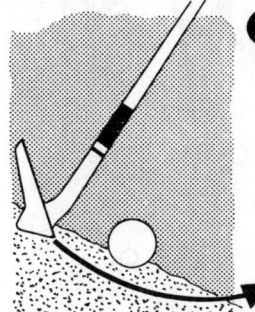

VARY CLUBFACE WITH LIE OF BALL IN SAND

A good way to standardize your sand play is to vary the facing of your club according to the depth of the ball in the sand.

I suggest that when the ball rests on top of the sand (top illustration) you face the club slightly to the right of your target. Face it at the target when the ball is slightly depressed (middle illustration), and to the left when the ball is buried (bottom illustration).

The more you aim the clubface to the left, the deeper it will cut into the sand, which is just what you need when the ball is low in the bunker.

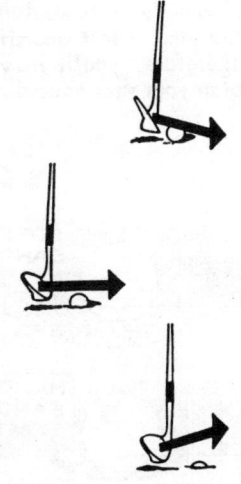

HOW TO PLAY THAT LONG SHOT FROM SAND

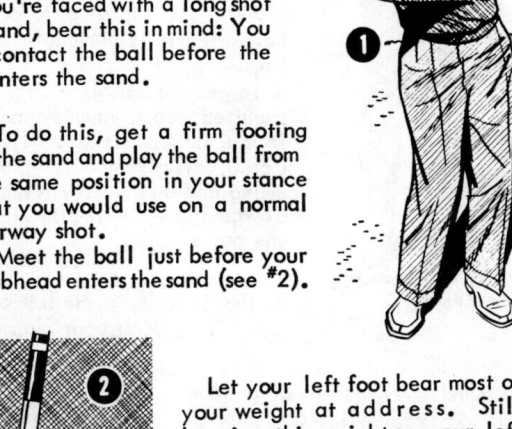

If you're faced with a long shot from sand, bear this in mind: You must contact the ball before the club enters the sand.

To do this, get a firm footing in the sand and play the ball from the same position in your stance that you would use on a normal fairway shot.

Meet the ball just before your clubhead enters the sand (see #2).

Let your left foot bear most of your weight at address. Still keeping this weight on your left foot, swing largely with your arms (see #2).

The important thing here is that your body movements be kept at a minimum.

TRY PRACTICING SAND SHOTS IN SLOW MOTION

Fear and tension cause many golfers to rush their sand shots. They are so anxious to get the shot out of the way that they unconsciously increase their swing tempo, and thus fail to make the shot as planned.

I think the average player would be wise to swing in slow motion when practicing sand shots. Then try to duplicate this rhythm in actual play. Just focus your attention on the spot behind the ball where you wish your club to enter the sand, and swing slowly – but firmly.

A side benefit also accrues from a slow sand shot swing. By swinging slowly the golfer will minimize chances that his feet will slip in the sand, as they might on a faster swing.

6—SAND SHOTS

BURIED SAND SHOTS DON'T CALL FOR BRUTE STRENGTH

Here is a simple way to pop the ball when it is buried in a sand trap.

To get the upright swing plane required, cock your wrists early in the backswing (see #1). This action will give you a high backswing and a sharply descending downswing that will cut well under the buried ball.

At address, toe your clubface so that it looks to the left of target. Then, when your club enters the sand (#2), its leading edge will cut readily into and through the sand.

You will be surprised how easily your club will pop the ball from a buried lie if you make these two simple swing adjustments.

THE LONG AND SHORT OF SAND SHOT PLAY

There is one objective on all sand shots: to return the ball to the fairway or the green. But beyond this general objective, we have two varying goals on different types of shots. On long fairway sand shots, the object is to hit the ball a long distance. On short sand shots from around the green, the object is to hit the ball high enough to clear the lip of the bunker and settle near the flagstick.

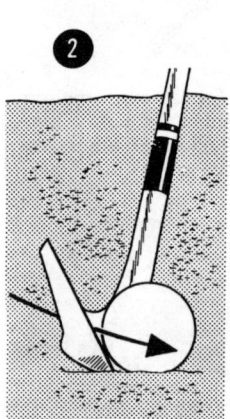

In illustration #1, we see the action of the club on short sand shots. Note that the clubhead cuts into the sand well behind the ball. This lifts the ball out of the bunker on a cushion of sand and deposits it softly on the green. You play this shot well forward in your stance—opposite your left foot—so that the club will enter behind the ball.

In the fairway sand shot (illustration #2), the club contacts the ball first, then the sand, just as it contacts the ball first on fairway shots. This action gives you the distance you need. Play this shot well back in your stance—just as you would a fairway shot.

THE SAND SHOT AND THE FIRM LEFT WRIST

The shallower the cut on a sand shot, the better. A deep cut would slow the clubhead's progress through the ball.

Cutting too deeply is mostly caused by closing, or hooding, the clubface in the impact area. When the clubface is closed, so it faces left of target, it cuts too deeply downward.

To assure yourself of a shallow cut, slice the clubface beneath the ball on a path from outside to inside the target line, with your left wrist quite firm throughout the downswing (see illustration). It is almost impossible for the club to cut deep if the left wrist remains firm until the ball is well on its way.

FIRM OR SOFT SAND? SWING TECHNIQUE MUST DIFFER

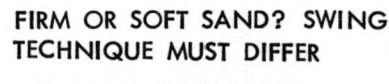

Your sand shot technique should differ with the texture of the sand.

For example, if the sand is wet, hard or shallow, your clubhead won't cut into it as deeply as it would when the sand is soft and sifting. Therefore, you'll have to plan your shot accordingly.

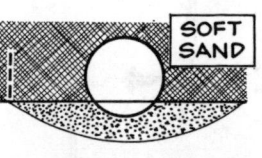
SOFT SAND

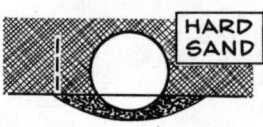
HARD SAND

If the sand is soft, try to dig in about 2 inches behind the ball; but when the sand is hard, wet or shallow, penetrate it about 1 1/2 inches behind the ball.

One last thing: Since firm sand will slow down your club considerably, give your swing a full follow-through. Don't quit on the shot.

6—SAND SHOTS

ALTER STANCE WHEN SAND IS WET

When hitting shots from soft sand, your club will encounter a minimum of resistance from the sand. You can cut fairly deep under the ball—thus avoiding a "thin" shot—and still pop the ball out readily.

However, when the sand is wet and heavy you will need a shallow cut through the sand. If you cut too deeply, you won't get the club through the sand with enough speed to pop the ball out.

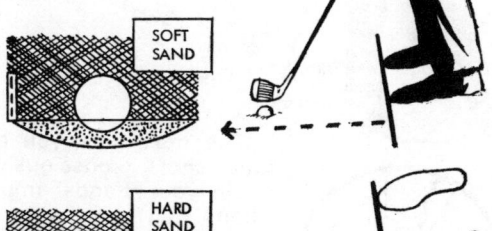

Thus you need a deep cut through soft sand and a shallow cut through deep sand.

You can make this change in the depth of your cut simply by changing your stance slightly (see illustration). The more you pull your left foot back and thus "open" your stance, the shallower will be the cut your club makes in the sand.

So use your normal stance in soft sand, but go to a more-open stance in wet sand.

PLAYING SAND SHOTS FROM HILLY LIES

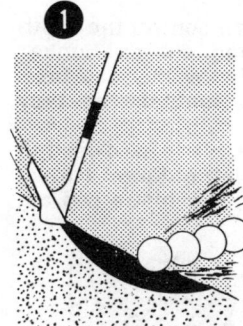

Too many golfers panic when they find their ball resting on a downhill or uphill slope in the bunker. A little knowledge about these shots can save you strain —both mentally and financially.

All you must remember is that, on downhill lies, your club will encounter less sand than normal; on uphill lies, it must plow through more sand (see illustrations #1 and #2).

Because your club meets less sand on downhill lies, the normal tendency is to hit these shots too "thin." You must offset the lack of sand resistance by cutting farther behind the ball than normal. Do this and your shot will react as it would from a level lie.

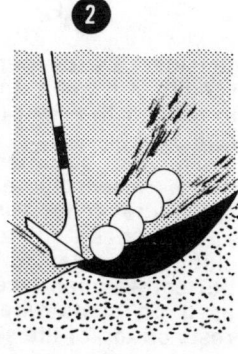

On uphill lies, you must offset the increased sand resistance. Hit the sand closer to the ball than normal so that ball will pop out as readily as it would from a level lie.

SETTING UP IN SAND

The wise golfer realizes that the success or failure of a sand shot is determined largely by the manner in which he sets up to the ball. In the illustrations, I show the proper address position for the normal explosion shot from sand.

You will note that my feet are positioned in an open stance with the left foot pulled back farther than the right from the ball. This open stance

pre-turns my whole body to the left so that it will turn readily in this direction on the downswing. Without this pre-turning it would be too easy to lose balance in the uneasy sandy footing.

You will note too that I have laid back the clubface. This increases the club's loft so that I get the necessary height on the shot. With the blade laid back there also is less chance that it will cut too deeply into the sand and thus lose momentum.

"SIT DOWN" ON SAND SHOTS

If you were to pay close attention to the better sand shot players on the pro tour, you'd find that most of them show a lot of flex at the knees as they address the ball.

It almost looks as if they were preparing to sit down on a stool (see illustration).

Then they swing with only a minimum of leg and foot work. They move the club largely with the arms and shoulders so as to avoid slipping in the loose sand.

By pre-crouching, as shown in the illustration, then swinging largely with the arms, you will be less likely to raise or lower your body on your downswing. You will find it easier to make the clubhead enter the sand in exactly the position you had anticipated.

6—SAND SHOTS

SLIDE KNEES ON SHOTS FROM SAND

The thing we want to avoid on sand shots is cutting in so deeply that the clubhead loses most of its speed.

We avoid this by making sure that our knees are ultra-flexed throughout our swing. They sort of slide toward the target on the downswing and follow-through. This knee action tends to keep the clubhead moving through the sand on a somewhat level path.

What we must avoid is stiffening the left leg. When the leg stiffens, the left shoulder raises. The other shoulder must then lower, and this forces the clubhead too far into the sand.

"SQUARE" CLUBFACE ON BURIED LIES

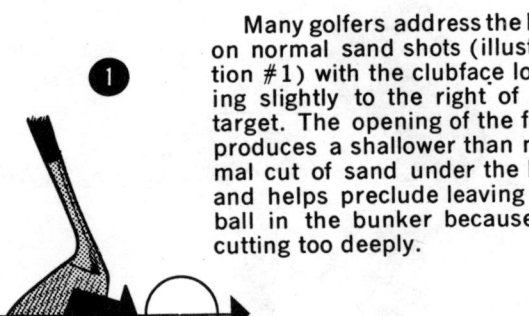

Many golfers address the ball on normal sand shots (illustration #1) with the clubface looking slightly to the right of the target. The opening of the face produces a shallower than normal cut of sand under the ball and helps preclude leaving the ball in the bunker because of cutting too deeply.

When the ball is resting low in the sand, however, the opened clubface is not suitable. The clubface should be either square to the target line (illustration #2) or slightly closed. This will cause the club to cut deeper into the sand so that the head will move well under the depressed ball. Striking a ball in a buried lie while using an open clubface could cause you to cut into the ball itself and to blade the shot well past the target.

AVOID CROSSING OVER HANDS ON SAND SHOTS

Cutting too deeply into the sand on shots from bunkers often occurs because the golfer allows his right hand to "crawl" over his left too soon on his follow-through (see "incorrect" portion of illustration). Actually this crawling over is merely an indication that the player was starting to close his clubface while the clubhead was moving through the sand. The closed face cuts too deeply; weak shots result.

INCORRECT

The next time you practice sand shots, consciously try to retain your hands' impact position well into your follow-through. Keep your right hand facing the target until the ball is well on its way.

This will keep your clubface square to the target line and a thinner cut of sand will result. I would suggest, however, that golfers who already consistently hit their sand shots past the target disregard this advice.

CLUBFACE ANGLE DETERMINES DEPTH OF SAND CUT

Golfers can control the depth of their sand cut on bunker shots merely by the way they position the clubface as they address the ball.

When the blade is closed to look to the left of target (drawing at left), the blade will cut

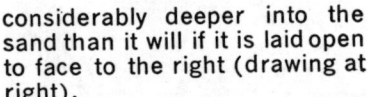

considerably deeper into the sand than it will if it is laid open to face to the right (drawing at right).

Thus it becomes apparent that a closed clubface will best serve the golfer who finds he needs a deep cut to move the clubhead under a ball that is buried. An open face should be used on shots where the ball rests on top of the sand.

6—SAND SHOTS

HOW TO ESCAPE FROM SAND ON FIRST TRY

How often have you left the ball in the hazard when trying to escape from sand? And how often have you criticized yourself for hitting too far behind the ball in so doing?

Quite probably you did hit behind the ball too far and, thus, left it in the trap. However, it may be that your position of contact with the sand was correct. Perhaps you left the shot in the bunker because your club cut too deeply. This cause of "left" sand shots is all too common.

Your clubhead cuts too deeply into the sand if it "closes" in the impact area. Even a slightly closed clubface will cause you to come up short on these shots. If your hands have turned over on the shot (illustration #1), you will probably have cut too deeply with a closed clubface.

On sand shots it is vital that your hands continue to face the target until the ball is well on its way (illustration #2). This will help assure a normal depth of clubhead penetration.

USE SUFFICIENT LOFT FROM DEEP BUNKERS

One of the most frustrating experiences in golf is to hit an otherwise excellent sand shot into the side of the bunker. This happens all too frequently... and simply because the golfer fails to select a club with sufficient loft.

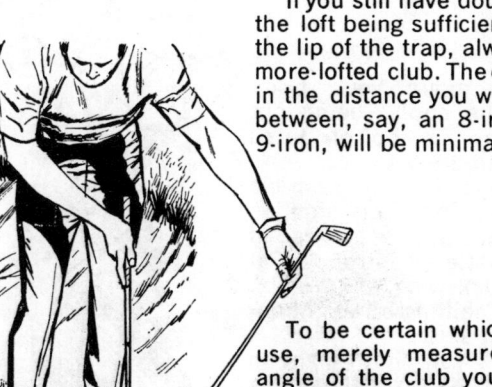

If you still have doubts about the loft being sufficient to clear the lip of the trap, always use a more-lofted club. The difference in the distance you will achieve between, say, an 8-iron and a 9-iron, will be minimal.

To be certain which club to use, merely measure the loft angle of the club you are considering as I am doing in the illustration. Just be sure that you do not ground either club in the sand, thereby incurring a penalty.

PLAY LONG BUNKER SHOTS AS IF FROM FAIRWAY

Many golfers make the mistake of playing long sand shots in the same way that they play the normal bunker shots. That is, they try to slide the clubhead under the ball. This slows the clubhead severely and prohibits the shot from carrying the necessary distance.

Play these long sand shots in the same fashion that you'd use on similar shots from the fairway. Make certain that the clubhead strikes the ball before contacting the sand. Play the ball a bit back in your stance to achieve this result.

Be sure to choke down a bit on the club. This shortening of the shaft-length will offset the fact that your feet are set down into the sand.

SAND PROBLEMS INTENSIFY ON WET COURSE

Most golfers find it especially difficult to play from wet sand, not only because they have trouble judging how to make the shot under such abnormal conditions, but also because balls tend to bury or plug in moist sand.

Shots from deep grass are also problems when it's damp. The moist grass really cuts down your ability to control the ball's action.

When the course is wet, the safe way is the best way. When you approach to a green that is guarded by a bunker, for instance (see illustration), shoot away from the hazard. It's well worth sacrificing a chance for a birdie to assure yourself that you will not bogey or double-bogey.

6—SAND SHOTS

TURN OUT LEFT TOE ON SHOTS FROM SAND

Because of the loose footing you can expect on sand shots, it becomes a bit of a problem to properly turn the lower body to the left on your downswing.

If you toe out your left foot on these shots, you will find it

easier to move your body through the shot. Toeing out in this manner sort of pre-turns your hips to the left.

Toeing out also restricts your backswing. This, too, is desired on sand shots as an aid for better control. A restricted backswing will prohibit too much shifting of weight onto the right side.

The less you shift weight on sand shots—short of stifling good rhythm, of course—the less chance you will have of losing your balance.

HOW TO JUDGE THE DEPTH OF YOUR CUT ON SAND SHOTS

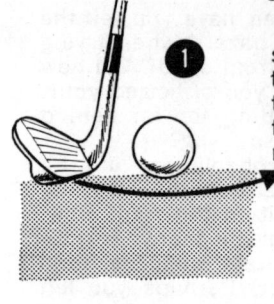

A basic principle of play from sand has to do with the angle of the clubface when it cuts into the bunker. Once you learn how the angle of the clubface determines the depth of the cut, you will be better able to execute the shot you need at a given time.

For instance, on a shot from a good lie in the sand you will want to make a shallow cut.

Therefore you should "open" or lay back your clubface, since this will avoid cutting too deep into the sand (illustration #1).

On shots to dislodge a slightly buried ball (illustration #2), you should go to a square clubface position so as to cut well beneath the ball.

However, on shots with a buried ball (illustration #3), you must close your clubface so that you will get maximum penetration into the sand.

HIT SAND SHOTS TWICE AS HARD

Middle and high handicap golfers must get tired of hearing experts tell them how easy it is to play sand shots. From what I've seen, most golfers on this level find sand shots anything BUT easy.

The biggest problem these golfers face is judging how hard to strike the sand on a give shot.

If you experience the problem, take a few balls into the sand trap and play them out and toward a nearby green. Strike the sand **twice as hard** as you would strike the ball if it was a pitch shot of similar length.

In other words, select a target that is behind the flagstick and twice as far away. The merely strike the sand as if you were pitching a shot to that distance. Observe whether your shots finish short or past the real flagstick. Then simply modify the force of your blows accordingly.

WHERE SITUATION ALLOWS, HIT SAND SHOTS AS FAIRWAY IRONS

Blasting from sand usually is necessary when you are near the green, when you have a low lie, or when the bunker has a big lip.

However, most professionals find it easier to hit sand shots almost as they would fairway irons whenever the situation allows. If the ball is sitting up well in the sand, and if the bunker hasn't much lip, I suggest you try playing the shot just as you would from the fairway.

Play the ball well back in your stance so that the clubhead strikes it before contacting the sand. Then swing largely with your arms, so as not to disturb your balance in the sand.

It is vital to avoid hitting the sand first. Therefore, choke down on your club and keep your left arm fully extended at address. Choking down and extending the arm will compensate for the fact that your feet are lower than normal in the sand.